D0891782

THE LAST JEWS
IN BAGHDAD

Nissim
Rejwan

THE LAST JEWS
IN BAGHDAD

Remembering a Lost Homeland

FOREWORD BY JOEL BEININ

 UNIVERSITY OF TEXAS PRESS
Austin

The publication of this book was aided by the generous support of the Jewish Community Association of Austin and the 21st Annual Jewish Book Fair.

An earlier and shorter version of "Bookshop Days" appeared in *The Literary Review,* Fairleigh Dickinson University, Madison, New Jersey, winter 1994.

First edition, 2004

Requests for permission to reproduce material from this work should be sent to Permissions, University of Texas Press, Box 7819, Austin, TX 78713-7819.

♾ The paper used in this book meets the minimum requirements of ANSI/NISO Z39.48-1992 (R1997) (Permanence of Paper).

LIBRARY OF CONGRESS
CATALOGING-IN-PUBLICATION DATA
Rejwan, Nissim.
The last Jews in Baghdad : remembering a lost homeland / Nissim Rejwan ; foreword by Joel Beinin. — 1st ed.
        p.   cm.
Includes index.
ISBN 0-292-70293-0 (cloth : alk. paper)
1. Rejwan, Nissim.   2. Jews—Iraq—Baghdad—Biography.   3. Jews—Iraq—Baghdad—Social life and customs.   4. Jews—Iraq—Baghdad—Social conditions—20th century.   5. Baghdad (Iraq)—Ethnic relations.   I. Title.
DS135.I713R447   2004
956.7'47004924'092—dc22
                                                      2004004110

To the memory of
Elie Kedourie,
dear friend and literary mentor.

And in remembrance
of youth companions and soul mates
Najib al-Mani',
'Adnan Raouf,
Buland al-Haidari,
Isaac Khedhouri (Bar Moshe),
and
all other members of the shulla.

Because you were foolish enough to love one place,
now you are homeless . . .

LOUISE GLÜCK, "ADULT GRIEF"

CONTENTS

FOREWORD

Jews as Native Iraqis: An Introduction

JOEL BEININ

*N*issim Rejwan tells us, quoting W. H. Auden, that he always fought for the right to remain "a private face in a private place." Readers of good faith will want to respect his declared intentions. Yet those who have found their way to this memoir are, like the author himself, unlikely to have avoided the bruising impact of the powerful political forces that overwhelmed the private interests and aspirations of most Iraqi Jews and terminated centuries of Muslim-Jewish coexistence.

Over a century of Arab-Zionist conflict has made it difficult for those with no direct experience of it to imagine Jews like Nissim Rejwan as an indigenous, indeed a vital, presence in Arab and Muslim societies and cultures. Nowhere were Jews more deeply rooted and culturally assimilated than in the Tigris-Euphrates Valley. The profound Jewish symbiosis with the other communities of what was constituted as Iraq after 1921—Sunni and Shi'i Muslim Arabs, Kurds and Turcomans, Assyrian and Aramean Christians, and Yazidis—is the indispensable point of reference for understanding the cultural and political context of *The Last Jews in Baghdad.*

The modern state of Iraq was formed out of three provinces of the Ottoman Empire: Baghdad in the center, Mosul in the north, and Basra in the south. During the nineteenth century the Jewish communities of these provinces, and especially the city of Baghdad, grew dramatically in number and prosperity. In the early nineteenth century there were about 10,000 Jews in Baghdad and less than 1,500 in Basra. By 1908 Jews constituted 53,000 of Baghdad's 150,000 inhabitants.[1] The last Ottoman yearbook for Baghdad enumerated 80,000 Jews among the city's 202,200 residents in 1917.[2] By 1947, according to the national census, Jews comprised 118,000 of the total Iraqi population of 4.5 million (2.6 percent; unofficial estimates range as high as 130,000). Jews were highly concentrated in the largest cities with 77,500 in Baghdad, 10,500 in Basra, and 10,300 in Mosul. Smaller Jewish communities resided in every province of the country. The dramatic increase in the size of the Iraqi Jewish community complemented the enhanced prosperity of its commercial and financial elite and the cultural prominence of its intelligentsia.

Jews served as the bankers of the governors of the Ottoman provinces of Mesopotamia as early as the eighteenth century. From the second half of the nineteenth century to the 1950s they also dominated long-distance trade from the Tigris-Euphrates valley to India and Europe. The rise of the Jewish merchants of Baghdad and Basra was enabled by the end of the commercial monopoly of the British East India Company in 1813, the expansion of the port of Basra, and the opening of the Suez Canal in 1869. Members of Jewish mercantile families settled in Bombay, Calcutta, Rangoon, Singapore, Shanghai, Hong Kong, and England. Jews residing in Britain and its colonies came under British protection, giving them legal and economic advantages over Muslims that facilitated the establishment of commercial networks extending back to Mesopotamia. The presence of family and trusted community members abroad allowed Jews to engage in banking and financing of long-distance trade more easily than Muslims and Christians without such connections. Jewish merchants, although they traded mostly in Indian and British goods, were not simply compradors. They competed with British businessmen more often than they collaborated with them. The extent of Jewish commercial dominance is expressed by their preponderant presence in Baghdad's leading commercial and financial institutions. In 1938–1939 ten of the twenty-five "first-class" members of the Baghdad Chamber of Commerce were Jews, and Jews comprised 43.2 percent of the chamber's 498 members. In 1936, thirty-five of the thirty-nine bankers and money changers in Baghdad were Jews.[3]

The Sassoons were the most prominent of the Jewish business families. "The Rothschilds of the East," as they were known, maintained a far-flung commercial, agricultural, and textile-manufacturing network with interests in India, Iran, China, Japan, and England in addition to Iraq. Families like the Sassoons constituted only 5 percent of the Jewish community. The great majority, like their urban Muslim and Christian neighbors, were either poor or small merchants, artisans, and white-collar employees of middling income.

Britain occupied Mesopotamia in 1917. That conquest was legitimized by a League of Nations mandate, and Britain remained the ultimate power in the country until Iraq gained independence in 1932. The elite elements of the Jewish community prospered during the British mandate; their business and political interests were generally compatible with British overlordship. Britain remained a substantial factor in Iraqi politics until 1958 through its military bases and dominant role in the petroleum industry.

The British installed Faysal I as king of Iraq in 1921. He was committed to forging a new, civic national identity which would unite Sunni and Shi'i Muslims, Christians, and Jews as Iraqis. Prominent Jews enjoyed good relations with the monarchy. The constitution of 1925 guaranteed the equality of all before the law, freedom of religion, and the right of minority communities to maintain schools in their own languages.

Elite Jews accepted Faysal's vision of a civic Iraqi identity, and several of them occupied high political offices in the mandate period. A smaller but still significant number remained politically prominent in the first years of independent Iraq as well. Sassoon Hesqel, one of the most prominent men of Baghdad in the first half of the twentieth century, served as minister of finance from 1921 until 1932. Ibrahim al-Kabir served as director general of the Ministry of Finance. Da'ud Samra sat on the High Court of Appeal from 1923 until he retired in 1946. Jews won five parliamentary seats in the 1925 elections—two each from Baghdad and Basra and one from Mosul. Menahem Salih Daniel (1925–1932) and then his son Ezra Ben Menahem Daniel represented the Jews in the Senate.

The Arab-Jewish communities of Yemen and the Tunisian island of Jerba continued to write primarily in Hebrew or Judeo-Arabic (Arabic in Hebrew script) into the twentieth century. Many Jews of North Africa and the Levant used French as their lingua franca. In contrast, Iraqi Jews spoke the Baghdadi Jewish dialect of Arabic at home and, from the late nineteenth century, adopted standard Arabic as their language of culture.

In 1864 the Jewish community of Baghdad opened the first modern school for boys in the three Ottoman provinces of the Tigris-Euphrates valley. Administration of the school was entrusted to the Alliance Israélite Universelle—an organization of French Jews which espoused a *mission civilisatrice* to Europeanize Middle Eastern Jews by providing them with a French, secular education. The Alliance opened a girls' school in Baghdad in 1893 and two more schools for boys in the early years of the twentieth century as well as schools in Basra, Mosul, and several smaller cities. Many Iraqi Jews developed a fondness for French and English and sometimes positioned themselves as translators from these languages to Arabic. But by and large the Jewish communities rejected the Alliance's policy of adopting French as the sole language of instruction. Most Jewish schools retained Arabic as the language of instruction, and their students attained high levels of mastery. The Alliance lost the struggle over the language of instruction, and all but the first two Baghdad schools reverted to administration by the local Iraqi Jewish communities during the mandate era.[4]

The network of schools established after 1864 enabled Jews to become, on the whole, better educated than their Muslim neighbors in the first half of the twentieth century. The influence of the Alliance promoted the secularization of the Jewish community. While many Jews became more cosmopolitan than their neighbors because of their exposure to English and French, the majority remained in the Arabo-Muslim cultural orbit.

The economic and social prominence of the Jewish elite, their integration into the newly established Iraqi state, and the community's embrace of Arabic were the basis for the "Iraqi orientation" adopted by the great majority of Jews. Most saw Iraq as their homeland, and many sought to contribute to building up the new state and society, while differing widely on how this should be done. The Iraqi orientation of the Jewish community enabled members of its intelligentsia to become significant figures in the formation of modern Iraqi Arabic culture.

More than a decade before the first Arabic press, Baruch Moshe Mizrahi established the first printing press in Baghdad in 1853.[5] Several other Jews established presses in the second half of the nineteenth century. These early presses published works in Hebrew and Judeo-Arabic. But soon after the turn of the century use of Hebrew became restricted to religious purposes. The secularization of the Jewish community was well underway, and Arabic was becoming the preferred language of the Jewish intelligentsia.

The 1908 Young Turk revolution consolidated the inclination of the Jewish literati to write in standard Arabic. Many Jews throughout the Ottoman Empire embraced the ideal of equality of all religious and ethnic groups on the basis of a common Ottoman civic identity that the new regime advocated. The abrogation of censorship and the restoration of the Ottoman constitution produced a flurry of new periodicals in the Arab provinces. Among them were three Baghdadi newspapers with substantial Jewish participation. The first two appeared in late 1909: the bilingual Arabic-Turkish *al-Zuhur,* edited by Nissim Yusuf Somekh and Rashid Effendi al-Saffar, and the Arabic *Bayn al-Nahrayn,* edited by Ishaq Hesqel and Menachem 'Ani. The bilingual *Tafakkur,* owned by Sulayman 'Anbar, appeared in 1912.[6] The first book in standard Arabic written by a Jew was *The Ottoman Revolution* (Baghdad, 1909) by Salim Ishaq, a lawyer and secretary to the chief rabbi, Ezra Dangoor.

The first works of Arabic fiction in Iraq appeared after World War I. By then there was a critical mass of Jews who were both well-educated in Arabic and familiar with Western literature, which they brought into conversation with emerging forms of Arabic literary modernism. The following paragraphs offer brief summaries of the accomplishments of many Iraqi Jewish writers of fiction, poetry, drama, cultural criticism, and journalism as well as actors and musicians. Those unfamiliar with this cultural phenomenon may find the detail overwhelming. I felt it important to mention these names (many others have been omitted) in order to demonstrate the extent of Jewish participation in modern Iraqi Arabic culture.

In 1922 Murad Mikha'il (1906–1986) published one of the first Arabic short stories in Iraq: "He Died for His Country, She Died for Love" ("Shahid al-watan wa-shahidat al-hubb").[7] Mikha'il also wrote poetry, and his innovative free verse was noticed by major Iraqi poets like Ma'ruf al-Rusafi. Over a dozen other Jewish writers made their debut in the 1920s, including Anwar Sha'ul (1904–1984), Ezra Haddad (1909–1972), and Salman Shina (1898–1978). Shina, a lawyer and member of the Iraqi parliament, established the Arabic language Jewish newspaper al-Misbah (The Candelabrum), which appeared regularly from 1924 to 1927 with a few issues in 1928 and 1929.

Anwar Sha'ul, a graduate of the Alliance school in Baghdad, was the outstanding member of this group. He was a lawyer and the legal advisor to the private treasury of the royal household from 1935 to 1949. In the 1940s he defended Jews charged with being Communists. His literary works include translations of two volumes of Western short stories as well as French and English plays into Arabic. Although he served as the first editor of al-Misbah, Sha'ul, like the other Jewish authors of his generation, generally did not address specifically Jewish concerns. This first generation of Jewish literati wrote as Iraqi patriots. Sha'ul opposed the British mandate, wrote poems praising the monarchy, and supported the emancipation of women and human rights.[8] In 1929 Sha'ul established a weekly literary journal, al-Hasid, which featured articles by many young Jewish and non-Jewish authors, including Sha'ul's wife, Esterian Ibrahim, and five other women until it ceased publication in 1938.

The appearance of al-Hasid marked the development of a second generation of Jewish authors. Shalom Darwish (1913–1998?) published his first short stories and critical essays in al-Hasid in 1929. Two volumes of his collected stories appeared in the 1940s. Both Muslim and Jewish critics consider Darwish to be the most talented of the first two cohorts of Iraqi Jewish short story writers and a significant figure in Iraqi literary history.[9] In addition to his literary accomplishments, Darwish was an activist in the National Democratic party.

Trained as an economist, Me'ir Basri (b. 1911) edited the journal of the Baghdad Chamber of Commerce from 1938 to 1945. Although Basri was not a major poet, he was among the first Iraqis to write sonnets and free verse. Ya'qub Bilbul (1920-2003) succeeded Basri as the editor of the journal of the Baghdad Chamber of Commerce (1945-1951). Bilbul and Basri both revived the Andalusian strophic forms of poetry known as *muwashshahat*. Bilbul published his first book of short stories in 1938 after graduating from the Alliance school. He is considered one of the first writers of social realist fiction in Iraq.[10]

The first modern Arabic play in Mesopotamia was written in 1888 by a Christian and performed in Mosul the next year. Jews had their own traditional theater based on the religious calendar. The Alliance schools introduced modern drama to the curriculum. *Queen Esther,* which debuted in 1908, was apparently the first play performed at the Baghdad Alliance boys' school. It may also have been among the first Arabic plays performed in Baghdad; previously plays in Turkish were offered by visiting troupes. Just before World War I Khadduri Shahrabani organized a Jewish company that performed theater pieces in Arabic in Basra and India. He resumed his theatrical activity in Baghdad after the war. Before World War I most of the dramatic productions by Jews were staged before mainly Jewish audiences. Because drama is usually performed in dialect, the existence of distinct communal dialects in Baghdad delayed the integration of the pioneering theatrical activities of Jews into the common Iraqi culture. But by the 1920s Jewish actors and directors were performing for mixed audiences. There were many well-known Jewish actors in addition to the preeminent Khadduri Shahrabani. In 1926 Prime Minister 'Abd al-Muhsin al-Sa'dun attended an Arabic production of Corneille's *Le Cid* directed by Shahrabani and featuring actors of the Literary Reform Bookshop. Sa'dun was so impressed that he recommended that a second performance be arranged in honor of King Faysal. The king attended and gave his approval. The texts of only a handful of plays written by Jews survive. *Loyalty and Betrayal* (1927) by Salman Ya'qub Darwish and *After His Brother's Death* (1931) by Shalom Darwish were published as was Anwar Sha'ul's Arabic translation and elaboration of Richard Sheridan's *Wilhelm Tell.* Others exist only in manuscript form. Shmu'el Moreh, an Iraqi Jew and professor of Arabic Literature at the Hebrew University of Jerusalem who has written extensively on Arabic literary production of Iraqi Jews, could not locate copies of the published works of Eliyahu

Khadduri, Hesqel Ibrahim Nissim, and Eliyahu Smira. Smira's student, Salman 'Abd Allah, wrote two plays in the Muslim Arabic dialect, but only the text of one in the Jewish dialect, *The Wedding in Baghdad,* is preserved.[11]

Jews were active in the revival of the classical Iraqi *maqam,* which was promoted by Prime Minister Nuri al-Sa'id and other prominent figures of the mandate and early independence period. The Iraqi *maqam* is a musical suite—a complex local variant of the musical form common in Arab, Turkish, and Persian cultures with origins in the 'Abbasid period (750–1258). Salman Moshe (1880–1955) and Hesqel Qassab were well-known *maqam* singers. Among the female vocalists who became popular in the 1920s was Salima Murad (1900–1972)—the Jewish wife of Nazim al-Ghazali, a Muslim and the student of Muhammad al-Qubbanchi, the leading Iraqi *maqam* singer of the twentieth century. Most Jewish *maqam* artists were instrumentalists, not vocalists. Many Jews performed in the ensembles that accompanied *maqam* singers known as the *tchalgi Baghdadi.* In 1932 al-Qubanshi appeared at the Cairo Music Congress, the first international Arabic music festival. All but one member of the *tchalgi Baghdadi* that accompanied him were Jews. Hesqel Mu'allim accompanied the Egyptian diva, Umm Kulthum, when she performed in Iraq in the 1930s. The brothers Salih and Da'ud Kuwaiti were the best-known Jewish *maqam* musicians.[12]

Jewish participation in Iraqi culture and politics diminished somewhat in the mid-1930s. King Faysal I died in 1933 and was succeeded by the weak King Ghazi until he died in a car crash in 1939. During those years Nazi propaganda disseminated by the German Ambassador found an audience among pan-Arabist army officers who fiercely opposed Britain's continuing influence in Iraq. A series of military coups beginning in 1936 undermined the liberal promise of the 1925 constitution. In 1935 the teaching of Hebrew, except for the Bible, was proscribed.

Despite these pressures, Jews remained a prominent presence in Iraqi cultural life. In 1937 the foremost Iraqi neoclassical poet, Muhammad Mahdi al-Jawahiri (1900–1997), wrote a newspaper article criticizing the decision of the Jewish community to raise the tax on kosher meat and expressing his support for poor Jews who would be burdened by the increase. The military government arrested him for inciting communal strife. In jail he wrote a satirical poem criticizing the government and referring to this affair using the Hebrew word *kashair* and its opposite, *taraif.*[13]

Al-Hasid was forced to close in 1938 by a combination of economic and anti-Jewish pressures due to its outspoken anti-Nazi stand. It was the last of the Jewish-owned Iraqi periodicals. But many Jews remained active in Arabic journalism and letters in the 1940s and 1950s, writing and editing for periodicals owned by Muslims or Christians.

The Jewish journalists and authors of the post–World War II period constitute a third generation, which was, on the whole, more sharply politicized than its predecessors. Communism was the most popular political current among young Jews in the 1940s. Its greatest rival was Zionism, which became significant only after the 1941 anti-Jewish riot known as the *farhud*. The mildly social democratic National Democratic party, the populist al-Ahali group, the centrist Liberal party, and the People's party all won adherents among the Jewish intelligentsia. These were democratic and Iraqist, not pan-Arab, political tendencies. Many Jews were eager to be Iraqi Arabs. But like most Arabic-speaking minorities, they were suspicious of the romantic and racialist aspects of pan-Arabism. Moreover, in Iraq pan-Arabism was associated with the continuing dominance of the Sunni Arab minority.

The proclamation of the state of Israel in 1948 and the participation of the Iraqi army in the failed Arab effort to block its establishment increased pressures on the entire Iraqi Jewish community, even though only a minority actively supported Zionism. The beginning of the end of prominent Jewish participation in Iraqi journalism was signaled by the removal of the two Jewish editors of the daily *al-Barid al-Yawmi* in 1948 following their arrest without charges. Yet many remained in the profession, some even after the mass Jewish emigration to Israel in 1950–1951. Na'im Tuwayq worked at the daily *al-Ahali* from 1934 to 1937 and resumed work at the paper in 1942 when it became the organ of the National Democratic party. From 1938 to 1963 he worked for the daily *al-Zaman*. Menashe Za'rur was the editor of *al-Iraq*, owned by Razzuq Ghannam, and then of the evening daily *al-Hawadith* till he left for Israel in 1955. Murad al-'Imari worked at the daily *al-Sha'b* from 1944, the year of its appearance, until 1946 and then for the National Democratic party's *al-Ahali* until 1952, when he became a reporter for the English-language daily the *Iraq Times,* where he remained until 1963. He also worked as a radio broadcaster from 1944 to 1946. Menashe Somekh sat on the editorial board of *al-Sha'b* until he left for Israel in 1950. Suhayl Ibrahim (Edward Sha'ul, b. 1918) edited *Sawt al-Ahrar,* the journal of the Liberal party, until he too left for Israel in 1950. Salim al-Bassun sat on the editorial boards of many papers, including *al-Sha'b, al-Bilad, al-Siyasa, al-Istiqlal,* and, after the overthrow of the monarchy in 1958, *al-Jumhuriyya.*[14]

Nissim Rejwan belongs to this literary generation. From 1946 to 1948 he wrote movie and book reviews regularly for the *Iraq Times*. He frequented a left-leaning, modernist literary circle centered on Al-Rabita Bookshop where he worked. The proprietor of Al-Rabita, 'Abd al-Fattah (Abdel Fattah) Ibrahim, had been a leader of the *al-Ahali* group in the 1930s and founded the small and short-lived Marxisant National Union party in 1946. Al-Rabita Bookshop was closed in 1948, and Rejwan left for Israel in 1951.

The most prominent Jewish authors of the post–World War II era are Sami Mikha'il (b. 1926) and Shimon Ballas (b. 1930), both members of the Communist party, and Naim Kattan, Esperance Cohen (b. 1930), Yitzhak Bar-Moshe (1927–2003), Nir Shohet (b. 1928), Sasson Somekh (b. 1933), Shmu'el Moreh (b. 1933), David Tzemah (1933–1998), and Samir Naqqash (b. 1937). They are indelibly marked by the decisive rupture between Jews and the rest of Iraqi society—the mass emigration of all but some five thousand to ten thousand Jews to Israel in 1950–1951. The demise of the Jewish community of Iraq was the result of a complex dynamic involving the pro-British and promonarchical sympathies of the Jewish business elite, the corrosive effects of Nazi propaganda in the 1930s, the delegitimization of the monarchy because of its links to British imperialism, pan-Arab nationalism, and the Arab-Zionist conflict.

Several Iraqi Jewish authors did not leave in 1950–1951. Anwar Sha'ul and Me'ir Basri considered themselves Arab Iraqis of Jewish faith. They continued to write poetry glorifying Iraq and the Arabs. In 1968 the Ba'th came to power and began to persecute Jews harshly. A show trial culminated in the public hanging of twelve Jews on fabricated charges of spying for Israel in January 1969. Basri was arrested without reason. Sha'ul unsuccessfully appealed for his release, but to no avail. One day a leading figure in the regime, Salih al-Mahdi, heard one of Sha'ul's poems in praise of Iraq recited on television. Its opening lines are:

> Though it be from Moses that I draw my faith,
> yet I live shaded by the followers of Muhammad.
> The tolerance of Islam is my salvation,
> the wisdom of the Qur'an is my inspiration.

Al-Mahdi was so impressed with the poem that he ordered Basri's release.[15] Even after this incident Sha'ul continued to write panegyrics to Arabism. At the Conference of Arab Writers in Baghdad in April 1969 he recited:

> My heart beats with love of the Arabs, my mouth speaks
> their language proudly . . .
> I love my precious homeland, and those who ennobled
> me with their love.[16]

Nonetheless, between 1971 and 1974 Sha'ul and Basri as well as the journalists Salim al-Bassun, Murad al-'Imari, and Na'im Tuwayq left Iraq. Basri went to London; the others to Israel. Nissim Rejwan's friend, Naim Kattan, left Iraq in 1946, immigrating to Canada. Their departure brought an end to the Iraqi orientation of the Jewish community.

The discrimination and denigration of their culture that Iraqi Jews faced in Israel—slyly alluded to by Nissim Rejwan's pithy account of being dusted with DDT on arriving at Lydda airport—do not justify a triumphalist Zionist attitude toward their history. Nostalgia has been a popular genre for the recovery of Iraqi Jewish culture. But nostalgic representation alone risks trivializing Iraqi Jewish culture as a minor folklore ancillary to "mainstream" Israeli Hebrew culture. Tragedy evokes the sense of loss, but disregards cultural endurance and adaptation.

Although the physical connection to Iraq was broken, Iraqi Jewish culture was not extinguished when the great majority of the community immigrated to Israel. Shimon Ballas, Sami Mikha'il, and Sasson Somekh continued to write in Arabic in the press of the Communist party of Israel. Although they eventually shifted to writing in Hebrew, their work is permeated with Iraqi influences and themes. Ballas and Mikha'il have both written novels critically portraying the disdainful attitude of the Zionist and Israeli authorities toward the culture of Middle Eastern Jewish immigrants and their inequitable treatment in Israel: Ballas's *The Transit Camp* (*ha-Ma'abara*, 1964) and Mikha'il's *All Men Are Equal—But Some Are More* (*Shavim ve-shavim yoter*, 1974). Neither is available in English. Mikha'il's *Refuge* (*Hasut*, 1977), one of the few Hebrew novels by a Middle Eastern Jew to be translated into English, draws on his experience in the Communist party of Iraq. Ballas became a professor of Arabic Literature at Haifa University and continues to write occasional literary essays in Arabic. Sasson Somekh became a professor of Arabic Literature at Tel Aviv University and has written about Egyptian and Iraqi Jewish Arabic writers. Yitzhak Bar-Moshe and Samir Naqqash still write only in Arabic. The other Iraqi Jewish immigrant writers adopted Hebrew as soon as they could. Eli 'Amir (b. 1937) was born in Baghdad and left for Israel with his family in 1950. He was sent to school in a kibbutz. His autobiographical novel—available in English as *Scapegoat* (*Tarnigol kaparot*, 1983)—

evokes the humiliation he, his family, and his friends faced as they attempted to integrate into an Israeli society dominated by European Jews who did not imagine that Arabic speaking Jews could have a culture worth preserving.

In the 1950s and 1960s Middle Eastern music was considered "primitive" in Israel; more recently it has become quite popular. For the last eighteen years elderly Iraqi Jewish musicians have gathered every Monday to play at Pardes Katz.[17] Yair Dallal, born in Israel in 1955 and trained as a classical European violinist, has achieved international recognition as an 'ud player. He preserves the Iraqi Jewish musical heritage and brings it into dialogue with other regional musical traditions through his performances with various Middle Eastern artists.

No single mode can capture the full variety of the Iraqi Jewish community's experiences and the diverse understandings of those experiences by differently positioned individuals. The linguistic range of the efforts to recall and record it exemplifies this diversity of experience. Anwar Sha'ul published his autobiography in Arabic, even as he lived in Israel.[18] Naim Kattan wrote an autobiographical novel in French while living in Canada.[19] Sasson Somekh has written several newspaper articles in Hebrew, which herald the appearance of a full-length memoir.[20] All three wrote in Arabic when they lived in Iraq. Finally, Nissim Rejwan offers us this memoir in English. The multiple languages used by the authors of these texts throughout their careers exemplify the hybrid cosmopolitan cultural identities that simultaneously made Jews an integral part of Iraq and ultimately excluded them from it.

Notes

I would like to thank Orit Bashkin and Lital Levy for their bibliographic assistance and comments on this essay.

1. Hanna Batatu, *The Old Social Classes and the Revolutionary Movements of Iraq: A Study of Iraq's Old Landed and Commercial Classes and of Its Communists, Ba'thists, and Free Officers* (Princeton: Princeton University Press, 1978), 248.

2. Sylvia G. Haim, "Aspects of Jewish Life in Baghdad under the Monarchy," *Middle Eastern Studies* 12, no. 2 (May 1976): 188. These statistics must be regarded as estimates, hence the inconsistency between the 1908 and 1917 figures.

3. Batatu, *The Old Social Classes,* 244, 246, 250. "First Class" members were the wealthiest with a "financial consideration" (capital and business volume) of 22,500 to 75,000 dinars.

4. Zvi Yehuda, "Iraqi Jewry and Cultural Change in the Educational Activity

of the Alliance Israélite Universelle," in Harvey E. Goldberg, ed., *Sephardi and Middle Eastern Jewries: History and Culture in the Modern Era* (Bloomington: Indiana University Press, 1996), 134–145.

5. Dafna Tzimhoni, "Kavim le-reshit ha-modernizatzia shel yehudei bavel ba-me'a ha-19 'ad shnat 1948," *Pe'amim* 36 (1988): 31–32.

6. Nisim Kazzaz, *Ha-yehudim be-'irak ba-me'a ha-'esrim* (Jerusalem: Mosad Ben-Tzvi le-Heker Kehilot Yisra'el ba-Mizrah, 1991), 147.

7. Sasson Somekh, "Lost Voices: Jewish Authors in Modern Arabic Literature," in Mark R. Cohen and Abraham L. Udovitch, eds., *Jews among Arabs: Contacts and Boundaries* (Princeton: Darwin Press, 1989), 14. The division of Iraqi Jewish authors into three generations is based on this article.

8. Myer Samra, "Shaded by the Followers of Muhammad: The Poet Anwar Sha'ul and the Jews in Iraq," *Australian Journal of Jewish Studies* 7, no. 2 (1993): 127–129.

9. Nancy Berg, *Exile from Exile: Israeli Writers from Iraq* (Albany: State University of New York Press, 1996), 36–37.

10. Shmu'el Moreh, "Arabic Literary Creativity of Jewish Writers in Iraq," in Shmu'el Moreh, ed., *al-Qissa al-qasira 'inda yahud al-'iraq / ha-Sipur ha-katsar shel yehudei 'irak / Short Stories by Jewish Writers from Iraq, 1924–1978* (Jerusalem: Magnes Press, Hebrew University of Jerusalem, 1981), 23.

11. Shmu'el Moreh, "Ha-te'atron ha-yehudi be-'irak be-mahatzit ha-rishona shel ha-me'a ha-'esrim," *Pe'amim* 23 (1985): 64–98.

12. Neil van der Linden, "The Classical Iraqi *Maqam* and Its Survival," in Sherifa Zuhur, ed., *Colors of Enchantment: Theater, Dance, Music, and the Visual Arts of the Middle East* (Cairo: American University of Cairo Press, 2001), 321–335.

13. Sasson Somekh, "Rhyme and Reason at Café Baghdad," *ha-Aretz,* September 10, 1999.

14. Moreh, "Arabic Literary Creativity of Jewish Writers in Iraq," 19–20.

15. Samra, "Shaded by the Followers of Muhammad," 131–132.

16. Reuven Snir, "We Were Like Those Who Dream: Iraqi-Jewish Writers in Israel in the 1950s," *Prooftexts* 11, no. 2 (May 1991): 155.

17. Aviva Luri, "Buena Vista Baghdad Club," *ha-Aretz,* June 23, 2000.

18. Anwar Sha'ul, *Qissat hayati fi wadi al-rafidayn* (Jerusalem: Rabitat al-Jam'iyin al-Yahud al-Nazihin min al-'Iraq, 1980).

19. Naim Kattan, *Adieu, Babylone* (Paris: Julliard, 1976); translated into English as *Farewell, Babylon* (New York: Taplinger, 1980).

20. For example, articles in *ha-Aretz,* September 10, 1999; September 17, 2001; October 5, 2001; January 18, 2002. The memoir was published just as this volume went to press: *Bagdad, etmol* (Tel-Aviv: Ha-Kibutz ha-Meuhad, 2004).

PREFACE

On Taking Stock

Dear Chava,

Karl Barth once wrote that every autobiography is perforce a dubious enterprise. This, he explained, is because the underlying assumption of autobiographical writings is that "a chair exists in which a man can sit down and contemplate his own life, to compare its phases, to survey its development, and to penetrate its meanings." To be sure, he added, every man can and ought to take stock of himself. But he cannot survey himself "even in the present moment, any more than in the whole of his past."

How true. But you, my friend, take things much more easily. "Start right at this point in time," you say with that peculiar finality of tone that is all yours. You are, though, perhaps right. A work of autobiography can be written in any one of a hundred different ways, and my question as to where to start telling this rather partial, very inadequate tale was at best rhetorical, at worst evasive.

"Here and now," you say. But which of the "heres" and which of the "nows"? The external or the internal? The intellectual or the emotional? The public or the private? These divisions and oppositions are, of course, largely fictitious. What finally makes what one is, what determines one's attitudes, one's predilections, one's outlook on life, and one's beliefs is no doubt the result of both external and internal, intellectual and emotional, public and private factors — influences and events that are extremely hard to capture in any order or chronology.

As I believe you know by now, I have always fought for the right to remain what Auden, in one of his poems, terms "a private face in a private place." The ways in which this simple wish was frustrated, and the circumstances at play there, constitute the subject of these fragments of a life . . .

* * *

Please note that Arabic names, when transliterated, can be spelled a variety of different ways. The same individual's name may be spelled one way in the foreword and another way in the main text.

* * *

Throughout the many years the writing of these memoirs took, I drew on the knowledge and experience of various relatives and friends. My thanks to all of them. Special thanks are due to my dear wife Rachel, for her understanding and support through thick and thin. My thanks too to the directors and staff of the Harry S Truman Institute for the Advancement of Peace for their hospitality and day-to-day assistance.

THE LAST JEWS
IN BAGHDAD

Chapter 1 | *I*N OLD BAGHDAD

*I*t has often been said that New York is a Jewish city. I think one can safely say the same about Baghdad of the first half of the twentieth century. At the time of writing, barely twenty Jews, most of them elderly, live in my hometown. The one monument these Jews have left is a synagogue where, as their ancestors did from time immemorial, they keep praying for "the welfare of the city," as Jews in the Babylonian diaspora were bidden to do by the Prophet Jeremiah some three millennia ago. For those who, like myself, were born, grew up, and lived in Baghdad in the years preceding the mass exodus of Jews from Iraq in 1950–1951, this state of affairs is extremely hard to imagine.

To have an idea of the city's demography and the position of the Jews there in those five decades, it is enough to glance at these few facts of statistics: In 1904, the French vice-consul in Baghdad gave the number of Jews in the then Ottoman *vilayet* as forty thousand, out of a total population of sixty thousand.

In 1910, a British consular report estimated the number of Jews in Baghdad as ranging from forty-five thousand to fifty thousand. In October 1921, a British publication quoted these population figures for the city as given in the last official yearbook of the *vilayet:* Total number of inhabitants, 202,200, of whom 80,000 were Jews; 12,000 Christians; 8,000 Kurds; 800 Persians; and 101,400 Arabs, Turks, and other Muslims.

A proclamation issued by the British military governor early in 1919 fixed the number of sheep to be slaughtered daily in Baghdad East (al-Risafa, the more populous half of the city) at 220 for Jewish butchers and 160 for Muslim and other butchers.

In 1926, the year the Baghdad Chamber of Commerce was founded, five of its Administrative Council's fourteen members were Jews, four Muslims, three represented British merchants, one represented the banks, and one represented the Persian merchants.

This was the Baghdad in which I first saw the light of day, and in which I spent the first twenty-six years of my life. However, while demographically the picture did not change in any significant sense up to 1951, a number of basic changes took place in almost all other aspects of the city's life throughout those three decades.

One such aspect was especially pronounced—the Jewish religious scene. The community, and the family, into which I was born can be described as observant in the strictest sense of the word, though perhaps not "orthodox" in the sense in which European Jews in general and East European Jews in particular use the term. Up to the age of ten I used to take my father, who had lost his sight many years before, to the synagogue every Saturday morning, on Holy Days, and on the various feasts. On Friday evening, Sabbath candles were lit, the table set, the *kiddush* recited, and the *esheth hayil* chanted in unison by all the males of the family. Saturday mornings, after the service, I used to run to the neighborhood Muslim teashop with an empty pot to get, for free, boiling water for the tea that was such an indispensable part of breakfast. No money was seen and no deals struck.

As for the socioeconomic status of my family, it all depends on the way one considers the overall economic and social scenes. In the conditions prevalent in Iraq in those days, economically the Jewish community was in the forefront, although viewed as a whole it was not wealthy. In the British consular report of 1910 cited above, the Jews are classified economically as follows:

1. A rich and well-off class, mainly merchants and bankers, 5 percent.
2. A middle class consisting of petty traders, employees, etc., 30 percent.
3. A poor class, 60 percent.
4. Beggars (hailing mostly from the north), 5 percent.

If one follows this somewhat arbitrary classification, my family can safely be said to have belonged somewhere between the 30 percent of the middle class and the 60 percent poor, with periodic shifts between the two, mostly in the latter's direction.

COMMERCE AND TRADE

The world outside the home was brought to a virtual standstill on Saturdays and on Jewish holidays. The bazaars were practically empty, and all commercial activity in the city's main street ceased, with only a few scattered shops open. Not only did the Jews, who owned the overwhelming majority of shops and stores, close their business premises and refrain from doing any shopping themselves; non-Jews too followed suit, refusing to make purchases on Jewish holidays lest the owners of the few shops open take advantage of the situation and overcharge them for the goods they bought. There were also many cases of non-Jewish shop owners closing on these days for lack of customers.

This was the position so far as the large bazaars and the main street were concerned. In those neighborhoods in which Jews predominated numerically — although no single neighborhood was ever exclusively Jewish — business life tended to come to a total standstill, what with non-Jews closing their shops, peddlers refraining from business, and petty farmers staying home rather than bring their fresh fruit and vegetables to bazaars where no "serious" buyers were to be found. These farmers, incidentally, used to bring their best and choicest produce to town on Fridays and on the eves of Jewish feasts, taking due note in fixing their prices of the seasonal needs of the Jewish inhabitants on these holidays — as, for instance, on the few days preceding the Feast of Tabernacles (*Succoth*) and Rosh Hashanah (the Jewish New Year) when certain fruits and vegetables were essential for the *berakhot*.

An idea of the extent to which the role the Jews played in Iraq's commercial activity and in the Iraqi economy was dominant can be had from the fact that, in 1935–1936, nine out of the total of eighteen members of the Administrative Committee of the Baghdad Chamber of Commerce were Jews. So dominant was this role, indeed, that Jewish holidays affected even some socioreligious aspects of the daily life and mercantile activity of the Shi'is in Baghdad and the adjoining Shi'i townlet of Kazimayn, and this despite the fact that the Shi'is were notorious for boycotting Jews to the point of considering them untouchables.

In his book, *The Shi'is of Iraq*, Yitzhak Nakash cites the following traveler's report: "Visiting Kazimayn in 1934–1935, the Lebanese Shi'i *mujtahid* (scholar) Muhsin al-Amin noted the practice of the Shi'i merchants of Baghdad of visiting the shrines of the imams in Kazimayn on a Saturday instead of a Friday, although Friday, as the Muslims' official as well as religious day of rest was the preferable day for the weekly visitation of the shrine. He explained that the business activity of the Shi'i merchants depended on the service of the Jewish merchants and brokers who dominated Baghdad's trade; hence, like the Jewish merchants, the Shi'is had to take their weekly day off on Saturday."

Ten years later, when I was in my late teens, much was to change in

Iraqi Jewish religious life and practices — as did so many other things. Indeed, the capacity of human beings to change and to adapt, taking things in their stride as if change, drastic change, was the most natural thing in the world, is something that has always made me wonder. The difference between the kind of world in which I was born in Baghdad of the mid-1920s and that in which I attained my maturity, in the late 1940s — not to mention the world in which we live now — was so great it would strain the imagination just to try to grasp it or to account for it.

In my own case, it is true, the change may have been all the greater since I happened to have changed my habitat somewhere in mid-life, moving as I did from one country to another, from one culture to another. To be sure, in certain crucial cases the differences between the two societies was not all that shattering; but the change in the sheer pace of life and activity was considerable enough to make a big difference.

The fact, however, is that in Iraq as well as in Israel, the two countries where my first fifty-three years were fairly equally divided, things did happen during these six decades — enormous, unsettling things that have changed the face of society; social and cultural changes of the most significant and crucial nature have taken place.

The result was doubly unsettling: By the time I was twenty-five Iraqi society as a whole and the socioeconomic structure of Iraq's Jewish community had changed almost unrecognizably, while moving to Israel meant something of a "culture shock." During the past fifty years, moreover, Israeli society itself has undergone a number of radical changes, which, of course, have had their impact.

BEIT LULU UM EL-BIGH

The relatively poor quarter where I was born was called Abu Shibil (father of a lion cub), named presumably after the (Muslim) strong man or chief landlord of the neighborhood. In Abu Shibil, as in the majority of Baghdad's neighborhoods, taps for running water were available only to a few selected homes, either because of the great expense of installing new pipes and connecting them to the main pumping station or because of some administrative difficulty. The poorer neighborhoods had two ways of getting their supplies of fresh water — residents could go to the neighborhood mosque, where there was always one or more large taps from which they could draw as much water as they could carry, or depend on the *saqqa* for their supplies. (The mosque water, which was available for all, was called *sabeel*, free, like in "freeway.")

In the house in Abu Shibil in which we lived as subtenants a tap was installed by virtue of the fact that it had a well that also served as a ritual bath, and the services of the *saqqa* were needed only when some technical mishap intervened and the house was left without clean drinking water, something which happened not infrequently. I remember vividly the neighborhood *saqqa* peddling his wares—a man with a heavily weighted donkey usually carrying three or four whole sheepskins brimming with water. The skins were especially made and adapted to contain the water so that only little of it gets lost in the inevitable drips, and the *saqqa* always knew where he was taking his donkey; he had regular clients with standing orders and usually refused to sell the water to other households.

Whether drawn from taps or brought by the *saqqa* directly from the banks of the bountiful River Tigris, which ran right in the middle of the city dividing it into its two parts—Al-Risafa to the east of the river and Al-Karkh to its west—there remained the problem of where to keep the water clean and relatively cool. This was the easier part. On its arrival, the precious liquid was poured directly into a huge earthenware container usually standing in a prominent place in the inner courtyard. The *hib*— that is how it was called in colloquial Iraqi Arabic—was a center of attention and of a significance second only to that of the kitchen. Placed strategically in the shade, it was always carefully covered with a wooden top to keep away flies, mosquitoes, and other natural intruders from the air.

The *hib* was a many-faceted device. Apart from keeping the water clean and fit for drinking it also served as a kind of primitive refrigerator. The water was always cool thanks to the breeze which, no matter how burning hot it was itself, always managed to cool the outside of the *hib* by contact with its damp walls. Moreover the *hib*, which was rounded and with a very narrow base, was placed on a sturdy wooden "cage" with small holes that, while permitting the draught to circulate inside and out, kept the place out of reach of scorpions, cockroaches, snakes, and certain other intruders from land. It was in this "cage," *qafas*, that some of the most valuable necessities were tucked away. Besides the special jug that was placed right under the *hib*'s base to gather the water dripping therefrom, there was ample space in it to accommodate pots, bottles, and plates containing cooked meals, milk, yogurt, liquid medications, and fruit and vegetables, which were preserved in reasonable coolness through the sweltering heat of summer and kept out of harm's reach. The *qafas* also prevented the cats from reaching the meats and the milk products. Ice and ice boxes were introduced only in the 1930s and were used in the better-off households to preserve meats, vegetables, and fruits.

It was rare in those days for a house in Baghdad to be free of scorpions and snakes, and in many households it was customary for the head of the family to go to bed only after he had inspected the holes in the walls for snakes. Although destroying scorpions was a duty, killing or harming a snake was strictly forbidden. Usually ground dry leaves of the nice-smelling *butnaj* were spread on the floor in the belief that snakes cannot stand the smell and consequently refrain from intruding any further. In certain households, again, the mistress of the house left a plate of milk around so that a snake drinking it would become pacified and friendly to members of the household. In such cases the mother chants, "O snake of the house, do not do us harm and we won't harm you!"

One day when I was about four years of age, the head of some little snake somehow came out of one of the holes in a wall in the inner house. Panic reigned; no one dared either to push the snake inside or bring it out. In the end, a certain "professional," a Muslim living in the neighborhood, was brought to the scene. Upon seeing the snake, he asked for an empty bottle, and with his bare fingers he extracted the snake, its mouth tightly shut, straightened it, and deftly put it in the bottle, tail first. He then corked the bottle carefully, put it in his pocket, said *salam,* and went. No money was involved; the snake itself was apparently ample reward.

Almost next in importance to getting and preserving water was the problem of the disposal of wastewater and sewage. Central sewerage systems were totally unknown and unheard of; domestic wastewater usually went into drains, of which there were always more than one in the house, dug deep somewhere right in the middle of the inner courtyard. There was also a separate hole in the ground directly linked to the toilet, which used to be a kind of glorified latrine. Toilet paper was not known since the Jews, following the custom of their Muslim neighbors, used water to clean themselves, for which end a special bottle was left in the toilet.

The work of clearing the drains and the toilets was considered—and in fact was—the most menial of all menial jobs. It was undertaken almost exclusively by Christians from a certain small town in the north of Iraq called Talkeif, but there were also Jews who engaged in the work; but never, never a Muslim. As small children, we used to dub every Christian *nazzah,* the name Baghdadis gave a man who cleaned drains and toilets. And Iraq's immortal popular poet and versifier Mulla 'Abbud al-Karkhi had an unforgettable poem in which he asks, among scores of other rhetorical questions: "Yimkin Mislim yisir nazzah? Yimkin yehudi yisir tchar-khatchi?" (Is it possible for a Muslim to be a latrine cleaner? A Jew to be a night watchman?)

Not only a Jew cannot ever be a night watchman; for some reason the night watchmen roaming the alleys of Baghdad were invariably Muslims. It seems though that some of these failed to do their job properly, if not worse. In the late 1920s, in fact, the authorities discovered that a number of thefts that took place in certain neighborhoods were actually made possible by some secret understanding between the *tcharkhatchis* and the contractors who supplied them to the authorities. The result was that the work was eventually entrusted to *paswaniyya* (sentries) who received their pay from the Treasury. They also had to get their rifles every evening and return them the following morning, seemingly to prevent them from using the weapons for other purposes.

It is interesting to note here, in parentheses, that in Iraq—and presumably in other parts of the Arabic-speaking world—in those days the appellation *Arab* was never used to define a person's identity, and the Jew-Arab opposition we constantly encounter today was never used either in writing or in daily discourse. A Baghdadian was usually said to be a Jew, a Muslim, a Kurd, a Christian, Armenian, Turk, Persian.

An explanation for this is not hard to seek, I think. The so-called "national" identity of a man or a woman was not only of no relevance but the concept itself was not known, and in those cases in which you needed to know a person's identity in the wider sense of citizenship or geographical location you simply said he or she was a Syrian, an Egyptian, a Yemenite, an Iraqi, Palestinian, Turk, Persian, English—or, as in the case of our *nazzah*, Talkeifi.

The day the *nazzahs* came—and they used to work in pairs or threes so that they could finish the work as quickly and as "cleanly" as possible—was a memorable one for us children. Depending on the ground's capacity to seep more of the wastewater, the event took place at least three times a year, and for us it was quite a sight to watch. One of the men descended right down into the drain to clear the muck after the easier part of the job had been finished with the help of buckets tied by ropes and lowered manually to draw the waste water, and eventually the big jars and tin containers were loaded on sturdy donkeys with desultory looks and taken only the devil knows where.

Many Baghdad houses in those days had private wells, from which they drew water for washing. In the house we lived in, the well was so built as to serve as *miqwe* (*mikve*). This particular *mikve* was for women only and had to be operated by a woman, and as the name of the lady who managed the *mikve* was Lulu, everyone in the neighborhood knew her as Lulu um el-bigh (Lulu of the well), and the house her family owned as *Beit Lulu um el-bigh*. It was a fairly prosperous *mikve* business, what with the strict observance in those days. Lulu's *mikve* also was renowned for its cleanliness, and a great deal of work went into keeping and maintaining the establishment, which entailed among other things heating the water in winter on the days the *mikve* was open.

While her husband and older sons were all gainfully employed, mostly in petty trading and money lending, Lulu was the real boss not only of the ritual bath but of the house as well, including the various details and activities related to subletting and subtenants like ourselves. Indeed I have always marveled at the fact that all the houses we lived in in the 1920s and 1930s were named after the women of the households rather than their husbands. From *Beit Lulu um el-bigh* we moved on to *Beit Dina,* then to *Beit Rahel*—and it was only starting with the late 1930s that most of the houses in which we lived as subtenants were named after male owners.

Chapter 2 | $\mathcal{T}$HE REJWAN TRIBE

here are two theories concerning the etymology and origin of the name Rejwan. According to my late father, one of his ancestors was so red in the face that people used to remark: "He's as red as *rejwan*" — the word *rejwan* being colloquial Iraqi Arabic for purple, crimson, or red, the original word in classical Arabic being *urjuwan*. In those days people did not usually have surnames, men and women being known either by their nicknames or patronymics; but in the lifetime of that ancestor of mine a law or custom appeared whereby people were required to have a family name — and it thus came to pass that my family's surname became Rejwan. Incidentally, one of the two Hebrew equivalents of *urjuwan* is practically identical to the Arabic, namely *argwan* — the other being *argaman*. On and off since the mid-1950s I have used the name N. B. Argaman as a pen name when it seemed to suit my purposes.

This was the standard explanation I used to furnish for the benefit of those who were curious enough to inquire about the history and etymology of my family name. A friend of mine, however, who is also something of a linguist and an Arabist, once drew my attention to the fact that Rejwan could well be a deviation not of *urjuwan* but of *rajwan*, an Arabic word derived from the verb *raja,* meaning "to hope," or the noun *rajaa,* meaning a wish or hope. In this context, he explained, *rajwan* would mean "one who hopes" or "one who has a wish."

Plausible though this second explanation may sound, I choose to opt for the first since it is in the nature of a family tradition. It is also more picturesque and attractive. After all, everyone is "hopeful" or has a wish of one kind or another. Not everyone's face can be as red as *urjuwan!*

Apart from being generally red in complexion the Rejwans seem also to have been hot-blooded and quick-tempered — and rather easily excitable. The story is still told by my surviving cousins and other relatives in Israel of one of our ancestors who was once so vexed with the local rabbinate that he actually took the drastic step of proclaiming his conversion to Islam, as a public act of protest.

The tale goes like this. Haron (Aron) Rejwan, a respected and fairly well-to-do member of the community, was an official of the Ottoman sultan in some administrative capacity. One Saturday morning, mindful of the kitchen supplies, the family's cook-maidservant, a Christian, found there were no dried pomegranate seeds left. Now these seeds were an essential ingredient for any *bamya* (okra) dish, especially when it was prepared for the rich—the idea being that they were better and tastier than mere lemon juice when it comes to giving the *bamya* dish that measure of sourness so essential to it.

The woman then duly made her way to the Shorja bazaar nearby and bought the seeds—reportedly not to cook them on the Sabbath but just to store them for the next time the family ordered her to prepare the *bamya* treat.

As luck would have it, however, the servant was spotted—and recognized—by an employee of the Jewish Community Council, and this watchful public servant promptly reported the felony to his superiors, devout and rather strict rabbis to a man. A case was brought against Haron Rejwan and eventually a decision was taken to excommunicate the man— a verdict customarily proclaimed in all synagogues. What made things much worse was that all this was done without the man's knowledge and without his being asked for an explanation or given a hearing of any kind.

Haron heard of the verdict and the public excommunication while he was sitting with friends in the neighborhood coffee shop, upon which— so the story goes—he stood up and announced his decision to become a Muslim in protest against the rabbinate's arbitrary verdict. Then and there he recited the *shahada*—a simple enough proclamation to the effect that there is no god but Allah and that Muhammad was his Messenger (*la ilaha illa-llah wa-Muhammadun rasul-ullah*).

Now my excitable ancestor had many Muslim friends, some of them were present in the coffee shop, and there was no easy way for him of going back on the *shahada*, which is the only act a person wishing to convert to Islam is asked to perform. And so Haron Rejwan remained for some time a nominal Muslim, although secretly he continued to lead the life of a Jew. Eventually, however, the rabbinate was to relent. It publicly acknowledged its error and our man somehow got a proper Jewish burial while the religious status of his wife and children remained unaffected.

RICH REJWANS AND POOR REJWANS

At a very early age I began to be made aware that the Rejwan tribe—there was and continues to be only one family with that name in this world—included some rich people as well as the poor and middling sort with whom I had come in contact within Father's own branch of the family. Especially well-off, and showing it, were two brothers, cousins of Father's, who had made it on the import and wholesale business of tea and sugar. So exclusive was their domination of the tea market, indeed, that they were individually called *Abul Tchai*—the tea dealer.

The two brothers Rejwan owned two very spacious residences, virtually twin buildings, with what were undoubtedly the most imposing exteriors and doors in the whole of downtown Baghdad. The two houses were situated in the posh neighborhood of el-Sinag, directly on al-Rashid Street. In the matter of seeking help from our wealthy relatives, Father used to go through some agonizing doubts and procrastinations, weighing the pros and cons for days and weeks, before submitting to Mother's pleas and deciding to approach one of the brothers—apparently the more generous-hearted or the older of the two. This usually happened when some financial calamity or other hit the family—and there was no dearth of these. Like when my parents had finally decided to give the hand of one of my sisters in marriage and had therefore to provide a dowry. Or like when brother Eliahu, the sole breadwinner of the family, had "liquidity problems" and was on the verge of bankruptcy. Or like when things were so bad we couldn't pay the rent or even pay our grocery bills.

As a matter of course, it was always I who had to take Father—who had lost his sight some years before I was born—to the home of his wealthy cousin, quite some distance from where we used to live in Old Baghdad and always to be done on foot. I recall especially one of these occasions. It was noon or nearing noon when we arrived. We were let into the house and left to sit there in the *tarar*—a kind of internal balcony giving on to the courtyard and the small *baqtcha* (garden) in the middle—waiting for the master of the house to arrive for his lunch break and siesta. Besides the cook—a middle-aged male—there were two or three maidservants. Since it was lunchtime, food was immediately served—delicious dishes to which I was not accustomed. On his cousin's arrival, Father would tell him the current tale of woe—and after a very short stay we left. I don't quite recall the contents of that particular tale, nor do I remember the nature of the answer or the promises made to Father. But I don't think that particular call went in vain ultimately.

In sharp contrast to these two rich cousins, Father's own brothers were rather poor though never as poor as we were generally. '*Ammu* (Uncle) Yaaqub, Father's senior by a good many years, was a cobbler by profession. He had a hole of his own for a workshop, which seemed to me to have been literally carved into the outer wall of *el-midrash* (Midrash Talmud Torah, a school for Torah study roughly equivalent to the East European Jewish yeshivah though run as a school of six forms or more). The shop barely sufficed to contain him and the piles of old shoes and sandals currently brought to him for repair—and he used to sit there, bowed for lack of space, driving nails or making stitches, depending on the kind of footwear he was mending.

Though obviously not one to whom to go for material help of any kind, '*Ammu* Yaaqub nevertheless contributed something to the family. He did not charge for services rendered to us, and would anyway have gained nothing had he done so. I used to take those shoes and boots and sandals to him, sometimes for a third, fourth, or tenth time, and I recall how he used to remonstrate with me to take them back since there was nothing in the world he could do to make them of use again. I don't know whether it was by chance or by design, but I remember that on those frequent visits to '*Ammu* Yaaqub's shop there were occasionally other rewards to be had. Literally next door to the shop was the gate of *el- midrash*—and as often as not there was some sort of treat, ranging from a portion of *halawa* (flour, oil, and sugar pudding) rolled in a piece of bread, or some fresh *kitchri* (kedgeree) with bread.

Father had another brother, Abraham. Though he and his family had emigrated to Persia just after I was born, '*Ammu* Abraham was destined to become the father-in-law of two of my sisters, Najiyya and Simha. Like the rest of the family, Abraham was at best a middler as far as material means were concerned. But he was a born leader and was easily and naturally chosen to be the *mukhtar* (elder) of the neighborhood in which he lived. In that capacity, he acted as a natural link between the inhabitants and the government of the day.

With no known profession or trade, '*Ammu* Abraham nevertheless managed to raise a large family—and shortly after the British came to Iraq he packed his things and crossed the border to Kermanshah. It was from there that he and his wife Sarah decided that my sister Najiyya was a good match for their eldest male child, Eliahu. One day in the spring of 1934, Sarah arrived at our home with one of her other sons, unannounced— and the match was concluded in a matter of minutes, my sister becoming betrothed to Eliahu sight unseen by either of the two parties.

Father's sisters, my aunts, were generally more fortunate. There were only two of them. Tuffaha, the younger, was the more impressive. Sturdy, tall, eminently good-looking, she was married to a member of the Birshan family whom she survived by close on fifty years. The house of Rubain Birshan, 'Amma (Auntie) Tuffaha's firstborn, hosted all the important events of the Jewish year — the *hatheema* on Pentecost, the all-night long *Hosha'na Rabba* closing the Feast of the Tabernacles, the various death anniversaries. Father attended these regularly, and as his guide I too was always there. There were also shorter visits, which Father made on occasions where some kind of help, financial or other, was needed and the rich members of the tribe were carefully chosen to approach, as, for example, when a daughter was being married off, or when Eliahu was declared bankrupt and imprisoned.

My other aunt on Father's side, 'Amma Hanina, lived with her family in another part of Iraq and I seldom had a chance of seeing her. Eventually, however, like so many other Jewish families from the provinces they were to move to Baghdad, but by that time I was fairly grown up and ceased to accompany Father on such social visits though I continued to take him to the synagogue on Saturdays and on the various feasts and holy days.

COPING WITH FATHER'S BLINDNESS

I was probably not much more than three years of age when I was taught to take Father to the synagogue, the barber, and various other places to which he used to go. In those days and in that particular society, to be blind was a kind of social affliction as well as a physical disability. Moving about the house and even giving a helping hand to mother in her daily chores posed no difficulty for Father; he also subsequently used to help me with my homework, especially in Hebrew and arithmetic. But to go out alone in the alleys and narrow streets of Baghdad, even for the shortest distance, was out of the question — not to speak of actually taking a job or otherwise trying to make a living.

Father was born around 1880 and married Mother at the turn of the century, when she was barely fourteen. The couple's firstborn was a baby boy who came to the world in 1903 or 1904. He was named Eliahu after my grandfather on Father's side and was fortunate enough to have been spared the bitter fate of those Iraqi subjects of the Sultan who in the course of World War I were hastily conscripted and sent to their almost certain deaths marching on foot, with a very few managing to reach the battlefront, not to speak of returning to their homes. After Eliahu, Mother gave birth to seven children—four daughters and three sons. However, of the three male babies born before me, only Eliahu was to survive, the two others—both named Nissim—dying shortly after birth. The daughters survived. Left thus with a family of three daughters and only one son, my parents made two other attempts comparatively late in life to add to the family's male population. It was thus that my younger sister Simha and I came to be born, with an interval of exactly three years.

The conditions in which I was born, late one night in December in Abu Shibil, a largely Muslim neighborhood of Old Baghdad, would today be impossible to describe as being anything other than destitute. Compared with many others, however, my family's situation was not exactly of the worst. With my birth, we became a family of six—father Baruch; mother Lulu; brother Eliahu and sisters Na'ima, Gurjiyya, and Najiyya; and myself. My eldest sister Na'ima had been married just less than three years before I was born.

Eliahu was my senior by a bit more than twenty years and, given Father's condition, was the sole breadwinner of the family. Right then he was doing fairly well; in partnership with a far relative, he had opened a store in a central location in Baghdad selling shirts and other articles of clothing and haberdashery, mainly to members of His Britannic Majesty's forces of occupation.

The precise circumstances in which Father lost his eyesight were related to me sometime in the 1970s by my eldest sister Na'ima, who was about nine years of age when the calamity fell. It all happened very suddenly some ten years before I was born. One late afternoon Father went to the house of Aunt 'Aziza's daughter Rosa to fetch Na'ima, who had been sent there by Mother on an errand and was rather late in coming back. On the way home, Na'ima remarked: "Baba, your eyes are extremely red, so red they seem to be burning!" That same night Father complained all the time of terrible pains in the head and the eyes—and next morning his eyesight was gone.

For what they were worth, all attempts on the part of the Meir Elias Hospital's staff to rescue Father's eyesight failed. But whereas the eye doctors pronounced the cause of blindness to be "acute inflammation," older members of the family insisted that the real cause lay somewhere else. The fact is that Father was a carpenter by profession and the Jewish Community Council at that time—the early 1910s—was still engaged in putting the finishing touches to a modern community hospital somewhere near Baghdad, the famous Meir Elias Hospital. Construction work and gardening called for the felling of a good number of old trees on the site, and Father was one of those assigned to do the work. It was as a divine penalty for engaging in this kind of work, so the lament went, that Father was blinded in both eyes, felling trees being a forbidden pursuit.

Despite the loss of his eyesight, Father managed to continue to work as a carpenter for a brief period; among other places, he worked in a carpentry shop near the Alliance school. He also had the idea of opening a grocery shop in which ten-year-old Na'ima became the person in actual charge. But World War I put an end to all this, what with so many of the able-bodied Jews being conscripted and herded for the long march through the desert from which virtually no one was to return—the so-called *safarbarlugh* in which the Ottoman Empire threw in everything in an abortive attempt to check the advance of the Allies.

Father had a fine analytical mind, was literate, and a true intellectual in his own way. A stoic by temperament, he was severe, self-disciplined, and craved order. Either because of an intrinsic liberality of approach or out of a realization that he lacked real authority over his children and the household generally, he was very tolerant with us children and took things rather philosophically.

Eventually Father started gradually to withdraw, realizing at last that his word no longer carried weight and that he was powerless really to influence things. What must have made matters even more difficult was the rapid and rather radical changes taking place all around—in the Jewish community, in the country as a whole, and inside our restricted family—and all this while he was rendered virtually a prisoner by his blindness. His visits to the synagogue became less frequent, as did his calls on relatives and friends. In fact, he had very few friends outside the extended family—relatives, in-laws, distant cousins, and such.

I never asked Father how and where he got his schooling. He knew the Torah and parts of the Prophets almost by heart, as well as the prayers, the *Haggadah,* and the various *berakhot* (blessings). He continued to preside over prayers and readings on all festive occasions—the Sabbath night *kiddush,* the two nights of the Seder of Passover, the festive night of Rosh Hashanah with the multitude of *berakhot* to be recited, the blessings said on Yom Kippur eves with the slaughter of sacrificial chickens, and the complex series of *berakhot* recited in the *succah,* which he himself used so expertly and elaborately to build in the days preceding *Succoth* (the Feast of Tabernacles).

Father was also the source of all the stories I heard in my childhood years. The tales ranged from straight accounts of Bible stories to ancient mythology. My acquaintance with the story of the Creation, Noah's Ark, Abraham and Esau, Isaac and Jacob, Joseph and his brethren, Moshe and the daughter of Pharaoh, and the first spy story ever concerning the occupation of Jericho—all these I first heard from Father in those long and extremely cold winter nights. But apart from biblical tales Father was also an unfailing source of lengthy stories full of strange creatures ranging from witches, good or wicked, to real giants and monsters. In retrospect I now feel sure those tales could not have been invented—and I keep wondering who had recounted them to Father in the first place.

| $\mathcal{M}$OTHER AND THE
PLACEBO EFFECT

$\mathcal{H}$ad she been a social scientist or a cultural anthro-
pologist, I am sure Mother would have become
a great advocate of the theory known as "the self-fulfilling prophecy" and
would have been the first to elaborate the theory, even before William I.
Thomas and Florian Znaniecki proposed it in their classic, *The Polish
Peasant in America and Europe.* Thomas and Znaniecki advanced the
thesis that in our study of man it is essential to find out how people define
situations in which they find themselves, since "if men define situations
as real, they are real in their consequences."

This, precisely, was the essence of Mother's philosophy of life, which
she never tired of repeating, always as a ready explanation for something
we kids complained was wrong. Apart from the usual traditional fear of
"making an opening for Satan," Mother's philosophy also taught that if
one ignored certain annoyances one would not be affected by them.

Usually, the doctrine was applied largely to psychological phenomena;
but at times it was extended to day-to-day physical complaints and afflictions. When, for instance, I or someone else in the household complained
of being "under the weather," of having no appetite for food, or that he
or she couldn't sleep, work, walk, or perform some little errand, Mother
would say something to the effect that "Well, naturally if you go on saying
that and believing in it, then in the end you will in reality feel unwell and
won't be able to do a thing. Better ignore it and try to persuade yourself
that you are perfectly all right!"

This conviction was so deeply ingrained in her approach to things that
Mother actually believed that if you wished something ardently and per-
sistently enough your wish would come true. This part of her philosophy
I never was able to accept or adopt. But I have grown to be a fairly firm believer in the workings of the self-fulfilling prophecy, also known to some
sociologists and in a different context as "the vicious circle"; whether
under her influence or not I have no way of knowing. In light of what I
came to learn in later years, I also started to see a close relationship be-

tween Mother's convictions in this regard and what one could call the placebo effect, which, as a number of recent studies had found, can palliate symptoms of a great variety of physical afflictions, ranging from asthma to congestive heart failure and even cancer.

I don't know whether it was some sort of extension of her overall philosophy of life, but there was a perpetual argument between us, which, although it took various forms and was caused by different factors, remained virtually the same. In the matter of food, for instance, Mother only rarely seemed to add the right amount of salt, pepper, lemon, sugar, or any of the other seasonings and ingredients in the meals she prepared. And so naturally the complaint was either that the food was too salty, too sharp, too sweet, or that it was not sufficiently seasoned. And Mother's standard reaction to this was something on the following lines: "Well, one really doesn't know what to do with you kids or how to conduct oneself in this household! Yesterday there was too much salt, today there's too little of it! Why can't you make up your mind? What do you want me to do?" It seems never to have crossed Mother's mind that this was a plausible state of affairs and that in both cases there was simply not the right amount of seasoning in the food.

Since it was almost always I who dared make those remarks and objections about the food, Mother decided to dub me *abu'l-triyya wil-mayazeen,* which, translated literally, means "the one of the chandelier and the scales." The reference, however, as I was to learn later, was to stars visible to the naked eye at nights, in this case Libra, for the scales; and one of the six visible—out of seven—stars of the Pleiades, for the chandelier. *Abu'l-triyya wil-mayazeen* (as *mayazeen* is plural of *mizan*) is said of one who procrastinates endlessly and doesn't seem to ever make up his mind, in addition to being extremely hard to please.

The story behind the saying tells of some newly married young man who, like all Baghdadis, had his bed moved up to the roof of the house in summer for a breeze of cooler air at nights. Lying on his back next to his wife, the guy stares at the stars and complains that he cannot possibly fall asleep right under the *triyya,* as the folks up there, charged with lighting the chandelier, might be tinkering with it, and it might fall smack on his head. So the wife duly switches places with him, but he immediately gets up moaning that the *mizan* (Libra) was right above his head and what would happen if one of the guys weighing the fares dropped a weight, or the whole scale for that matter, right on his head? The same, of course, happened when the wife patiently moved the whole bed to this side or that side of the roof! Hence *abu'l-triyya wil-mayazeen.*

With the passage of time, Mother's reactions on those lines became something of a family joke in which she sometimes shared, however reluctantly. Even I, with the notoriety I had earned for myself early in the proceedings as an insufferable perfectionist and splitter of hairs, got quite used to it and greeted the inevitable answer with nothing more serious than a smile and a shrug.

MOTHER

When I try to find words with which to describe Mother's features and her general bearing I can think only of the words "classic" and "noble." Socially, hers was a family mainly of merchants and in this respect seems to have been a little higher in status than my Father's. In those somewhat haphazard days, what with dowries being an inseparable part of any respectable match and with daughters being universally considered something of a burden to their parents, it was not uncommon for a good family with an impeccable "pedigree" to give their daughters' hand in marriage to young men hailing from families of a humbler social status.

Any one of a number of factors can be at work here: a sudden turn for the worse in business or some other economic setback that makes an offer of a suitable dowry unthinkable; the girl's homeliness or some other physical disadvantage or disability that tends to overshadow even a sizable dowry; or a status which the young man in question had acquired thanks to his own effort and which had raised him to a much higher social position than his origins would have justified. Until the 1940s, the other factor that would naturally come to mind in considering these socioeconomic "intermarriages," namely love and elopement, was hardly heard of.

In my parents' case, as far as I can gather, it was "pedigree" that decided the issue. To be sure, economically Father's immediate family was not of a status quite compatible with that of Mother's; but it seems that what the family lacked in terms of money and worldly possessions it appeared to have more than made up for by its social status — and thus the match was made and a young man of as indifferent a status as that of carpenter was taken in as a son-in-law.

I was named after my mother's father, Nissim Ezra Nissim. It is the custom among Iraqi Jews to name their children after dead parents, grandparents, and close relatives. (Naming a newborn after a living grandparent is not allowed since it is considered a bad omen — vaguely precipitating the death of the namesake.) A strict hierarchy is followed. First comes the paternal grandparents, the firstborn being always named after the dead grandfather or grandmother; then the maternal grandparents; and when all of these happen to be still alive the name of some close dead relative is chosen.

In later years, with the onset of independence and the increasing integration of Jews in educational and other national institutions, it became fashionable to give a child two names, one Hebrew and one Arabic. Thus the first son born to my brother Eliahu after Father's death was named Baruch/Farouq. This custom has been continued after the exodus to Israel. Modern, better-sounding, and more fashionable "status-names" such as Yoram, Tamar, Batia, Yigal, Ilan are usually appended to ancient Hebrew and biblical names such as Ezekiel, Shmuel, Rivka, Esther, Nehemia, Shlomo, and others — with the result that the child is later invariably identified by the more fashionable name and the other name is totally neglected. In our own household, for instance, we never call our firstborn Baruch but always Rony, although the first of his two names is Baruch, after his paternal grandfather's name.

My maternal grandfather and namesake was a merchant of some standing in the city, and his sons, the four who survived the uncommonly high infant mortality rate, all had some schooling. By the time I was old enough to understand these things, Mother's eldest brother, *Khalu* (uncle) Yuseif, had four grown-up sons of whom two were in business while the eldest, Yamein, was an officer in the Iraqi army and hence nicknamed Yamein el-Dhabit (the army officer). Uncle Menashe had moved to Abadan (El-Muhammara) in Persia and all I knew of him was a name. The two others, Ezra and Ephraim, both worked as accounts clerks in the country's leading transport firm, owned by Hesqail Nathaniel.

During a certain phase in my early childhood, when Eliahu was declared bankrupt and we had absolutely no money to subsist on, I used to go to the Nathaniel offices every Friday at noontime, where I would be handed a rupee, a contribution shared equally by the two uncles. I must add that in those days a rupee, which was equal roughly to two English shillings, used to buy enough subsistence food for two or even more days and I remember vividly how welcome it was in the house. Throughout that whole period, by some mishap or other, my uncles failed to give the rupee only once — and it was quite a sad day for the household and a great annoyance to me personally since I was suspected in some way of being responsible for the misfortune. The complaint, I think, was that I was "too damn proud and haughty" to ask. In fact I was both too shy and too proud to say a single word; I merely showed up, made my presence felt, waited patiently until one of the uncles had collected the other's share, took the rupee and left without so much as saying bye-bye, not to speak of "thank you" or any such civility.

SABBATH EVE HEN

For all her foibles and idiosyncrasies, Mother was a hard-working home-maker though a little too fussy sometimes. Being in charge of the house-hold, she tried very hard indeed to make ends meet. How she succeeded I don't know exactly; but the dishes she prepared, though poor in substance and ingredients, were tasty enough though seldom served in sufficiently large portions.

Mother was especially good at making the best of a bad or middling situation, putting to maximum use food ingredients which today would appear to be dismally little and inadequate. In later years—to give one notable example—when I had time or occasion to reflect on such things, I never managed to find a satisfactory explanation for the phenomenon of the Sabbath eve hen and the number of dishes extracted from it.

For one thing, the Sabbath eve chicken always posed a problem in our household because of its relatively high price. It is amazing how the prices of various foodstuffs and meats differed, both in relation to each other and in absolute terms, from what they are today in most countries of the world. In the Baghdad of my childhood and youth, for instance, the prices of beef and mutton were considerably lower than that of poultry.

Also, poultry was never sold by weight; it was sold by the piece, and the fatter the hen the higher the price it fetched. Incidentally, a tasty chicken had to be a hen since cocks were usually lean and devoid of all fat. The only occasion on which cocks were slaughtered in a self-respecting Jew-ish home was the eve of Yom Kippur, when the males of the family had to have a cock each for ritual sacrifice—and what used to save the day for us then were the females, who were privileged to have a sacrificial hen each.

The day for purchasing the Sabbath hen was Thursday, and there was always a good deal of weighing of pros and cons. First there was the crucial question as to the sum to be spent, everything else considered. Then when the bird was finally purchased and brought home, always by Mother, there would be some agonized guesswork as to its worth in terms of the price paid, the amount of fat it had in it, whether there were inside it some yet unformed eggs—and whether Mother had made the terrible but not un-common blunder of mistaking these egg yolks for a precious piece of fat usually to be located in the same vicinity — and which for some reason was called *waqqa*, the colloquial Jewish pronunciation for *waraqa*, Arabic for "sheet" (of paper). A hen's *waqqa* was so crucial an issue that the word was also used to denote something's or somebody's real worth — like in *binu*, or *biha, waqqa* (it, or he/she, has substance). It had, of course, to be a live hen; there never was any question of somebody selling or purchasing a slaughtered hen or part thereof.

Usually the first to examine the bird was Father, who after a good deal of examination and sizing up, would pronounce his considered verdict — a fat and fleshy bird at a reasonable price was the verdict that gave Mother most satisfaction. But when the verdict was unfavorable — and Father seldom erred in his estimates — Mother would say with the maximum of confidence she could muster but evidently mixed with doubts: "No, you're mistaken this time — and you will see . . ." The hen was then set free in the courtyard to await its encounter with the neighborhood *shohet* Friday morning to be properly slaughtered.

In anticipation of the good things to come throughout the following two days, Thursday's lunch and main meal invariably consisted of kedgeree and bread. A dish of Indian provenance, kedgeree was prepared in a number of different ways, but in Jewish Baghdad homes the ingredients were mainly rice and lentils, sometimes cooked with tomato slices but mostly without. After the rice and lentils were cooked, sesame oil was boiled in a separate pan, and after adding garlic and cumin and letting them fry to capacity, the contents of the pan were carefully added and the dish was ready to serve.

But this was the simplest and cheapest category of a kedgeree meal, the one we always had. The less poor used butter instead of sesame oil, while the really well off always had it either with two fried eggs a head, a cupful of yogurt, or both. They also had large enough portions not to need to eat it with bread. This kind of kedgeree meal I had only very occasionally, and this only at the homes of some well-to-do relatives.

Although Sabbath meals had to include fish and a bit of mutton, Mother must have been a genius judging by the way she managed to make a poor lone hen suffice for at least two whole meals for all the seven of us — and some more. Slaughtered on Friday morning, the bird was first cleaned and salted, then after the required interval it was carefully skinned, with the breast, the wings, and sometimes the lower back preserved so that the whole skin remained as intact as possible. The skin thus extracted was a most important part of the hen, not only because virtually all the fat was preserved therein but also because it was essential for preparing Sabbath day's main meal called the *t'beet,* which, roughly translated, means an overnight dish.

After being washed and scrubbed again and again, the skin — with only the wings and the breast left intact — is filled with rice, tomato slices, turmeric, salt, pepper, and slices of whatever meat there was in the hen's stomach, then sewn and put aside. That would make the meatiest and largest *hashwa* (stuffed skin). Other smaller pieces of skin, mainly that of the neck, are somehow rescued and similarly stuffed, though never so richly and generously. When every venue has thus been explored and all the precious stuffed portions prepared, a large pot is put on the fire and is suitably oiled with either sesame oil or — if you could afford such a luxury — with chicken fat. And when this is boiled, the stuffed chicken and the other minor *hashwat* are added, then a little water and tomato juice, then a quantity of rice and finally more water and seasoning. When the whole contents of the pot are half or quarter cooked, it is usually shifted to a very small fire, on a kerosene cooker or, better still, on live coal. Then, after covering the pot with a multitude of specially made rough cushions and rags, it is left right there until Sabbath noon, a remove of at least twenty hours.

The *t'beet* was usually served at lunchtime on Sabbath, but in winter when the weather was very cold an exception was made and it was served late in the morning, directly after the men had returned from their prayers. In those cases, more water would have been added to the pot and the stuffed chicken usually swam in a kind of very thick rice and tomato soup.

The other main chicken dish was served on Sabbath eves, and the ingredients were the legs, the skinned neck and some other bits and pieces skillfully preserved from the hen. The liver however had to be prepared separately, always by grilling it, since, because of the amount of blood it contained, it was forbidden to boil, fry, or prepare it any other way.

Now the way in which the *t'beet* was kept, the state of the fire on which it spent the night, and the extent of the cooking that had gone into it before it was laid to bed were all tricky matters that no housewife could hope to juggle in such precise coordination as to be certain of the quality of the finished article. It was a haphazard affair, mostly a matter of luck, and often there were hitches. The flame was not exactly the right height and then the *t'beet* was either not well done or not sufficiently steaming hot or both. Or there was too much rice inside the chicken for the precious contents to be sufficiently cooked — or too much water, or heat, or any one of a score of things for the dish to be cooked just right and taste just right. When any of these mishaps happened and some member of the family—usually I—was cheeky enough or inconsiderate enough to make a comment, Mother's reaction was uniform. She would shrug a shoulder and say, *n'seeb el-Shebbath* (the Sabbath's lot)—implying that there was nothing anyone could have done about it.

Compared with other days of the week, we must have spent a small fortune on Sabbath meals. Beside the fried fish and the chicken soup and rice, the Sabbath eve meal had to include certain other fairly expensive items whose nature depended on the season and the weather. In later years, when I was old enough to ignore these customs and after Father's death, I came to miss these and other festive occasions very much indeed—and was always delighted to partake in one of them when there was an opportunity. These came mostly when I happened to be visiting at the homes of Eliahu or Na'ima—my brother and sister and both my seniors by more than fifteen years; but later we were to attend them at the home of my wife's parents, where a crowd always gathered on the eves of the main feasts, especially the two Rosh Hashanah eves and the Seder nights.

Almost in spite of herself and certainly not out of choice, Mother became the decision maker in practically everything affecting the household. What with Father being homebound and often even something of a burden to her, my brother out all day earning us all a living, my sisters and myself being too little or too unimportant to count, Mother had to take charge of things—and in order to make ends meet she had to be rather strict and extremely prudent where the spending of money was concerned.

This became a habit with Mother, a second nature almost, and when my elder brother finally married she couldn't part with the habit. At first things went smoothly, but with the passage of time and after a short period of apprenticeship my new sister-in-law Hella started asserting herself, if for no other reason than that she was the wife of the sole breadwinner in the household. Arguments started, usually over small things, and soon Eliahu became involved, having to listen to the complaints and supposedly act as a judge between the combatants. Mother's main disadvantage in this running quarrel was that her daughter-in-law had all the time in the world to relate to Eliahu her own, allegedly distorted version of what had happened the day before, while she, poor soul, had virtually no access to her own son.

The rift became worse immediately after Hella gave birth to her first baby—and although it was a girl and therefore nothing much to boast of, she became increasingly impatient with a state of affairs in which a mother-in-law seemed to dominate the arena—not to mention a homebound father-in-law, two fast growing sisters-in-law, and one rather spoiled brother-in-law. Apart from the sheer cost of feeding five superfluous mouths there was the problem of crowdedness, which must have made life extremely difficult for the new mother. I am sure that the one decisive factor which prevented a final breach and consequent physical separation was the economic difficulties such a separation would have posed, since it meant that Eliahu would maintain and support two households, and we were altogether too poor to afford that kind of luxury.

Chapter 4 | $\mathcal{N}$A'IMA

a'ima, my eldest sister, died peacefully in her
sleep one night in November 1980, aged seventy-
seven. A few years before her death, I made a habit of visiting her in her
tiny immigrant housing flat in Netanya, where I usually stayed a night or
two. Na'ima's memory was phenomenal. For hours on end she used to
answer my queries about those early days, describing the conditions in
which our family lived before and just after my birth. One day she recited
to me this old rhymed saying of the Jews:

> *Hayi lulayi aghdha khfifi*
> *'Ala walad id lat'shilon*
> *Akel mamghatta la-taklon*
> *U'ala shein maysigh yimmighdon.*
> (This is a land whose ground is shaky. Never raise a
> hand to a child; don't eat anything that has been lying
> uncovered; and never get worked up no matter what the
> cause.)

Na'ima was a very energetic, highly intelligent, and extremely practical
person. Since the age of nine, when our father was blinded, she never
stopped working. Shortly after that disaster, Father decided to open a
small neighborhood grocery shop—and for the two or three years it took
him to go broke it was Na'ima who managed the place—keeping an eye,
doing the accounts, weighing, dealing with the cash, and so on. Our
brother, Eliahu, who was her senior by a year or two, tended, like all Jewish male children of those days, to be spoiled and he did not so much
as lift a finger—the more so because he was attending the Midrash Talmud Torah, while Na'ima stayed home like the majority of her female
contemporaries.

Na'ima's wedding took place in the fall of 1919, five years before I was born. Things then looked quite ominous in Baghdad, what with the British occupation and the imminent arrival of King Faysal I, who was eventually enthroned as King of Iraq in August of 1921. Na'ima related that the wedding was not properly attended, since many of the relatives and friends who were supposed to come failed to do so as they were apprehensive of leaving their homes.

It was a good match by the standards of those days. The bridegroom, Salih Tahhan, came from a solid background though he was not of what the Jews then would have termed "good family." The Tahhans were a typical family of thoroughly acclimatized Baghdad Jews with very deep roots in the place. They lived in the Dihidwana quarter, which like Abu Shibil, the quarter in which we lived as subtenants, was predominantly Muslim with a few Jewish households scattered all over. The word *tahhan,* from which the family's name derived, means "grinder," and the family owed its name to the fact that in their house in a far corner of el-Dihidwana they had for years operated a wheat grain-grinding device, extremely primitive in its design and working with the indispensable aid of oxen. Immediately after the Great War, with the coming of the British, larger and more "modern" mills were introduced and business for the Tahhans became so slack they decided to close down shop.

It did not take the Tahhans long to acquire new skills — and the brothers managed to rent a small workshop-cum-jewelry store in the Bazaar of the Goldsmiths (suq el-siyyagh). The dominant figure in the family was Salih's elder brother Khedhouri, who in addition to opening the jewelry business also rebuilt the old grinding mill site plus residence, and it was in this new house that the families of both Salih and Khedhouri lived for many years. Khedhouri was a wily fellow and a true survivor. During the years of World War I he actually managed, with the help of money or gold he had on him as well as of his sturdy constitution, to escape to safety, and came back to Baghdad shortly after he was conscripted with thousands of other unfortunates who were sent to the front after a panicky campaign of general mobilization, the so-called *safarbarlugh (seferberlik),* from which hardly one of the conscripts managed to return to his family.

Next door to the Tahhans lived Abraham Habba, whose wife Farha was the famed *Hanna el-qabli's* (Midwife Hanna's) eldest daughter. About the Abraham-Farha match a story used to make the rounds in Mother's close family circle. Gossip had it that Farha, shortly before her marriage, used to work as domestic help in the household of some rich Jewish merchant with a great reputation for lewdness and lechery. Although married and with several children, he was said to have managed to seduce and bed practically every good-looking maid who happened to have worked for the family—making some of them pregnant.

Young and highly attractive, Farha did not escape that fate—but the man was a clever manipulator and he always managed to find some honorable way out. In most cases, the stratagem was simple enough and it always worked. Since the girls in question were poor and since no Jewish girl in those days could possibly find a husband, however humble himself, without paying some kind of dowry, our lecher simply helped in marrying his pregnant housemaids off quickly enough for the whole affair not to come to the open. He also took care of the expense that the virginity problem entailed. It was exactly thus, so the story went, that poor Farha was spared a fate worse than death.

THE TAHHANS' HOUSEHOLD

My visits at the Tahhans' household were pretty frequent. At the age of five to eight our economic situation was already deteriorating and I often went to Na'ima for an occasional meal, sweets, dessert, or some fruit since her family was relatively well off. Na'ima, her husband, and her first four children then lived in a section of the Tahhans' household, in which the whole Tahhan family lived—the ageing but still fairly active parents, Khedhouri their first-born and his family of five, my brother-in-law Salih and his family, and his two younger brothers who were still unmarried.

It was Khedhouri, however, who was the undisputed master of the household. He was the first-born and Salih's senior by several years, and his sons were grown-ups by then, with the eldest already helping his father in the business and the second, Naji, studying to be a doctor. It is difficult nowadays to impart the kind of awe the word *doctor* used to evoke in those days; there was a kind of challenge, of defiance even, in the very fact that a boy who had been raised in those circumstances and those surroundings would so much as dream of becoming a medical doctor. But Khedhouri was a man of will and determination—and according to Na'ima's account he had vowed to make of his son Naji a doctor come what may. In the event, indeed, Naji proved to be a little too thick-headed and, despite the superhuman effort he made to master his subjects, it was only by using his various wiles and his authority as a father that Khedhouri finally managed to be the proud father of a real doctor.

Needless to say, Naji's studies—the fact alone that he had to study and prepare his lessons — made him a privileged member of the Tahhan tribe. Alone among them he had a room of his own, with a large inner balcony which he used to stroll endlessly back and forth while memorizing his difficult material. And when Naji was at his studies we children were ordered to keep quiet lest we disturb him or distract his attention.

Meals at the Tahhans' household were normally prepared collectively in huge pots and pans, and as was the custom in Jewish homes in those days certain dishes were made on certain days of the week, especially the last three days of it: kedgeree on Thursdays; sour-sweet *kibba* (meat balls cooked with vegetables) on Fridays; and the inevitable *t'beet* (chicken cooked with rice and kept overnight on a small fire) on Saturdays. Midday — and main — meals during the rest of the week depended largely on the material situation of individual families, with the main question being largely whether or not meat would be an ingredient.

Usually, there was one day for fish — for poor and rich alike since fish in those days was far less expensive than meat. In this context it is interesting to add that the organized Jewish community's finances came largely if not wholly from the taxes it levied on kosher meat (*lahem kashair*), a circumstance which made the prices of meat at the Jewish butcher much higher than those charged for the same meat at Muslim butchers. Nevertheless, in all my experience of life in Baghdad no Jewish household even thought of buying nonkosher meat (*lahem taraif*) — not even those with no tradition or desire to observe *kashrut* laws. The paradox was that members of some of these same families, while not hesitating for a moment to eat out of a tin of imported nonkosher corned beef or some other food with meat ingredients, would not come near to a local nonkosher butcher.

I don't remember spending much time during these visits at the Tahhans' household. Apart from the meals and the goodies — the former were always plentiful and fresh from the pot, the latter a simple matter of luck and good timing — I had little to do there. Khedhouri's male children were too old for me, while Na'ima's were too small; and there always was this annoyance of having to keep quiet, since Naji seemed to be ever there, studying and memorizing his impossible lessons.

But my attachment to Na'ima and her household was to continue for a long time. As usual in such cases, the two Tahhan brothers were shortly to feel obliged to live separately — whether because of the growth of the two families or some other difficulty I don't know. They also set up separate businesses, remaining, however, in the same line — gold and moneylending. In the course of the coming years, Na'ima and her family alternately lived with us as subtenants (when we were still living with Eliahu's growing family), first tenants, or separately. But somehow the links remained strong, and throughout it was Na'ima who usually extended help to us in one way or other—food, small cash, and services.

Na'ima's family of seven immigrated to Israel in 1951, the year of the Jews' exodus from Iraq. A few weeks after their arrival she was to lose one of her three sons, who was shot accidentally while in military training. Some two decades later, with her children all married and settled, Na'ima spent the last ten years or so of her life living alone in her flat in what became a slum area of Natanya. When we were living in Ramat Gan, we often used to invite ourselves to a festive meal of *pacha* (lamb stomach and intestines stuffed with meat and rice) on a Saturday; but after Salih died and there remained no one to make it to Tel Aviv to buy the ingredients from the Tikva quarter butchers, we used to go in summer to stay for the day—and later when we moved to Jerusalem and my wife couldn't always accompany me because of the children, I made a custom of going to see Na'ima for a long weekend or a few days during the week, which I used to divide between mornings on the beach and afternoons and evenings for long and interesting accounts of my childhood and our family, which Na'ima with her fabulous memory recounted with tireless enthusiasm. I used to take notes for my projected memoirs of Baghdad—and by the time Na'ima died in November 1980 I had managed to recapture much of that distant past.

SIGHTS, SOUNDS, FLAVORS, SMELLS

Another attraction at the Tahhan-Habba complex was the *m'tayyirchi* next door—a fully grown man probably in his thirties who kept a flock of pigeons, tending and feeding them like they were his own offspring. At certain hours of the day he would shoo them with his long pole and they would take off, roaming the sky where he directed, with him watching with admiration and fascination and some visible anxiety. It was only years later that I learned the reason for the man's anxious look: Our *m'tayyirchi* neighbor—presumably an Iraqi equivalent of what in the West is known as a bird-watcher—was actually engaged in a kind of mock warfare with adversaries from near and far, the war aim being limited to attracting pigeons from the enemy's flock and then adding them to his own. How this was accomplished—how pigeons from one flock were drawn to join those in another, or to one particular one amongst the lot—remains a mystery to me.

Complaints were often made to the police by *m'tayyirchis* who had suffered heavy losses in their unwieldy wars. The trouble, however, was that
the testimony of a *m'tayyirchi* was not acceptable to the courts owing to
the bad name members of the band had earned for themselves. The result
was that such complaints were looked into only if the complainant managed to provide outside witnesses. These and various other difficulties
notwithstanding, however, the art of the *m'tayyirchi* was practiced widely
enough and the number of such bird-watchers was sufficiently large for
a few specialized vendors roaming the alleyways of Baghdad shouting,
"*Z'arti, z'arti*, where are the bird owners?" — *z'arti* being the choice feed
for their birds.

It was also during my frequent visits in the Tahhans' household that I
caught my first glimpses of the highly colorful and variegated life of the
more downtrodden neighborhoods of Old Baghdad. This was partly because, while a few comparatively well off and fairly prosperous Jewish
families of the status of the Tahhans and the Habbas chose to stick to
their own houses deep in places like the Dihidwana quarter, these overwhelmingly Muslim neighborhoods were fast deteriorating owing to the
departure of their original inhabitants, their gentry so to speak.

The roads themselves, indeed, which I had to tread walking to Na'ima's
house, were full of sights and sounds and curiosities that were to leave
indelible impressions in the imagination of an observant and searching
young soul. The shouts themselves, the endless disputations and arguments and the extremely juicy curses — these encounters were in the nature of veritable revelations. Even the ways of speech, as well as many of
the expressions, were often a surprise.

To be sure, the Jews of Baghdad had their own Arabic vernacular which
they used in their own houses and in their daily contacts with each other,
while at the same time managing to speak with their Muslim neighbors in
the latter's own colloquial Arabic. The fact, however, was that people in
every neighborhood and of every ethnic and/or religious sect and class
in Baghdad had a slightly different way of expressing themselves. This
was true even where the Jewish community was concerned, what with
differences in class and education being so marked and the fact that there
were certain neighborhoods where certain groups of very poor and illiterate Jews used to live, especially those who in the course of the years came
to Baghdad in search of work and a better life.

These usually engaged in the most menial of occupations — porters,
domestic help, latrine cleaners, washerwomen, garbage collectors. They
almost invariably hailed from the north of the country, sometimes from

further north, as far as Persia, Afghanistan, Kazakhstan, and Georgia. Curiously, some of these were considered models of beauty, mostly, of course, the females. The Georgians especially had the singular distinction of an adjective coined in the name of their native land. As a mark of their special beauty — light complexion, blue or green eyes, usually small and delicate features, especially their mouths and noses — the words *gurji* and *gurjiyya* (masculine and feminine for "beautiful" as well as for "Georgian") actually became popular proper first names. This is not surprising in a community where light complexions and small facial features were celebrated.

The sounds, too, were a veritable celebration. Passing through the Hinnuni bazaar, you heard the shouts of the peddlers and the small shopkeepers and the dozens of strolling packmen in praise of the wares they usually carried on their heads, some of the more prosperous accompanied by donkeys that carried the loads. Many of these used to come from surrounding towns and villages where they grew fruit and vegetables in their small farms — apples, oranges, lemons, sweet lemons, apricots, pears, grapes; onions, garlic, cucumber, potatoes, cabbage.

Toward the end of the morning — which in these cases was long before noontime — those of the peddlers who failed to sell all their wares in the bazaar turned to chant the praises of their wares through the lanes and alleys, where people who could not or would not take the trouble of going to the *suq* to shop would appear in their doorsteps to engage in lengthy arguments about prices and finally take what vegetables and fruit they needed for their households. It was always men who were seen dealing with these peddlers, especially where Muslim households were concerned. No self-respecting Muslim woman would want, or be allowed, to show her face to a total stranger.

There were also the vendors who settled in selected strategic spots in the neighborhoods shouting their rhymed praises of their goods: "stork's eggs" (*beidh el-laglag*, a large, colorful sweet that melts at a mere touch of the tongue), sugared sesame-seed pancakes (*sumsumiyya*), boiled salted chick-peas (*lablabi*), fried dumplings (*kahi*), boiled turnips (*shalgham*), string beans, broad beans, bride's fingers, and fresh and dried fruits of all provenance — apples, apricots, grapes, plums, pears, figs — all advertised either by province or country they come from or by their quality and degree of freshness.

Handymen and petty professionals also roamed the quarters of Baghdad peddling their services, some of them looking foreign. There was the knife sharpener (*tcharrakh*); the so-called china "tailor" (*khayyat far-*

furi), who mended broken china and earthenware plates; the dealer in old articles of clothing and household utensils (*abul bai'*); and one who felled trees and chopped wood for heating (*kassar khashab*).

Suq Hinnuni was, of course, a mixed bazaar, even though the Jews were more prominent owing to their numbers as well as economic predominance. However, Jewish shopkeepers seldom dealt with agricultural produce, unless they happened to own larger grocery shops that sold certain fruits, in which case they made their wholesale purchases at the *'alwa* not far away, where wholesale prices were charged and sales were made by auction. But in the Hinnuni bazaar all the butchers were Jews, owing to the *kashrut* problem, Jews naturally not being allowed to purchase their meats from a gentile. These butchers took their live sheep, which they had purchased from Muslim farmers, to the slaughterhouse where it was seen that they were properly slaughtered, their insides duly examined; they were then skinned and the mutton taken to the shops to sell. In case some of the sheep slaughtered proved deficient, nonkosher, the butcher sold them to his Muslim counterpart at a much lower price.

Altogether, the price of mutton at a Jewish butcher was at least one-and-a-half times, sometimes twice higher than the nonkosher variety. Cows were never slaughtered for sale in kosher shops; beef was indeed considered inferior to mutton, partly because it had less fat. Only the poor amongst the Muslims ate it. Altogether the price scale of meats of all kinds was the exact opposite of what it is today: beef was cheaper than mutton, mutton considerably cheaper than poultry, and fish was the cheapest of all.

Also, as the morning progressed and noontime approached, butchers reduced their prices since, with no refrigeration of any kind available, meats could never be stored overnight, in summer not even till evening. Dealers in fish were in the same unhappy situation, and only those who sold fowl were in a position to maintain reasonably stable prices since no one ever sold or consented to buy a slaughtered hen or cock. Licensed kosher slaughterers were always near at hand in that section of Suq Hinnuni in which fowl was sold.

In this respect eggs presented quite a difficulty. Not a few of the eggs purchased proved to be bad or partly bad owing to the heat or some other natural cause, and it was a long and rather risky procedure when an egg had to be returned to the grocer or peddler, since in order to prove the egg was bad you had first to take it home, break it into a frying pan or boil and peel it — and only then could you take it back to the grocer and ask for a replacement or for your money back. In case your egg was already in the pan or half-boiled there was always the problem as to what, precisely, constituted a bad egg, with the grocer insisting that it was only the yolk that got broken, got a mere dot of red or black—and that that doesn't make a bad egg!

And there always were the porters, who invariably spoke in a language only they understood. The fact is that virtually all good porters were Kurds hailing from the north. Sturdy, strong, and patient as mules, they seemed capable of carrying unlimited weights. Their strength and their power of endurance were so phenomenal that a saying used to make the rounds in Baghdad, laying it down that "were it not for the Kurds the donkeys would've perished" (*lawla al-Akrad la-halaka al-hameer*).

In Baghdad in those days donkeys were widely used as a means of transportation of goods of all kinds, and in certain cases the owners rode them to get from one place to another. Owing to the huge burdens they were made to carry and the long distances, these long-suffering creatures often showed signs of slackness and refused to keep the pace their owners chose for them. The result was either heavy strikes dealt with long, sturdy rods or deep insertions with especially large needles, or both. The practice was so widespread that the Baghdad municipality (*amanat al-'asima*) issued strict orders forbidding the use of needles and, worse still, limited the length of the rods used to a mere thirty centimeters. This made it unbearably difficult for the drivers to make their point to their beasts of burden, what with the short rods often causing less pain to the beaten than to those who did the beating. It was then that bitter complaints were often heard, made by tired and profusely sweating owners while prodding their donkeys with their inadequate tools to keep going. Addressing their poor donkeys, some of these drivers would cry, in a somewhat low voice: "Get you going, fellow, suddenly you have acquired new uncles and caring relatives!" (*Dee, imshi! Tul'olak e'mam wu-khwal!*)

Some donkeys, however, received special treatment. Those of a breed called the Hassawi, for instance, were considered too good or too "intelligent" to carry such stuff as garbage, and were used only to carry fruit, watermelon, dates, honey, and people, while the dirty work was left for those of the Shamiyya breed to do. The females of the Hassawis, unlike those of the Shamiyya variety, were also said to give birth only once in a lifetime. Another specialty of the Hassawis is that they wouldn't enter an alley or a side road with which they were not familiar, but would stop short waiting for their owners to lead the way.

Needless to say, all these were aspects of life in Baghdad in which foreign travelers from the West could see nothing but dirt and squalor. To give one example, this is how Miss Freya Stark, a British lady who traveled and wrote extensively about the Arab world—and who was usually considered "pro-Arab"—had to say about her initial impressions of Baghdad. "What you first see of the Caliphs' city," she wrote in *Baghdad Sketches,*

> is a most sordid aspect; a long low straight street, a dingy hybrid between East and West, with the unattractiveness of both. The crowd looks unhealthy and sallow, the children are pitiful, the shops are ineffective compromises with Europe; and the dust is wicked, for it turns to blood-poisoning at the slightest opportunity, and bears out the old Babylonian idea of an atmosphere inhabited by Demons.

And so on. Naturally, this certainly is not my idea of the Baghdad of my childhood and youth, though the words were written at roughly the same time I was capable of taking in and absorbing the city's sights, its sounds, its flavors, and its smells. Sigrid Nunez, a gifted American novelist writing about one of her characters—the American-born daughter of a Chinese father and a German-born mother—captures the essence of it in this brief exchange about the father:

> He always wanted to go back. He always missed China.
> But he was only ten years old when he left.
> Yes, but that's what counts—where you spent those first years, and your first language. That's who you are.
> *A Feather on the Breath of God* (HarperCollins, New York, 1995)

BAGHDAD'S FAMOUS BAZAARS

A few years later, when I was about ten, Eliahu's business moved to Suq el-Saray, in the center of the commercial hubbub and where almost all the bazaars were situated. It was also nearer where we happened to be living at the time. This made it easier for me to go there, mostly to stay when there was no school and every working day after school. My job was to take Eliahu's lunch, which consisted of three dishes placed carefully in a three-floor tin gadget with a satchel, one for cooked meat, one for the inevitable *plaw* (fried boiled rice), and one for the dessert.

On the way to the Suq el-Saray carrying Eliahu's lunch, I passed through Suq el-Bazzazin, Baghdad's largest marketplace, which specialized in cloths of all descriptions, to be designed and sewn at home later for clothes for members of the family, either by the mistress of the house herself or by a professional tailor (*khiyyata*), always a female who did the work at the owner's home and left at sundown.

Then there was Suq el-Safafir, where house utensils large and small were made, and where the din of hammers beating at the hot raw material would have been unbearable were it not for the songs and the funny tales chanted by the sweating laborers. Craftsmen in this particular *suq*, all Muslims, used to a man to close shop on Fridays—unlike other Muslim merchants and shopkeepers who, while the Jews predominated in the various lines of clothes and haberdashery, usually took their week's holiday on Saturdays.

While living in some other Muslim neighborhood, not far from the previous one, I used to pass through Suq el-Shorja on my way to Eliahu. The bazaar—also known as Suq el-'Atatir—was lined almost entirely of grocery stores where all kinds of cereals, dried fruit, spices, and jams were sold. Except for a few stores, and the confectionaries (which were all Jewish), the shops here were all run by Muslims. A few of the confectionaries, which generally made and sold the usual local sweets and cookies, specialized in *man el-sama,* a line in which the Jews predominated. The so-called *qadrasi* cookie was made from this raw material, which was imported from Isfahan, in Persia, in a fairly rough state and then boiled, compressed, and made into small round cookies, usually with one or two almonds thrown in.

It is interesting to note here that the name *man el-sama* itself (meaning *man* from the sky) is in the Jewish vernacular, *man* being a Hebrew word. The reason for the name is embodied in the story told in the Hebrew Bible (Exodus 16:13–21). It appears that, in their forty-year long wandering in the Sinai desert prior to their arrival in the promised land, the Jews who had been expelled from Egypt subsisted on something that fell from the sky especially for that purpose—a sweet, sticky, honeylike, heavy-dropped juice. As told in the book of Exodus (Revised Standard Version), observing the quails that came up in the evening covering the camp, and in the morning when the dew went up, "there was on the face of the wilderness a fine, flake-like thing, fine as hoarfrost on the ground." When the people of Israel saw this, "They said to one another, 'What is it?' . . . And Moses said to them, 'It is the bread which the Lord has given you to eat.'" In Hebrew, the question that the Israelites asked was "*man whu?*"—*man* for "what." Hence *man el-sama.*

Peddlers, vendors, and criers of all descriptions used to crowd Suq el-Shorja, usually offering foodstuff items brought by them from nearby

villages and townlets in the mornings and which they had to finish selling by evening. Scarcely any of the goodies I saw could I have afforded by
what little money I usually had on me, if any. Such sweets were usually
brought home Fridays by Eliahu when *he* could afford it.

In later years, when in my teens, I made the acquaintance of the city's
other bazaars, venturing to go farther west along the main street, Shar'i
al-Rashid. Apart from the variety of stores, teashops, restaurants, and
mosques, there were side streets and alleyways as well as *suqs* to ex-
plore. Just opposite Al-'Aquliyya quarter was the most colorful and best-
organized fruit marketplace in town. It offered the most expensive fruits
usually just arrived from Persia, Syria, and the north of the country.

A little farther west was Al-Mutanabbi street, which led to the main
government offices and ministries, and where in addition to the old houses
of the city's gentry were situated the offices of many lawyers and medical doctors as well as the editorial offices and presses of at least two daily
newspapers and three weeklies, the latter usually rather short-lived.

Walking a little farther west, passing through a number of the best restaurants (*mat'am el-shams* among others) and teashops (*gahwat Hasan
el-'Ajmi,* for one), we finally reach Suq el-Haraj (literally "the noisy bazaar"), the allusion being to the shouting auctioneers offering all and
sundry, from bags of goods to secondhand furniture being sold by owners
who needed the money for more essential purposes, usually subsistence.
It was in that *suq* that I used occasionally to have a dish of *kebab,* out of
sight because the meat was obviously nonkosher.

There were almost no places where you could buy a cold drink, let
alone ice cream. Ice cream and bottled cold drinks were unknown, and
ice itself was rarely available, except in the month of fasting, Ramadhan,
when those who could afford it drank cold juices on breaking the fast—
when the month happened to fall in the hot summer days, that is. By the
end of the 1920s, when ice started being produced in quantity, ice cream
became available, made usually of orange or melon juice, and occasionally of milk. It was only in the mid-1930s that soda and other bottled cold
drinks were introduced, this time by Syrians such as 'Abdu el-Shami,
who specialized in a variety of ice creams, and Hajji Khairi el-Halabi, who
came from Aleppo and was known especially for the *sherbet el-loz* (almond
juice) he made and sold.

Chapter 5 | £ARLY INITIATIONS

*F*ather was my only source of mental nourishment for at least the first seven years of my life. Homebound and with pretty little to do, he used to spend hours explaining things that used to perplex me and answering my nagging questions. I don't remember having asked any of the questions usually put to parents by clever and highly imaginative boys—such as the one as to whether a crocodile would overpower a tiger or the other way round. My questions—judging at least from the answers I still remember—were of a much "higher" character: What was in the sky and "further up"; the mystery that was the moon; the source of the sun's heat and why it had the habit of rising and then setting; the concept and precise nature of God, His possible shape and His ways of making decisions; the angels that dwelt in Heaven; the nature of Heaven and Hell and the good deeds and the bad that earned or denied one admittance thereto. To all these queries and bewilderments Father's answers were ready and very definite, at least at first; but under further pressure and nagging he would relent a little, adding however that at his age he would not want to entertain doubts of the kind I was insinuating.

Years later, in my late adolescence, I read somewhere about some rather novel concepts, variously called "the religion of nature" or the theory of evolution; when I confronted Father with the thesis that the universe and our world with it came into being without anybody's orders or whims, he would merely reiterate his old argument. All his life long, he would explain, he was guided and lived by the beliefs and doctrines he was taught to observe. He believed in God and in the account of the Creation given in the Torah, in the Ten Commandments, Moses' mission, resurrection of the dead, Heaven and Hell—and he was not now going to entertain so drastic a revision of these beliefs as was suggested by my outlandish reflections and "inventions."

For my part, apart from a very brief period in my adolescence years in which I became deeply religious, I was always an agnostic and remain one.

As far as religious observance was concerned, the general attitude in our home was one of tolerance, of live-and-let-live, although throughout the first sixteen years of my life no one dared openly to flout the requirements of Sabbath observance or the main precepts and prescriptions connected with other feasts and holy days. Yom Kippur was, of course, the holiest of all these holy days, and fasting was universal, except for children of up to age thirteen who were on "the step-by-step fast," *som el-daghaj,* and allowed to eat at midday. It was in my eleventh or twelfth year, however, that I voluntarily decided to have my first regular fast; this must have been during my religious phase. However, although I managed somehow to last the day I found the ordeal too great to bear. That was my last as well as my first full fast.

I don't think that my failure early in the proceedings to observe the Sabbath and to fast on Yom Kippur had anything to do with the fact that I never had a proper bar mitzvah ceremony. Indeed, what is now known throughout the Jewish world as bar mitzvah was in Baghdad called simply *libs el-tefillin,* "putting on the phylacteries." It was a simple ceremony performed in the synagogue, where the boy is called to the reading of a portion of the Law—usually the last portion (*maftir*), which gives him the opportunity of reading the prophetic lesson (*haftarah*). Except for the middle classes and the well to do, there were usually no accompanying celebrations or the kind of gaudy displays now associated with the event. For reasons I do not recall very clearly, but which must have had to do with the expense involved, I skipped the synagogue ceremony—and the first time I recall I ever put on phylacteries was when I was obliged to do so when attending morning prayers during the *shiv'a* for my mother in the mid-1960s.

I believe that Father, had he had the kind of authority which fathers used to exercise even in those early days of approaching modernity, would have insisted on my having a proper synagogue ceremony when I came of age. But by that time Father was fast losing control of things in the household and among us children. He simply was not in a position to influence events in the family any more in a meaningful way.

DINA AND HER DAUGHTERS

Sometime in the late 1920s, when brother Eliahu's business was relatively thriving and shortly before his engagement to Hella, we were living—again as subtenants—in *Beit Dina* (Dina's House), just off the main road of Taht el-Takya, a largely Jewish neighborhood. Dina and her husband Abraham were decent folks and strictly observant Jews, but for some unspecified reason all the children they managed to have were two daughters who were to give them no rest or peace of mind.

At the time, the two daughters were "nymphets" in their early teens, probably in their eleventh and twelfth years respectively. 'Aziza and Nazima were their names, and at first sight they didn't look at all related, the older one, 'Aziza, being a full-fledged brunette with dark eyes while her younger sister was much lighter in complexion. Also, judging by the kind of games they were capable of playing, and the cosmetic devices they occasionally insisted on using despite their mother's protestations, the two sisters must have been of a very special breed indeed.

'Aziza and Nazima were to play a decisive role in my sex education. For the fact is that, for better or for worse, being the only male about with whom they thought they could take some liberty I became the focus of their interest and devotion. For the rest of the house—my parents and theirs, and Eliahu and my three sisters—there naturally seemed nothing special in all that. It was deemed quite natural for two young girls with no brothers of their own to pamper and to spoil a handsome boy of four.

But the sisters had other designs—and soon enough they managed to make me a willing party to these. In his essay on infantile sexuality, Freud somewhere speaks of the regular existence of a sexual instinct in childhood. He criticizes those of his colleagues who, though admitting occasionally that small children can engage in precocious sexual activities, regarded these as exceptional events, as oddities or as horrifying instances of precocious depravity. Freud, on his part, regards such manifestations—erection, masturbation, and even "activities resembling coitus"—as fairly common phenomena whose neglect by psychologists was to be explained partly by considerations of propriety.

Freud also speaks of the effects of seduction, which he defines as treating a child as a sexual object prematurely, teaching him in highly emotional circumstances how to obtain satisfaction from his genital zones. At their ages, and mine, it is now clear to me that 'Aziza and Nazima were engaging in full-scale seduction, complete with erection, partial penetration, and a climax remarkably resembling coitus. But it was not always easy to find an empty room in an overcrowded house to repeat the deed frequently enough, and other, more "independent" methods had to be found to bring about that sweet satisfaction which was so easily to be obtained from the genital zones.

Some years afterward, when, suddenly one night, the indulgence ceased to be "dry," I kept worrying about it and tended to curse my two childhood partners for the depraved deed they had done. But eventually, with the knowledge that came from reading about such matters, my fears and anxieties were assuaged. At one stage, indeed, I actually sought contact with the two sisters, stopping one of them in the street to say hello and "howdy." The response was always polite, to be sure, but there was never a hint of the good old days. But then I was a shy sort and the difference in age was considerable, at least by the standards of those days.

Like all Jewish women of her class, the two girls' mother, Dina, was a dynamic lady in her late youth — and, because her husband Abraham was something of a *talmid hakham* (diligent scholar), soft-spoken and vaguely lazy and impractical, the wife was the dominant figure in the house, which, in my own family chronicles, came to be known as *Beit Dina*. It was in *Beit Dina* that, besides gaining my first glimpse of normal physical sexuality, I also seem to have first opened my eyes on the world around me. It was in those years that I attended *l'estadh*, a kind of kindergarten in which instruction in elementary Hebrew and the Torah was given. Because we were very small, we were picked up each morning by the *khilfa*, whose job it was to herd us little brats to and from *l'estadh*. In most cases, the *khilfa* was something of a half-wit or made an effort to appear to be and to act like one. In later years I met one of my various *khilfas* in the streets of Jerusalem. Like many Iraqi Jews who immigrated to Israel, he had by then changed his calling and was now selling *Maariv*, one of the two local evening papers. It was in the early 1960s, when Egyptian president Nasser was at the peak of his unpopularity in Israel and was having difficulty maintaining Egypt's so-called merger with Syria — and my old *khilfa* was habitually playing the buffoon, howling, "Nasser *met*, Nasser *met—yimmah sh'mo*" (Nasser dead, Nasser dead — may his name be erased completely). I passed him by since I thought there was not a chance in the world he would recognize me.

BROTHER ELIAHU

My early recollections of my brother, Eliahu, my senior by more than eighteen years, are rather dim. I think the reason for this was that, since my birth, Eliahu had to work to support all of us and it was thus that I saw relatively little of him. In better days, when business was going well in the years preceding the Great Depression, he used to bring home of a Friday afternoon a small paper package full of "goodies," sweets and toffees and such—and these used to be carefully tucked away in the cupboard and rationed out to us children, hopefully lasting the week. But these good days did not last long.

Eliahu's engagement was announced in 1931. The matchmaker was a woman called Salha and the bride-to-be was from the townlet of Khanaquin in the north. Hella was a Cohen, and a Kurd to boot. Mother judged her to be "too skinny." I don't quite know how, what with all these drawbacks, the match was made in the end. Probably it was the dowry—which, though not so large, was in the end allegedly not paid in full or not paid at all.

In those years, beginning in 1928 or 1929, I used to take Father to the house of Haron Birshan, the eldest son of Father's sister Tuffaha and father of Shalom, David, and Reina. The house was spacious and clean and richly furnished, and it was situated a few houses from the Alliance school for boys. Haron's wife Sarah was an exemplary woman and did pretty little by way of housework, since the family had two live-in servants, a male cook and a maid—something unheard of in my father's restricted family circle. It was usually at the Birshan house that we went for prayer and Torah readings on the two mornings of Rosh Hashanah and *leilt el-hatheema,* the last night of *Succoth* (the Feast of Tabernacles), which was usually spent in reading and prayers by the men while the women busied themselves—and thus managed to keep awake—by making heaps of grain-size *sh'ighiyyi* from a specially made dough.

It was probably no more than a piece of wishful thinking, but sometimes there was a good deal of whispering and gossip in our family about a possible match between Eliahu and Reina—an event that, had it actually happened, would have proved to be a boon not only for Eliahu but for all of us. Eliahu had started a small business, a store on the main street near "The Bridge," shortly after the coming of the British late in 1917. It must have been in the summer of 1920, when he was barely sixteen. The shop was opened in partnership with a far relative, a young man by the name of Murad, nicknamed, for some reason connected with the famed authority and character of his mother, *ibn sit el-kil* (son of the grandmother of them all).

By the time he was eligible for marriage, in the mid-1920s, Eliahu had ended his partnership with Murad and established his own shop in the city's central bazaar, Suq el-Saray. Starting with the early 1930s, I used to go there early in the afternoon, taking his midday meal, since he worked all day long without a break and there were no kosher places to eat—and anyway nothing compared to a homemade dish. It seems that Haron Birshan had in some ways helped Eliahu stand on his feet, and there was no doubt that he had taken an interest in him as a possible match for Reina. But it was probably no more than the then natural tendency on the part of every father to see in practically every young man a prospective son-in-law.

It was probably only part of that piece of wishful thinking, as well as a kind of self-rebuke and a way of showing off—but I recall that, shortly after Eliahu's engagement to Hella, gossip had it that the mighty Haron Birshan was somewhat dismayed by the haste in which Mother allegedly decided to marry off her first-born. Indeed, I remember clearly the rumor making the rounds that Haron Birshan expressed himself rather sharply on hearing the news; but, of course, it could have been only a comment on the bride, the fact that she was a Cohen, or of Kurdish origin, or almost the same age as Eliahu—or all of these alleged shortcomings put together. Such is the power of wishful thinking, however, that his remark was immediately taken to mean that he had planned to have Eliahu for son-in-law, and Father and Mother were inconsolable.

In perspective, I think the chances of Haron Birshan's actually giving his daughter's hand in marriage to Eliahu were as good as nonexistent. Reina eventually was married to a lawyer from the house of Jiji. Her daughter Blanche married Yaaqub Bilbul, an aspiring young poet and short story writer who eventually was to become secretary of the Chamber of Commerce, and who in Israel changed his family name to Lev.

SHIFTING FORTUNES

Eliahu married early in 1931, and for the occasion and the need for more room we moved to a new house situated in a better neighborhood. Our landlord this time was an imposing, domineering Jew from some small town in the north who had come to Baghdad looking for and finding better employment. His name was as awe-inspiring as his bearing—Hesqel ibn Mulla Mardan. I have no idea where the man's father acquired the title *mulla,* the word *mulla* being the Persian equivalent of man of religion or religious leader that is usually used as a title only for Muslims. Most probably Mardan, an Arabic/Hebrew word meaning "rebellious," had been a rabbi of note and, alongside with the Muslims who might have gone to him for advice or cure and who no doubt called him *mulla,* the Jews too took to the habit and the word became part of his name.

By the family's standards, the new house was a marked improvement on anything we had known—certainly better than *Beit Dina*—and we occupied a whole half of it. Eliahu and his bride took one large room for themselves, while Father, Mother, my two sisters and I slept in the other room. We also had the use of the cellar—the *neem,* so essential for the almost mandatory after-lunch nap in summer—as well as one inner balcony on the ground floor—*tarma*—and use of the kitchen and what passed for a bathroom. The main wedding event, the *qiddus* that preceded *leilt el-dakhla* (literally, night of the entry), took place in the house, and one of the things that impressed me most was the fact that food was plentiful and that we had employed for the occasion not only a cook but a man also to manage, direct, and overview the whole event and who was called the *huwwash,* a word derived from *hosh* (house).

Leilt el-dakhla was an elaborate and rather complex affair—and was often accompanied by difficulties, punctures, and ugly scenes. In some cases, indeed, it ended in tragedy—at least in the social sense of the marriage being broken and the betrothal declared null and void. This usually happened in the extremely rare cases where the bride's virginity could not be verified—or where some other disability was discovered. On this particular occasion, however, everything went smoothly. Eliahu was taken aside in the course of the evening and was amply instructed by two or three of the older and more experienced members of the family. Unless the bridegroom had some previous experience, that was usually the first and only time a Jewish male received instruction in sex education. However, even with the most experienced among them it was essential to impart to them the knowledge and the technique of how to deal with a virgin.

After the "entry"—which really consisted merely of entering the room where the bride was all ready and groomed for the big event—the mothers of the newlyweds usually sat close to the door or just hovered about it, waiting for the word to come out, together with the conclusive proof of virginity in the form of a small handkerchief with pinkish blood signs on it. This was usually shown to the people most concerned and the closest of friends—so that no mistake be made or gossip start. After this double proof—first of the girl's virginity and second of the bridegroom's having actually deflowered the bride—the two were usually left alone to spend the night in peace. Within my experience in those days, the concept of "honeymoon" was totally unknown—and it was business as usual the very next morning.

A year or so after the marriage, with the world economic slump beginning to take its toll, Eliahu faced acute cash difficulties and we had to move from Ibn Mulla Mardan's house to other, far more modest accommodation as subtenants, this time in the home of the Gabbay family, with whom we shared the small house in the 'Aquliyya quarter. We stayed there a mere six months and in truly miserable conditions since there was no money to cover our barest needs. It was in this house that Eliahu was officially declared bankrupt and had to spend some time in prison.

By the spring of 1933 things deteriorated so much that we had to look for still cheaper accommodation and make do with a much poorer neighborhood. We then moved from the Gabbays' house to *Beit Rahel* in the Taht el-Takya quarter. By that time Eliahu and Hella had two baby daughters—itself a near disaster—and we had to be crowded into one large room, which obviously went to my brother's family, and a small attic (*kabishkan*) in which all the remaining five of us had to sleep in winter.

IN THE EYE OF THE BEHOLDER

If I were to give a rough approximation of the ideal of feminine beauty prevalent in Baghdad in those days—among Jews and non-Jews alike—I would probably have to resort to a comparative approach. Alberto Moravia once asked Claudia Cardinale: "What are your shoulders like?" "They are," she answered, "full, rounded, completely feminine, and graceful; not at all sharp and angular." Asked about her hips, however, Cardinale said she wished they were narrower. It is, of course, all a matter of individual taste; but I tend to think that, were they to express an opinion on the subject, none of my countrymen would have agreed with the Italian film star, especially where the width of her hips was concerned.

The fact is that the Arabs, both Muslims and non-Muslims, had throughout the ages formulated for themselves a special concept of feminine beauty, with strict and sometimes too demanding standards. Salaheddin Al-Munajjid, a well-known Arab historian, and the author of a book on the evolution of Arab ideas of feminine beauty through the ages, writes that the eclecticism of the Arabs' concept of beauty springs from the great variety of the aesthetic experiences that were open to them. Their flourishing civilization, he explains, "resulted in thousands of beauties offered for sale in Eastern cities and marketplaces every day."

According to Al-Munajjid, the widespread belief that the Arabs consider generous curvature the measure of feminine beauty is largely mistaken. True, he adds, the earliest Arabs used to prefer huge thighs and great protruding breasts; but preference for fatness in women is generally prevalent among primitive and backward peoples, and during the many centuries of their flourishing civilization the Arabs used standards of beauty that were very far from these — although they were to revert to preferring the bulky and the fat in later periods, "when they again became retarded."

I suspect that Al-Munajjid's use of words like "backward" and "retarded" in this context signifies a kind of concession to the prevalent Western concept of feminine beauty, as well as an attempt to correct what he considers an unfavorable impression prevalent in the West concerning the Arabs' taste and their sexual predilections. Be that as it may, he lists the following five requirements which he says the Arabs considered essential for a woman's beauty to be perfect:

1. The ideal woman should be tall, neither lean nor fat, and taut in body and muscle rather than slack.
2. The various parts and features of her body must be proportionate and shapely, so that they may constitute a harmonious whole.
3. Bust measurement must be equal or almost equal to that of the hips, while the waist should measure half of that or just a little more.
4. In addition to these general requirements, the Arabs insisted on "beauty of the soul." Feminine beauty is not merely a physical matter. Verve, delicacy of movement, coquetry, sweetness of conversation — all these contribute to a woman's attractiveness.
5. Arab experts have also laid down detailed requirements and descriptions of every one of a woman's features, but these are too specialized to be listed here.

As already indicated, I think Al-Munajjid here is considerably influenced by the standards prevalent in the West today. A more representative, and more accurate, appraisal was the one provided by Algeria's Emir Abd el-Qadir al-Jazairi (died 1883) who, before his surrender and exile, wrote in answer to a number of questions put to him by the French commander in Algeria, General Daumas, that "the beauty beloved by the Arabs requires woman to have [these seven sets of] four features: four black, four white, four red, four big, four small, four large, and four narrow. The black ones," the Emir elaborated, "are: the hair, the eyebrows, the eyelashes, and the pupils. The white: the skin, the whites of the eye, the teeth, and the nails. The red: the cheeks, the lips, the tongue, and the gums. The big: the breasts, the pudenda, the knees, the buttocks. The small: the ears, the mouth, the hands, and the feet. The large: the forehead, the eyes, the curve of the bosom, and the navel. The narrow: the nostrils, the ears, the waist, and the vulva." (It is worth noting here that Sylvia G. Haim, who wrote a highly instructive essay on the subject and is the translator of this passage, was careful to point out that "the coarseness which may appear in the translation of these texts is . . . due solely to the fact that word equivalents often have connotations in one language which do not exist in another," and that "the Arabic words as they are used here are empty of affective or emotive content.")

Where my own surroundings as a little boy are concerned, leanness in women was likewise not only not recommended or praised but was seen as a serious drawback. I recall distinctly that, on her return from inspecting my brother Eliahu's future wife—unaccompanied by the groom-to-be, needless to say—Mother reported that the young woman was basically okay, except for the regrettable fact that she was too slim—*jild w'adhem* (skin and bone). She consoled Father by adding, however, that his future daughter-in-law would no doubt gain weight once she got married and became pregnant.

This was roughly the view Iraqis in those days held on the subject. Jews, especially the women and famously the matchmakers, had a fairly incredible way of describing a beautiful bride: "The face is white and round like a full moon, the nose a clove, the mouth a cardamom." And the eyes? Here we encounter a problem in sheer proportions, for the ideal eyes were now "like almonds," now "like a cow's." Height, too, was much valued, and the proportions of a healthy young and beautiful female were said to be *el-tool shgha' wul-ghaqba dhgha'* (the height is that of a sail, the neck is a yard long).

At age seven or so, hearing my mother complaining about her future daughter-in-law's physical proportions, I tended to agree with her . . . What is important, for me, was and remains the requirement specified by Al-Munajjid—namely that a woman's features and the various parts of her body should be proportionate and shapely so that they constitute a harmonious whole whether slim, fat, or middling.

THE SCHOOL NURSE

One such "model" of perfect feminine beauty for me was the school nurse during my second or third year of primary schooling. She had red hair and was generally full of color—her face seeming fully painted though obviously she used no makeup. I took an instant liking to her bordering on blind passion. After my brief apprenticeship under the two sisters at *Beit Dina,* I had at the age of eight or nine become quite capable of taking care of my sexual needs, for what they were. But with the nurse at the Ras el-Qarya school it was a totally different matter—a new kind of yearning, a truly "platonic" kind of passion that had no definite physical object and was seemingly capable of being gratified through mere sight and contemplation.

The nurse, who was Jewish as almost all female nurses were in those days in Baghdad—the rest being Christian—was probably becoming fully aware of my eager, wide-eyed, almost frenzied staring. She must have lived in the same neighborhood we lived in—and when I spotted her walking to and from home I used actually to follow her. From a safe distance, to be sure, just to enjoy the sight of her figure and the movements of her shapely legs and hips. However, with the kind of education about "the facts of life" girls then were used to getting, I figure she did not suspect a thing. On my part, I was quite happy and content to keep my distance—and eventually lost sight of the young beauty, who I believe worked only on a part-time basis and left by the end of the school year.

I think that this brief experience of passionate attachment to what I took to be a beautiful woman was my first conscious encounter with feminine beauty. Ever since that time, I have never stopped being struck and awed by the sight of a truly pretty feminine face. For me it remains a mystery, a veritable miracle of craftsmanship and totally beyond explaining and analysis—how certain features combine to make a woman attractive and intensely desirable. Not that I had any particular preferences in this field. A woman can be white or black, a blonde or a brunette or a redhead or none of these things. She can have large features or small, with a full body or slim, her eyes large or small. The crucial factor is her overall appearance, the mysterious ways in which the totality of her features, her size, her weight, and her general bearing combine to produce what is generally called her "looks."

This somewhat eclectic disposition as to what constitutes feminine beauty tended to contradict all accepted opinion in those days—and not only in the milieu in which I grew up. In such an appraisal, the Algerian emir's seven sets of features don't seem to fit—not quite. Gentlemen in America and the West generally may have preferred blondes; they definitely did so in Baghdad. It is quite feasible, however, that a blonde can be allegedly not only "dumb" but totally uninteresting physically. And so could be brunettes, redheads, dark-skinned, and blacks.

SEX IN THE FAMILY

As far back as I can remember I never observed any signs of sex life between my parents. This was not only because lovemaking and love play were usually carefully guarded secrets performed in the dark of night. They were so, to be sure; but with my early knowledge of these matters and the physical conditions in which we lived in those days such goings on would not have escaped my notice.

In retrospect, this seemingly total absence of a sex life seems to me quite remarkable. After all, Father could not have been in his mid-forties when I was born and Mother not much more than thirty-five — and as far as begetting children was concerned, my parents' next, and last, baby — Simha — was born all of three years after I was. Did that mark the end of my parents' sex life? All I can remember with any clarity was a hint, a mere hint, of a refusal on Mother's part. Once, when I was probably six or seven, I caught my parents in the heat of an argument, and there was some reference to Father's possible request to perform his marital duties — and then I heard Mother hinting she would never, but never . . .

Since I hardly saw brother Eliahu except on Saturdays and other holidays — which anyway he spent mostly playing backgammon with his friends in some teashop — there were usually only my two older sisters to play with and learn from. And in that field, up to the age of six, I gained little knowledge or experience because after 'Aziza and Nazima we lived in households where the only young girls available were my sisters. Simha, of course, was no help. Gurjiyya, about eleven years my senior, was a very quiet sort, diligently attending to her embroidery which she had learned in the Atelier, a school for needlework and dressmaking founded by the community to train poor Jewish girls in a profession. She was also soon to be married off in what I thought was a rush, and the bridegroom — an opium-smoking and hot-tempered Persian Jew — took her with him to Kermanshah.

It was Najiyya, some nine years my senior, who was to play a part in my sex education — an unconscious though not insignificant one all considered. She was a lovely young girl all along, and it was in *Beit Rahel* that I first became aware of the extent of her knowledge in those matters. At age fourteen or fifteen, she was capable of engendering considerable allurement and excitement when she chose to do so. The object, of course, was not innocent little me but the fortunate Naji, our landlady's youngest son and at the age of twenty or so gainfully employed as a truck driver in a leading transport company. Because he worked nights sometimes and had to spend a few days at a go outside the house he had a lot of free time during the day and was thus in a position to see much of Najiyya. It was even rumored that they used to manage to meet privately outside the house. Naji was obviously attracted to her—and no wonder. What I kept wondering at was that she thought she had to work so hard to allure him—sitting in the inner balcony just next to the room where he slept and finding a hundred excuses for catching his attention. At times, watching from the alcove where I slept, I used to stare, for hours sometimes, carefully watching the movements that Najiyya always found excuses to make in order to be in various positions of partial exposure.

The only other glimpse I got of any sexual activity in the family was of Eliahu and Hella shortly after their marriage. It was in *Beit ibn Mulla Mardan,* where they had a whole room for themselves and there was no way for anyone to see or enter unannounced. Bedrooms, however, were on the second floor, where no living soul could stay in summer for any length of time. These rooms were completely abandoned in summer, people sleeping on the rooftops at night and having their siesta either in the *tarma* (open saloon) on the ground floor or in the coolness of the *neem.* It was in the *neem* one early afternoon that I got a glimpse of my brother and sister-in-law engaged in serious necking. I must add that there was nothing particularly exciting or even curious about this scene; at seven or so I was already well past learning much from the grown-ups around me.

THE MANSERVANT OPPOSITE

Judging by the length and height of its outside walls and the size of the gate, the house must have been large and spacious. However, considering the fact that seldom if ever had anyone been seen entering or leaving it, the house must have been virtually uninhabited. I was never to know for certain what sort of creatures did live in that building, whose door was directly across the road from *Beit Rahel,* and in the year or two we spent there I don't remember ever seeing a soul coming or going there. The only sign of any life was an old, white-haired manservant—and he too would probably have not shown his face were it not for his apparent weakness for very young females.

My sister Simha must by then have been five or six years old, but like the general run of poor and deprived children she was by far much wiser and wilier than many kids her age. And she and I were pals—at least in the sense that we tended to pool our scant resources to make ends meet. It was not above us to scheme for pinching a pear or an apple from the green-grocer—or, better still, such a rare delicacy as a banana. It was not mischief or anything like a childish urge to do things one knew were strictly forbidden. It was a nagging need to have and to taste certain things we saw daily displayed in the better shops and stores but that were never, ever brought into the house or seen on the table.

One day Simha surprised me by actually producing a bar of chocolate. It did not take much persuasion to find out about the source of the new bounty. It was the Muslim manservant opposite. At first I was angry and warned Simha I would tell on her if she dared do it again, then I demanded to know exactly how and why and in what manner the chocolate was given to her by the old man. It then transpired that, when he caught sight of Simha at the door—which was fairly often—he would beckon to her to come in with the bar of chocolate in his hand. The temptation was great but Simha said she resisted it for some time. Then this last time she gave in, entered the fearful house and was handed the chocolate. Okay, I insisted, but why did she have to go into the house if the thing was as innocent as it sounded from the story she told? This part too took some time and gentle persuasion coupled with threats to clear up: during the few seconds Simha was in, the old manservant would fondle her just a wee little bit and then part with the chocolate.

There is nothing like rationalization to make unacceptable things sound acceptable and finally be accepted. And there is nothing like hunger or any other variety of deprivation that is so inducive to rationalization. Okay, the old man was after all only an old man; and if he was foolish enough to dispense such precious things as sweets and a real bar of chocolate in return for something so innocuous and harmless, why the heck not!

And so for some time at least—until the man stopped appearing at the door with his irresistible goodies—we enjoyed the prosperity. As to the reason for his disappearance, this was to be as mysterious as the house itself in which he served. For all we knew he might have died, or fallen hopelessly ill, or have been sacked for reasons of old age. Or was he, after all, the real owner of that house and its sole inhabitant? Did he perhaps actually pass away somewhere in that spacious mansion, with no one to take care of him or even see to his burial?

Chapter 6 | SCHOOLING

A New York friend of mine, a writer notorious for her outspokenness, once wrote in a letter in the course of one of her periodic reprimands: "Why, Goddamnit, didn't your father and mother send you to the Baghdadian equivalent of *cheder?* Ideas of human values did begin, you know, before the Voltairian Enlightenment, and even the Enlightenment's ideas are Isaiah's."

But they did send me to one — well, to what was the Baghdadian equivalent of the East European *cheder* (which must mean "room"). It was called *l'estadh* (the master) and what that master taught us brats there was to read the Torah. To be sure, we all sat in a room, usually in the house, usually "the master's" own, and the solitary teacher simply made us repeat what he read. But I hardly remember having ever heard him or us recite any farther than the first few pages of *Bereshith* (Genesis).

Either I didn't stay there long enough or there was something radically wrong with the teacher. The fact remains that we never managed to go far beyond these first passages. The idea, I suspect, was just to keep us boys busy and out of the way, rather than to teach us the elements of Hebrew or reading the Bible.

But if *l'estadh* was not enough — and it certainly wasn't — I was also sent to the *midrash,* the nearest thing Baghdad Jews had to compare to the East European yeshivah. The *midrash* perhaps differed from the yeshivah only in that it embraced all ages and all levels of Torah studies, so that a boy could simply take there his very first steps in Hebrew and religious studies. But — need I say it — I managed to spend little if any time there. The crowdedness, the stench, the incredible regimentation, the sheer cultural poverty of both the place and the crowd — these simply made me hasten to leave the place like a man running for his life. I don't know at what age exactly I was then — nor would I be surprised had the official reason for my leaving the *midrash* been my own insufficient level of Hebrew and/or Torah study — or something to do with my own lack of discipline. What I do know is that my reaction was one of sheer revulsion—and that under no circumstances was I able to stay there even one more day.

To my ever-angry friend—who also happens to be a radical Jewish ethnic-nationalist and something of a fanatical anti-Arab—I wrote:

No, then; that was simply not the point—going or not going to the Baghdadian equivalent of *cheder*. Obviously it was something in the "culture" of the place and of the people. And what did the *cheder* teach those who did attend it anyway? Modern political Pan-Jewish nationalism—the mirror image of an ethnic-racial concept of nationality that was to be borrowed lock, stock, and barrel by the disillusioned assimilationist Jews of Central and Eastern Europe and latterly practiced with a vengeance by their followers in Palestine? And you have the heart— and the incredible intellectual carelessness—to call me "a son of the Enlightenment"? Who the deuce is who anyway? You know—or at least ought to know—who the "neglected and discarded sons of the Enlightenment" in Jewry are! Don't count me among them, thank you very much! I would rather be called—as I've indeed been called, and by a university professor to boot—a bloody "medievalist."

And you think you are clever. You think you have finished me off by merely paraphrasing my remark about German Jews. (And how about thanking you for "not exactly calling [me] a 'complete idiot'" and for being content with implying that I was a somewhat ordinary, harmless sort of idiot?) Wrong again—and doubly so! In the article you quote I wrote: "German Jews were complete idiots to have imagined—knowing any history—that they could be absorbed, assimilated or accepted as 'Germans first and followers of the Mosaic faith second!'" And you offer the facile counter-formulation: "Iraqi Jews were complete idiots to imagine—knowing any history—that they could be absorbed."

And so on. But dear, angry, impatient, and impulsive Chava, to start with, Iraq's Jews never, ever even wanted—let alone begged—to be absorbed or assimilated by or into the predominantly Muslim society in which they lived. I know that it is difficult for you and for people raised in a European Jewish surrounding to believe it, yet the fact remains that as far as the Jews of the Middle East and North Africa were concerned this whole question of acceptance, absorption, or assimilation simply didn't arise. Nor is there anything strange or remarkable in this: The fact was that, since the idea of ethnic-racial nationalism had no foundation in Arab history or Muslim thought in the first place, there was no need for people to go to any lengths in order to be "accepted" or admitted into the wider society. Indeed, "knowing any history," the Jews of Baghdad would have been complete idiots even to contemplate seeking such admittance — let alone actually consider it essential. But they were not idiots and they did not try.

So go on and have your own bit of fun! If it pleases you to liken me to a German Jew — something that I seem to recall you did in one of your recent letters — so be it! But there is no scope for making such an analogy and, so I hope, you are destined to continue to try and solve the unwieldy mystery that appears to you to be me. I wish you luck — in your next effort and the ones inevitably to follow.

A YEAR IN KINDERGARTEN

Apart from two or three years of attendance in one or other *estadh*, all I had behind me in 1936 by way of formal education was five out of the six years of primary school, received in at least three different Jewish elementary schools.

But it is of my one preschool year, spent in an obscure Jewish kindergarten not far from where we lived, that I want to speak here. My recollection of that year is however almost entirely confined to a rather painful experience I had with one of my classmates. This boy, too clever by half, systematically talked me out of all the cookies my mother used to stuff into my satchel — and this on the false pretence of "buying" them from me. But the deal was made on credit, the boy each day promising to pay me the accumulated sums "tomorrow."

The reason for my consenting to this rather unfair transaction was that cash for me was then in very short supply; it was something of a rule in our family that money should not be "wasted" outside of the house and its needs. There was also the added consideration that an ignoramus of five or six will inevitably squander any cash he or she gets on non-nourishing and expensive sweets and such. Instead, you got whatever you needed, including at times some of the things you wanted most — like sweets and chocolates — but you were not allowed to take hard cash.

But I wanted hard cash — and wanted it precisely to spend on non-nourishing things. Hence my accepting the offer to sell my cookies and go virtually hungry in the hope of laying my hands on some cash, however small. However, the result of my first attempt at salesmanship was dismal: a relatively huge sum of money that I thought I earned from selling those cookies remained totally theoretical. I never saw a penny of it.

All considered, I was something of a loner from an early age, given to moods and brooding and tending to be an object of practical jokes and ridicule on the part of my mischievous peers at school. I seldom participated in their games, and only on one occasion did I take part in their pranks against schoolteachers. It was at *l'estadh*, where we had gotten used to the half-crazy, poorly clad instructor with whose every move we were familiar and whose reactions we could predict with remarkable accuracy. One day this idyllic atmosphere suddenly ended: A new teacher, wearing European clothes, his face closely shaven, his shoes shining, and his voice mock-authoritative, was introduced to us as our new instructor. To cap it all, he spoke with a strange accent and we were told he was just back from Palestine where he had gone to study Torah and Hebrew.

He was haughty in appearance and addressed us with apparent arrogance, and a number of my naughtier classmates decided "to teach him a lesson." It was summertime and there were a lot of bad watermelons around, full of smelly juice and totally inedible. One day, having finished school and leaving as usual some minutes before he did, a few of us climbed over the roof of a building on the route we knew he would take. It was only half a watermelon but the impact and the confusion were great when it fell with precision on the poor fellow. I think my confusion and pity were far greater than my exhilaration, and I never took part in such pranks again.

Nor did I participate in the games that my peers usually played, mostly in the streets and alleyways near their homes. These games either required money to buy the equipment and often for bets, or they required physical fitness — and I was short of both. It was probably this that accounted for the fact that I never had real friends till the age of fifteen, when friendship could be struck on the basis of some intellectual pursuit or simple companionship. It is curious that even then, as far back as I can recall, my friends happened to be considerably older than me.

The fact that physically I was not quite fit for sports and exercise had nothing to do with the state of my health, although the general opinion in the family was that I was prone to catch colds and get tired too quickly and too often. This was to become apparent a few years later when, along with all Baghdadi boys, I was finally sent to a trainer to teach me to swim. It took me a mere two days to give up the attempt, having returned home on the second day with my nose bleeding and my limbs hardly capable of movement.

MADRASAT RAS EL-QARYA

On the whole, my schooldays up to the age of thirteen, when I left the Ras el-Qarya school immediately after finishing the fifth form, were ones of almost unrelieved anxiety, boredom, and unhappiness. As far as actual learning was concerned, I think the six years I spent at that school were extremely unproductive, although there were exceptions. Arabic and Arabic grammar were my favorite subjects and I can say I got a good grounding in them while at school. The only other subject I remember having had any appeal to me was geometry, which like grammar and inflexion, required systematic and logical thinking and in turn implanted in us an orderly frame of mind.

Madrasat Ras el-Qarya, named after the quarter in which it was situated, was a government-run school founded to provide primary education for Jewish boys who either could not afford a private school or proved to be too poor in attainments to be admitted to one of the better schools run by the Jewish community, or both. One such school was Al-Ta'awun, to which I was admitted earlier and which I had to leave because of my inability to cope, especially in English and arithmetic. One of the difficulties was that Al-Ta'awun started teaching its pupils English right from the first form, when government-run schools introduced English only in the fourth form.

From Al-Ta'awun I was transferred to Ras el-Qarya in the autumn of 1930. I had no difficulty whatever passing the examinations throughout the first three forms. I remember having earned a reputation at home that I was so clever and my memory so good I always absorbed my lessons in the classroom and thus had to do no homework or prepare for the exams. I don't know how justified these boasts were, but I know I did no homework or ever bothered to open an Arabic reader or a textbook outside of the classroom.

Real trouble started only after the introduction of subjects that not only required some preparation and memorizing but also entailed actual homework—arithmetic, history, English, and geography. Geography was the bane of my life in those days, involving as it did a number of most hateful endeavors. The trouble was that one had to memorize not only the capitals of all those godforsaken countries, but also their respective sizes, populations, and climates, and their main imports and exports. As far as Iraq's own geography was concerned, the emphasis in homework was put on listing the places, rivers, and other geographical spots passed by or encountered in imaginary journeys from one place to another—complete with maps. Though eventually I managed to learn some useful tricks—such as that the climate, main exports, and most imports of all countries, say, of Latin America or Southeast Europe were roughly identical—I had in the end to give up even trying, and duly failed in this subject in the end-of-year exams in my fourth form. The rule then was that provided you fail only in one subject you can have a repeat exam after the summer holidays and, if you pass that one successfully, you can move on to the next form. I did not prepare for the second exam, failed to pass it, and duly remained in the fourth form for an additional year.

Though it was a government school, all my teachers at Ras el-Qarya were Jewish except for Abdel Sattar Afandi, who taught physical training and anthems, and the mighty school principal Hasan Afandi. The principal, who at forty or thereabouts was the oldest member of the staff, was a great disciplinarian and a fervent believer in the benevolent use of the stick. My worst experience with Hasan Afandi was when I was caught with one tiny container of eau de cologne in my pockets. The container was acquired by my brother Eliahu in the course of his work as a broker and brought home for his wife to use. I don't remember whether I stole or was given it—I rather think the former was the case, judging from the enormity of the scandal that its discovery in my possession caused. Hasan Afandi was somehow informed of the existence of the scent, and on being apprised of the fact I immediately hastened to the toilet and threw the incriminating evidence safely into the cistern. But it proved of no use, since I seem to have used the thing and my whole body was reeking of the fragrance. In the end, not content with wielding his stick repeatedly and in full force, Hasan Afandi decided to assemble the whole pupil population in the inner courtyard and reprimand me publicly for my crime—so that it would be a lesson for them to remember.

Looking back, I now think that the possession of that tiny flask of eau de cologne was considered such a terrible felony owing to something I never came to realize at the time. Homosexuality among males was not unknown in Baghdad, although it had little in common with what is taken as homosexuality in the West, where it amounts to a physical affliction. Either by inclination or because of lack of female partners, a certain proportion of males tended to be attracted to members of their own sex, usually handsome and young ones. These men were almost without exception bisexual, and almost all of them eventually married and became fathers. In my experience, in fact, I never remember having met a "proper" male homosexual—and knew only one who claimed that he could not have sex with a woman. As a matter of fact, the sex objects of male homosexuals were in almost all cases normal youngsters who were cajoled, bribed, or tricked into a relationship with an older man of that inclination. There must, however, have been some male prostitutes around—or those who did it for money. These were considered the lowest of the low, far worse than female prostitutes.

I was considered quite handsome and therefore desirable sexually— and already in my early teens I realized I was being sought after physically. It was this, I think, that made my possession of a tiny flask of eau de cologne seem so terrible a crime. I do not know about Hasan Afandi, the principal, and his inclinations in that sphere of activity; but with Abdel Sattar Afandi, our physical training instructor, it was a different kind of story. I don't think I was the only boy to attract him sexually, since I used to hear it said that he "chases after boys" (this was the curious phrase by which those men were known in Baghdad—*yidawwur awlad*).

The stick was nothing unusual in the schools of Baghdad in those days—and it was used liberally in the best and "richest" of them. But never so liberally as in those of the schools where the pupils were known to come from disadvantaged families economically. Such a school was Madrasat Ras el-Qarya.

Winter in Baghdad is a serious affair; heating was a luxury we seldom could afford, and no amount of clothes seemed to offer enough protection against the biting cold. On top of it we children had to go to school in shorts. Since we always seem to have lived some distance from the school, by the time I finally reached the place I was freezing—bare hands, bare legs, scantily covered feet, a bare head and a running nose. And as luck would have it I was as often as not late for class—and that was an unforgivable sin. So serious a sin, in fact, that the principal himself dealt with the culprits.

However, despite the thousand vows one made—to oneself as well as to Hasan Afandi—"never to do it again," there was no way of not repeating it. For one thing, my brother Eliahu was the only member of the family in possession of a watch—and that watch was not always dependable. For another, something always managed to go wrong: a long line at the baker's, something gone bust with the kerosene stove, tea or sugar or both to be purchased that same morning. But even when I had had my cup of tea and a half loaf of bread—which was my regular breakfast except for Fridays and Saturdays—some school book or exercise book was mislaid, money needed to purchase a pencil or paper was simply not available or it was hard to part with without a thorough investigation, or some errand to have done with.

Of the Jewish teachers at Madrasat Ras el-Qarya I remember Salih Afandi, who taught arithmetic and used to insist on addressing us in the colloquial Arabic Muslims spoke, unlike his colleagues who managed to make do with a strange combination of classical Arabic and the Arabic spoken by Jews. Especially pompous was a young teacher by the name of Nyazi—an uncommon name among the Jews of Iraq—who taught us English in the fourth form. I remember him telling us that the correct pronunciation of the word *bicycle* was to rhyme with "behind" and "besides," the accepted pronunciation being completely wrong. He insisted on our doing it correctly and it was only some years later that I found out how nonsensical the correction was.

BOYCOTTING NAZI GERMANY'S PRODUCTS

Another unforgettable teacher, also a Jew, was Dawood Afandi, our Hebrew Bible teacher. When the Nazis came to power in Germany, at the end of January 1933, I was in the middle of the first term of the school year where I was spending my year in the third form. One day in the spring of the same year Dawood Afandi devoted practically the whole hour to a discourse on the situation of the Jews in Germany and how that country's new ruler Adolph Hitler was persecuting them. But it was not only information he wanted to impart. He had also an announcement and an appeal to make. Showing us how to locate the make of the goods we buy, he asked that nothing with the words "Made in Germany" printed on it be bought either by us or by members of our families. He also announced that a boycott on a far larger scale and more basic in nature was being organized—namely that no Jewish merchant or exporter-importer would henceforth deal with Germany or promote goods manufactured there.

Dawood Afandi's appeal was generally taken quite seriously and at least we boys refrained from purchasing any school stationery of German manufacture. The boycott as a whole proved quite effective in its own small way, what with virtually the country's entire export, import, and wholesale trade being concentrated in Jewish hands. However, there were rumblings on the part of the more conscious Muslims and Arab nationalist groups. The German Foreign Ministry records of the time contain reports sent to Berlin by Germany's envoy in Baghdad dealing with this subject. It transpires that in October 1933 Muslim Arab circles were showing signs of resentment against the boycott. It is doubtful whether the resentment, which was directed mainly against the Jews, was really caused by the boycott or even connected with it.

The German envoy, in a report to his superiors in Berlin dated October 25, 1933, told his superiors that the Muslim majority was becoming vocally and vehemently anti-Zionist in the wake of increasing immigration of German Jews into Palestine. The envoy quoted a cable sent to the German Legation by the Muslim Youth Association (*jam'iyyat al-shubban al-muslimin*) on October 23 of the same year protesting the rise in the number of visas granted by the German authorities to German Jewish citizens permitting them to immigrate to Palestine through the British authorities. In his report, the German envoy expressed satisfaction at this protest movement, on the ground that it helped represent the British as the archenemy and subsequently as bound to make an Anglo-Iraqi accord more difficult to reach. The envoy made it clear, however, that the Jewish communities of Baghdad, Basra, and Mosul were not attacked or mentioned in the newspaper articles published in protest against the immigration of German Jews to Palestine.

A SPLIT IN THE COMMUNITY

The call to boycott all commodities made in Germany was not the only time in my experience as a boy in which the Jews of Baghdad took what was a mass communal stand. A few years back, when we were living in the largely Jewish neighborhood of Taht el-Takya, a great and extremely noisy rift developed within the Jewish community, accompanied by an unprecedented campaign of slander and curses, claims and counterclaims, charges of "apostacy," and prayers for the damnation of "the heretics" in the opposing camp. The uproar was felt in every Jewish home in all the predominantly Jewish neighborhoods—Taht el-Takya, Hinnuni, Abul Sa'd, Kutcht Baher, and others. As a child I watched these goings-on without comprehending what the fuss was all about. Only decades later, when working on my book on the history of the Jews of Iraq, did I manage to get something like the full story.

It all seems to have started sometime in the mid-1920s but reached its peak only in the early 1930s. Formally evolving round the election of the chief rabbi, the rift represented something far deeper and its results were accordingly quite far-reaching, with the Jewish community greatly weakened and the powers to manage its own affairs materially restricted.

What happened was that by the late 1920s a whole new generation of

Iraqi Jews, mostly graduates of the various Alliance schools, sought to install a chief rabbi (*Hakham Bashi*) and a communal leadership more receptive to modern concepts and mores. The only course open to these was to infiltrate the community's institutions and work for change from within. They started with penetrating the community's "lay council," *Al-Majlis al-Jismani*, leaving strictly religious matters to members of its so-called "Spiritual Council," *Al-Majlis al-Ruhani*. This they managed to do by working hard, throughout the 1920s, to have their members elected to the lay council—and by the early 1930s they managed to secure the resignation of the conservative chief rabbi, Ezra Dangoor, replacing him with Rabbi Sasson Khedhouri as chief rabbi as well as president of the Spiritual Council.

But members of the *Ruhani* council fiercely opposed the election. Apart from objecting to the way Dangoor was removed from the council's presidency, they considered Khedhouri dangerously lenient in matters of religious observance and the preservation of *halakhah* (Jewish Law). Unable to prevent Khedhouri's election as the new chief rabbi, the conservatives resorted to the letter of the law, which empowered them to disordain a rabbi should he be found wanting. They proceeded to disordain the chief rabbi, on the ground that he held unorthodox views about the Torah. The result, they thought, was that Khedhouri could not continue as chief rabbi since he had been found not fit to be a rabbi in the first place. However, though strictly speaking they were acting according to the letter of the law—in this instance an old Ottoman ordinance—their action resulted in a further weakening of their authority and, ultimately, in depriving the communal institutions as a whole of much of their power to run the affairs of the community.

For what happened was that, responding largely to appeals from the "Westernized" members of the lay council, the government enacted a new law in 1931 regulating the affairs of the Jewish community. Under this law, a layman may preside over the community and not necessarily an ordained rabbi. Moreover, the elected head of the community (*Raees al-Ta'ifa*) had to have his election ratified by a royal decree. It was thus that Sasson Khedhouri became both head of the community and its chief rabbi, protests and shouts and curses and demonstrations directed against him notwithstanding.

From that point onward, the chief rabbi became virtually a government functionary and felt no longer bound by allegiance to representatives of the community. The reformists, on their part, felt alienated from an institution that they saw as anachronistic and practically defunct.

Chapter 7 | *T*HE GREAT CRASH AND US

I don't know how these things work—nor, I suspect, do professional economists. In later years, of course, I learned about the Great Crash of 1929; but then that happened in a distant land and to well-to-do folks. The precise effects that crash was to have on a tiny, primitive mercantile community in a provincial town like Baghdad—the mere fact that there could have been such effects—have always been something of a mystery to me. The fact remains, however, that it was only two years after the crash, and a slightly longer span of time after my brother Eliahu's marriage, that the world economic slump started to take its toll among members of Baghdad's business community.

Eliahu, for one, first "went broke" (*tala' kasser,* or *shabbar*) and was enabled to settle at a certain percentage his accumulated debts with whatever cash he possessed and/or was presumed to undertake to pay. Shortly afterward, he was officially declared bankrupt (*aflas*). One of the results was that we had to find another, cheaper tenancy, far more modest than the one we had.

It was at the Gabbays' house, situated in the fashionable 'Aquliyya quarter, that Eliahu was declared officially bankrupt and had to serve time in prison. At the time of the trial, Eliahu was so ashamed and felt so helpless that he attempted to take his own life, with the rather primitive device of drinking from a bottle of gasoline—upon which Father snatched the bottle and started drinking its contents himself. Among other unseemly things that happened to us there, at a time when everybody's nerves were on edge, Father once got so mad at something Simha—my junior by three years—had done that he tried to strangle her with his bare hands.

By the spring of 1932, we had to move from the Gabbays' house to *Beit Rahel,* situated in the much poorer neighborhood of Taht el-Takya. We had to be crowded into one large room overlooking the narrow street, which obviously went to my brother's family, and a tiny attic, over the room used by the landlady's youngest son Naji. It was at *Beit Rahel* that a romance of sorts was started between Naji and my older sister Najiyya.

After an interval of some months of utter misery and penury following his release from prison, Eliahu used to spend his days in one of the coffee shops in the commercial center, usually Qahwat Moshi, Moshe's teashop—and gradually he got into the business of brokerage, working as middleman between wholesaler and importer on one side and retailer on the other, in his own line of merchandise, haberdashery. Eventually, we were able to leave *Beit Rahel,* moving to the *diwankhana,* the part of the home originally built for the master of the house and his male friends, at *Beit Abul Juss* off the far more airy and fashionable Al-Mutanabbi Street. This was a two-story construction with a large inner court and a tiny plot in the midst of which one or two fig trees stood and gave fruit in season.

NAJIYYA AND NAJI

It was shortly after we moved to *Beit Abul Juss* that Father was to exercise his paternal authority for what must have been the last time. It was when he managed to have his way in the matter of Najiyya's betrothal. Naji one day paid us an unexpected visit, asking to speak to Father. Everybody guessed what was on the young man's mind. To be sure, following our move out of *Beit Rahel* no one knew exactly what went on—if anything—between those two, although all had their suspicions. Where they were seeing each other—if indeed they continued to do so—and the exact nature of their relationship no one knew for certain. Apparently some sort of contact was maintained in strict secrecy, and—such were the strange norms of those days and of that society—that in itself almost automatically ruled out any thought of a proper relationship past or future.

And so when Naji finally came—all by himself, with no matchmaker, elder relative, or mutual acquaintance—to ask for his daughter's hand in marriage, Father refused adamantly. His reply had a strange ring of finality to it that I still recall vividly. We are not, he assured the young suitor, looking for a husband for our daughter, "neither you nor anyone else." What maddened me at the time was that we must, almost as a matter of course, have been praying for a suitable match, and that the proposed one was not at all bad. In retrospect, I think what really irked Father was the suspicion that something wrong and vaguely sinful had been going on between those two—and that wasn't the right way for young people to enter into holy matrimony.

It must have been a traumatic experience for Najiyya, with whom I was to develop a special attachment in later years. Even though she did not mention that episode specifically, I could easily notice her bitterness and regrets, which curiously enough showed most pronouncedly in her attitude to the behavior of young women in the Israel of the 1970s. That behavior, especially in the case of Iraqi and other Oriental young women, their "modern" ways and their premarital activities, could easily seem licentious and would have been condemned as immoral and punishable even in the late 1950s. However, whenever the subject was raised, whether in connection with the behavior of some young woman of the family or of friends and neighbors, Najiyya would say something like why, by all means let them live their own lives, let them enjoy the years of their youth . . . She was especially pronounced on the subject as to who in the family had the right to decide whom the young daughter was to marry, and her liberal, almost libertarian, attitude went against the grain as far as men and women of her own generation were concerned.

It is not easy to describe the relationship between Najiyya and Naji in anything like contemporary terms. There was no doubt that the two were very attracted to each other, what today would probably amount to being "in love" with one another. The reasons why neither could be said to have "fallen in love" with the other, however, were social rather than emotional or psychological. In the Baghdad of those days, truly falling in love—obsessively thinking about the loved one, something in the style of, say, Goethe's luckless young Werther—was something that came nearest to a physical and mental affliction, an ailment. Indeed, in the popular mythology of the times, among Jews and Muslims alike, only a spell, a sorcery, administered by an established fortune-teller or sorceress, could result in such an obsessive preoccupation, whose victims almost invariably ended up in the madhouse. Unless, of course, an effective counter-spell was solicited from some even abler wonder-doer.

A DEATH IN THE FAMILY

A great tragedy befell the family while we were living in the *diwankhana* in *Beit Abul Juss.* My sister-in-law Hella, who had borne my brother two daughters, finally gave birth to a son. The joy was great and everybody congratulated everybody else, speaking of good omens and good fortune and praying the baby boy would be followed by six more baby boys, saved from the evil eye, and such heartfelt wishes. The *brit*—or *el mila* as it was called in the local Jewish vernacular—was not much of a celebration because Eliahu had still not quite recovered from the bankruptcy of a few years back.

For the first few months the baby seemed to be as healthy as any other newborn baby. But then he suddenly fell ill, and died in a matter of days. I remember a doctor being summoned to examine the baby — at great cost needless to say — but I don't recall that he gave a clear diagnosis and no one was to know the precise nature of the illness. My brother's grief was great, and I remember him moaning that he wished he himself had died instead. But the general attitude and the gist of the condolences extended by relatives and friends was that as long as the parents were alive and healthy, Allah would compensate them for the terrible loss.

It so happened, however, that during that same year, not long before the baby's death, Mother fell ill and had to undergo an operation at the Meir Elias Hospital. Though she never really recovered from that operation, in the course of which the surgeons made a silly technical mistake, she did come back home fairly sound of limb and officially healthy. The baby's illness and death occurred not long after Mother's discharge from hospital and, my sister-in-law being more superstitious even than the general run of Jewish women in Baghdad in those days, some like-minded friend or relative managed to convince her that there was some sort of connection between Mother's illness and her recovery on the one hand and the baby's death on the other. The theory was that the baby's death would have been prevented had there only been a *qurban* (sacrifice) for Mother after she had that operation — some lamb or even a hen slaughtered specifically as such a *qurban*. In the absence of such a sacrifice, the baby was "chosen" to be the required *qurban* and thus his death was inevitable. The elderly lady who described all this in great detail finally sighed, adding something to the effect that all the sorrow and the tears would have been spared had we thought of slaughtering a mere hen for Mother on her leaving the hospital.

The cause of the baby's death, needless to say, was a purely medical issue. In those days in Baghdad, births universally took place in the home. When the time came, the husband rushed to bring the neighborhood midwife, and she did all the work. Judged by today's standards, however, the methods employed were extremely primitive and the comparatively rather high death rate is now seen only as a result of lack of cleanliness and such. Sometimes, in certain Muslim neighborhoods, when the baby was stuck and all the midwife's efforts had not helped, one of the *muezzins* of the mosques nearby was approached for help, and he duly climbed to the top of the minaret and cried, "Ya-qarib el-faraj, ya-'ali bidun daraj, 'abdatka b'shidda w-tutlub minka al-faraj" (O Thou. Who Art our ready in trouble, O Thou, the most ladderless high, Thy handmaid is in sore trouble, asks for Thy deliverance).

We must have been in real financial straits during this period—or else were eager to earn a bit more money to ease our situation. One day in the following summer, my brother came from the marketplace with a novel proposition: Two enterprising young local Jews engaged in the export of fish to Palestine were looking for a place where their wares could be properly packed and loaded. They offered what then seemed to be very generous terms—a nice small sum of money in cash plus a bag full of fish for the family's use.

Never mind the chaos they created, the awful smell, the noise the few workers and porters made, the breaking of ice blocks into small bits so that the fish could be packed properly and reach Palestine before disintegrating; never mind, too, the amount of cleaning that was to be done in the inner courtyard where all the work had to be done. There was the money and the fish and they were enough compensation. This happened twice a week, but it was not to last for long. Two or three months later, the two young fish exporters gave up, either because they did not manage to get their wares all the way to the Holy Land while still in an edible state or they found a better transitory packing plant.

From the *diwankhana* we moved—late in 1933 or in the spring of 1934—to *Beit Yamein,* a spacious house that my brother himself rented this time and let parts of it to small families and couples who came and went while we stayed as virtual landlords. It was the first Baghdad home in my memory—and the last—in which I spent more than three years in succession. Yamein, after whom we named the house, was a cousin of mine—my maternal uncle *Khalu* Yuseif's eldest son. He spent his twenties and thirties serving in the Iraqi army after graduating from Iraq's military college. He seems to have retired early, and on retirement became a banker of sorts—money lending and mortgages and such.

The house which my brother rented from Yamein had been mortgaged to him by its Muslim owners, a rich and noble family of Turkish origin consisting now of an idle surviving son and inheritor—possibly an army officer but obviously a spendthrift—and two daughters, still unmarried though past their twenties. The world of the 1930s and 1940s in Iraq was a man's world and, unless they had family or female friends, the chances were that the two sisters had no social life of any kind and therefore there was no way at all in which they would find suitable suitors. My cousin let the house to us on a strictly business basis but left it for us to do what we wanted with it. If ever I can speak of my "formative years," it was in *Beit Yamein* that I lived them.

In the summer of 1934 I was coming up to ten, yet I was only finishing my third year of primary school. By then I had two unmarried sisters; Najiyya was my senior by about seven years, while Simha was six years old. By the standards current in those days, Najiyya at almost twenty was highly eligible for marriage, while Simha was a mere child.

KERMANSHAH

Of the six years I spent at Madrasat Ras el-Qarya—and in the course of which I managed only five grades—the most eventful for the family coincided with the two long years I had to sit out in the fourth form because of my refusal to prepare my lessons in geography. Shortly after the end of the first of these two years, less than two weeks before Rosh Hashanah in the summer of 1934, Mother, my younger sister, and I started on the journey to Kermanshah, to be present at Najiyya's wedding, whose hand had been given in marriage to my cousin Eliahu, Uncle Abraham's firstborn.

The match was made earlier that summer when, with no prior notice and almost out of the blue, Sarah—Abraham's wife and a Rejwan herself—came from Kermanshah accompanied by her younger son Siyyon looking for a bride for Eliahu. Among others, she saw Najiyya, declared herself satisfied, and the engagement was announced. Uncle Abraham's family had left Baghdad and settled in Kermanshah in the wake of the marriage of their daughter Rivka to a well-to-do Persian Jew from that townlet.

Kermanshah is described in reference books of the 1970s as the capital of the Kermanshah province, 270 miles west-southwest of Teheran at a height of 4,850 feet. Its population is composed largely of Kurds and in the 1966 census totaled 188,000. What distinguished the town was that it was a commercial and route center and very near the Iraqi border. It is also situated in a fertile agricultural region. In 1967, passing by the town while on a study tour of Iran, I had a glimpse of Kermanshah and realized that it was no longer the small town in which I, my mother, and Simha arrived one summer evening in 1934, where willy-nilly we also had to spend Rosh Hashanah and Yom Kippur.

It was in Kermanshah that I contracted a vicious left-lung pneumonia that was very nearly the end of me. As far as anyone knew, at that time there was only one doctor in Kermanshah, and he had only two medicaments to offer no matter what the luckless patient was suffering from. These were *sharbat* and *sihle,* the former being some concoction that probably had some material in it akin to what we now know as aspirin and the latter a very powerful and unswallowable digestive that was supposed to cleanse the stomach completely.

Obviously, no matter how good and what they were good for, these two prescriptions were not meant to cure something so serious as pneumonia, and it was left entirely to fate whether I would ever recover from my illness. However, after a few sleepless nights and terrible nagging pains I started to feel better—thanks partly, so it was said, to certain primitive methods of treatment such as rubbing the sick and painful side of the chest and abdomen with hot vegetable oil. But it took me quite some time fully to recoup my strength.

CONTEMPLATING WOMAN'S LOT

Back in Baghdad, a week or two after the school year started, I, of course, found myself sitting in the same classroom I sat in the previous year. That year was easily the worst of all my early years of school, bad enough as they all were. I don't recall having done any homework, not even in the days preceding exams. Not that I had done anything of the kind in previous years, but as subjects increased in number and scope it was no longer possible to rely solely on a good memory.

Things at home were also looking pretty unpromising, what with the seemingly endless quarrels between Mother and Hella over what appeared to be the silliest and least important of issues. To make things worse, I found I was taking my mother's side, occasionally even interfering with a remark or a request. The death of the baby son and the general shared feelings of loss and grief might have helped to make these verbal quarrels less bitter and less vocal, but that was only temporary. Even Najiyya's marriage, with one mouth less to feed, less crowdedness, less difficulties and gossip and complaints, failed materially to improve the situation.

With things at home so uninspiring, the world outside started to attract more of my attention. During the long additional year I had to spend in the fourth form, when I could read Arabic fairly fluently and knew a few phrases and blessings in Hebrew, my reading consisted exclusively of works for grown-ups. At eleven or thereabouts I became aware of the existence of newspapers and magazines and certain categories of books, especially historical novels. As a matter of fact, I don't recall ever having laid hands on a children's book, and as a little child I had never possessed any toys or games — and later on when boys my age were filling the neighborhood with their shouts and playing the various games boys used to play, I seldom joined in and on the very rare occasions I did I was almost invariably beaten and consequently became an object for pranks and ridicule. Mine, I realized early in the proceedings, was a lost childhood.

In sexual matters, too, maturity came rather early, and the touch or even the mere sight of young women ten or fifteen years my senior were capable of starting waves of physical excitement and a proper arousal. It remains a source of wonder to me, looking back now after so many years and such drastic changes in mores and attitudes, how a boy barely eleven years of age could have mustered the courage — and the cheek — of seeking actual bodily contact with women twice or three times his age by catching them unawares in certain crowded places and occasions — like when leaving a wedding ceremony or some other event held in a public place, usually a school or synagogue, or standing in line for cinema tickets, or caught in crowded bazaars. But this was partly how I managed to satisfy my limited sexual needs at that stage of my life.

Looking back, I cannot help wondering what could have made such petty transgressions and harassments passed over in silence, unpunished, presumably unnoticed. The answer, I believe, had to do with the general position of women in those days and the strict limits then imposed on their every gesture and movement — their attire, the way they had their hair cut, the cosmetics they used, even the way they talked and expressed themselves. In a way, indeed, women were treated in a manner that reduced them to easy prey given the least provocation. A woman who dressed in a certain way, had her hair exposed, her face made up and her lips heavily painted and earrings inviting, went out without a veil, walked with high-heel shoes — such a woman was liable to be an object not only of whistles and cries of admiration and erotic remarks but also of pronounced verbal and even physical harassment.

In this connection it is instructive to cite the case of foreign women travelers in Iraq roundabout the time I am writing about. Sometime in the early 1930s, the Iraqi Ministry of Interior issued an administrative order addressed to "European and American ladies in Iraq" and including what was described as "regulations regarding residence and travelling."

The regulations were issued for the benefit of "European and American ladies and ladies of similar national and social status," and it was made clear that ladies who did not comply with the said regulations "render themselves liable to the cancellation of their visas."

Among the things these traveling ladies were not supposed to do was to move around unaccompanied, the order taking care to add that "a lady is said to be 'accompanied' when one European or American member of a similar national and social status of the male sex is traveling with her."

And so on. This prompted one of these ladies to send a letter to the editor of the English-language daily, the *Baghdad Times,* in which she wrote, among other things:

What exactly is meant by a "Similar Social Status?"

It is quite difficult enough, in these days, to define a "Lady," but when she has to have a Similar Social Status as well, it becomes impossible without the help of some lucid official definition.

It is rather important, for I gather from the above-mentioned document that if she is neither a Lady, nor possessed of any Social Status in particular, the authorities do not really mind what becomes of her . . .

I take it that before accepting any invitation that may be made, she must also be very careful to look into the adequate Social Status of the European or American who is to accompany her. This is always judicious, especially when travelling abroad—and cannot be too carefully recommended. But a few hints as to how to decide on such a matter at short notice would be very useful. Socks and ties and an Oxford manner are apt to be misleading, and a short test that could be applied rapidly whenever an excursion or expedition is under discussion appears to be highly advisable.

EL-CHIFIL—THE GUARANTOR

The second time I was in Iran was some thirty-five years after our Kermanshah stay. During a study tour of Iran in the spring of 1967, our group stopped one day at a small town with a large and ancient mosque. The place was picturesque and imposing and, taking off our shoes, we went inside. Recounting the mosque's history and some other details, our Persian guide pointed to a tomb situated in the middle of the open courtyard and evidently well preserved. "And there," he said, "is the shrine of the Prophet Ezekiel, *'alaihi es-salam* (may his soul rest in peace)."

I was the only member of the group who came from Iraq—and I was thus the most shocked by the information. There was, of course, nothing very remarkable about a Jewish prophet from the early period of the Babylonian Exile being buried in any part of the Persian Empire, of which Iraq was an important part. But for me it was different; I knew that the tomb of the Prophet Ezekiel was situated in a holy place not far from Baghdad known to Jews and Muslims alike as El-Chifil. But there was no point in raising the question at the time and my murmurs of astonishment were hardly heard by the company. Two shrines of the same man, I kept wondering! Even if the man happened to have been an acknowledged prophet!

I had visited El-Chifil only once, as a little boy. The reason why I was not taken there regularly had something to do, I believe, with the expense involved. In Judaism there are three pilgrimage festivals — Passover, Weeks, and Tabernacles — but the tradition of the Jews of Iraq was that the pilgrimage to El-Chifil was to be made during Pentecost (*Shavu'ot* — Weeks), and on this occasion they used to recite the Scroll of Ezekiel. This tradition was so old and so entrenched that the name of the feast itself became the Feast of the Visit, or Pilgrimage (*'id el-zyagha*). But the pilgrimage entailed some expense, since it took more than one day and alms had to be given, accommodation paid for, and food bought and prepared. It was not that poor Jews did not make the pilgrimage; they did, and usually slept in the open or inside the outer courtyard of the shrine and probably lived off the leftovers from meals prepared by the well-to-do. It was that families of a certain standing and "pedigree," even though they might be the poorest materially, could not afford to be seen behaving like paupers.

And so it was that I never really had a good glimpse of the shrine at El-Chifil. In later times I came to regret it, because the place has one of the most fascinating histories and even its name had a bearing on a subject in which I was to become absorbed — namely, relations and mutual influences between Jews and Muslims in the Middle East generally and in Iraq in particular.

It is not generally known that the name El-Chifil is taken directly from the Koran, the holy book of Islam. The Prophet Ezekiel is mentioned in the Koran twice, but in neither case by name. In Surah XXI, The Prophets, 85, Allah orders His Messenger: "And mention Ishmael, and Idris (Enoch) and Dhul-Kifl. All were of the steadfast." In Surah XXXVIII, Sad, 49, Allah again enjoins Muhammad: "And make mention of Ishmael and Elisha and Abul-Kifl. All are of the chosen." In footnotes attached to the name Abul-Kifl in both cases the English translator of the Koran, Pickthall, states: "A prophet famous among the Arabs, whose story resembles that of Ezekiel."

The use of Dhul-Kifl instead of the prophet's name is because Ezekiel was known by that name, which translated literally means "He of the guarantee." Ezekiel, of course, earned this name through the prophecy he made in which he guaranteed the Babylonian Exile a reconciliation with God and the restoration of Jerusalem through their return. It was Ezekiel who, in a general mood of growing despondency and lack of hope, countered with his vision of the dry bones, a symbolic expression of faith and hope in Israel's ultimate regeneration. The precise circumstances in which the appellation Dhul-Kifl was passed from the Muslims to the Jews of Iraq, and the answer to the related question as to whether the composers of the Koran themselves did not borrow it from the Jews of Arabia, are not immediately known. I still find it remarkable that the Jews of Iraq should have borrowed the name from the holy book of Islam.

I have always wondered what Muslims would read into this remarkable coincidence—and whether they were altogether aware of it. I am therefore astounded to see that some kind of controversy went on about the subject not long ago in at least one Arabic newspaper. In its issue of August 1, 1981, the Kuwaiti daily *Al-Siyasa* ran an article by one of its columnists, Hasan el-'Alawi, an Iraqi émigré, with the peculiar title: "Is Ezekiel a Muslim or a Jew?" The gist of the piece is that Allah, by mentioning Ezekiel and praising him as "of the chosen" along with other upright men, showed some bias in favor of the Jews—especially that Ezekiel is given the name Dhul-Kifl because he promised them a return to Jerusalem and regeneration. Since this was unthinkable, 'Alawi implied, Ezekiel perhaps was in fact a Muslim and the place where his shrine lies is a mosque rather than a Jewish holy place.

'Alawi then tells the story of a certain Haj Dharb, who he claims was "mayor" of the town of El-Chifil in the days of the Ottoman Sultan Abdul Hamid. This good Muslim, irked by the mass pilgrimage of Jews to the shrine, wrote the *vali* protesting that the place was a mosque, witness the minaret therein from which the muezzin continued to send out his calls for prayer. The *vali* thereupon sent one of his subordinates to investigate the matter in person. But this official, having been generously bribed by the Jews, sat, in the shade of the minaret itself, and wrote out a report testifying that there was no such thing as a minaret in the mosque in El-Chifil! However, good Haj Dharb refused to give up, and promptly wrote the *vali* to say that the subordinate's report was a fabrication and that the *vali* himself can come and see that a minaret in fact stood there.

The *vali* didn't come but reported the affair to his superiors in Istanbul, who decided to send a special commission to enquire into the good Haj's claim. But the commission too was bought by bribes, "and probably by women too," and its members duly confirmed the Ottoman official's previous false report—and this without ever reaching the location. And thus a report was sent to the sultan: There is no minaret in the mosque of El-Chifil! Finally the Sultan died, the bribed officials died, and the *vali* died—and no one now remembers the good Haj Dharb who fought single-handedly for the Arabness of El-Chifil and the Islam of the mosque. "As for the minaret," 'Alawi concludes, "it still stands right there!"

This provoked David Khalaschi, an Iraqi Jew living in London, to give what he claims to be the Jewish side of the story. It transpires—according to this version of the story—that a minaret was indeed built there, on the orders of the same Sultan Ulgaitu who ordered the building restored. The minaret was built as a mark of respect for the Prophet Muhammad and was never used to call the believers to prayer. As to the allegation that Abdul Hamid's delegation failed to reach El-Chifil to investigate the matter as a result of the bribes paid its members by the Jews, Khalaschi explains that the delegation behaved in the way they did simply because they were convinced of the truth of the account given to them by three leading members of the Jewish community in Baghdad.

| *H*ESQAIL ABUL ʿALWA
HIRES A HELPER

*I*t was only toward the end of 1945, when I was almost twenty-two, that I finally got my secondary school certificate. It was a very narrow escape, so to speak, since in the final exams I failed in history and by some mistake or a miracle got 54 in mathematics. The problem of having to sit again for the history exam at the end of the summer vacation caused me a great deal of anxiety throughout the vacation, especially since I could not muster the will-power to really prepare for it properly. By that time I had cultivated so many friendships and my literary and intellectual interests had become so varied and ambitious that I could not just put everything aside and memorize the tedious dates, causes, factors, and consequences of all those distant events, especially since the textbooks were badly written and poorly organized. Finally, I did manage to make it in the so-called "complementary" exam, *ikmal,* getting the incredibly high mark of 70.

By the time I received the certificate, whose main advantage was exemption from compulsory military service with an indefinite "threat" of future recruitment in the officers corps, I had worked in a good number of places. The first job I ever had, as far as I can remember, was when I was nine, and my first employer was a man by name of Hesqail el-Hlali. It was a few months after our return from Najiyya's wedding in Kermanshah in October 1934, with me still convalescing from my terrible pneumonia, that el-Hlali came into my life. Hlali was married but childless, and he lived with his wife in one or two rooms in *Beit Abul Juss.* They were in the *haram* (ladies' quarter) of the two-house building, and we occupied the *diwankhana.*

Hesqail el-Hlali must have come originally from some village or small town in the south. He dressed, looked, behaved, and spoke like any Muslim farmer or landowner or tribal chief come to the metropolis on business or to see some senior official or minister. In certain parts of Baghdad, such as El Karkh (Baghdad west), men of his build, bearing, and dress were to be seen; but I don't remember having seen any Jew clad in the same way—complete with *kafiyya*, *'egal*, and *'abaya*. His occupation, an auctioneer in the vegetable and fruit wholesale market in Baghdad west—the *'alwa*—was strenuous though undemanding in terms of time and apparently quite rewarding financially. He had to be in the *'alwa*, a good half an hour's walk from where we lived, by 3:00 or 4:00 A.M. every day of the week except Saturdays and the various Jewish feasts, when anyway business was slack because the Jews on those days did no shopping. It was the time the grocers and vendors came to purchase their daily supplies of fruit and vegetables from the farmers who had spent the night bringing their wares to the *'alwa*, mostly on donkeys and often enough on their own backs or heads.

While Hesqail—who in our household came to be known as *Abul 'alwa*—was used to this kind of life, he could not possibly cope with the work alone. There were the wares to move from place to place and to put on display for everyone to see, then the auctioning itself, then when the price had been settled there was weighing to do and calculations to make and money to collect and then to pay after deducting the commission due. And as though that was not enough, there was the added work involved in taking and putting safely aside a certain tiny portion of the fruit or vegetable sold, the lot then to be taken home. By the standards of those days, *Abul 'alwa* was not young either: At forty or thereabout a man was usually considered, and probably he too considered himself, as coming on to old age. In short, he needed help. He approached my parents—or did they in fact approach him?—and the offer was readily accepted.

Not that I had any objection to work, especially that it gave me an opportunity to have some pocket money. But rising at such unearthly hours and undertaking the long march to and from the *'alwa* was too much even for an unspoiled child. Our financial situation, too, was not as bad as it had been in the early days following my brother Eliahu's bankruptcy though it was bad enough. But the reward was too tempting—all of twenty *fils* a day and, more important still, a generous and steady supply of free fruit and vegetables that was more than we were used to consuming. Thus my parents made it clear that I should take the job. But the ordeal did not last long. Following the school's spring vacation, throughout which I worked, it became obvious that I could not possibly do the job and attend school as well. Hesqail thus had to make do without me, and it was only when the summer vacation started that I took up the toil again.

I don't know if I was something of a weakling. (Mother used to say that the reason I was so "delicate" [*nazuki*] was that, when only a few weeks old, I had caught a very bad cold from exposure to the winds while sleeping on the roof of a summer night—an illness whose aftereffects allegedly kept afflicting me all my life.) I myself tend to attribute it to nutrition deficiency and "sexual exhaustion." The fact was, though, that following any real physical exertion my nose used to begin to bleed—and when that happened the line was clearly and firmly drawn. It began to happen after a few weeks of working with Hesqail during the summer months and it was decided that, the twenty *fils* and the bounty of vegetables and fruit notwithstanding, the arrangement with our neighbor must be terminated.

HASAN AND A SHAM SUICIDE ATTEMPT

I soon found a new job to last me the summer vacation. By then my brother Eliahu had gone into brokerage. Since I was very young and untrained, however, only small merchants would have me work for them—and such a one was Eliahu Cohen, a newcomer to Baghdad from Khanaquin in the north and technically a Kurd. He was one of three or four grown-up brothers and apparently the least successful of the lot, and he was helped to open a small wholesale business so that he would be gainfully employed on the one hand and gain the family some sort of foothold in the metropolis on the other. My job was simply to sit in a tiny room chock-full of cartons and bundles of underwear, socks, handkerchiefs, and such like items. Most of the time I spent in idleness, my work consisting of fetching now some cartons, now some bundles to show a customer; making packs of merchandise sold and counted; counting and checking merchandise received; and guarding the fort while the boss went to close a deal, have a meal, or go to the lavatory.

It was tedious and totally uninspiring work—were it not for two kinds of distractions near at hand. Eliahu Cohen's business was situated in a *khan* in Banks Street, so called because literally all the banks—Eastern Bank, the Ottoman Bank, and Zilkha Bank—had their premises there. The street also had the advantage of housing all the best coffee shops including Moshi's, a post office, and a good number of shops and vendors selling meals and snacks to the hundreds of businessmen, clerks, brokers, and idlers of all kinds who crowded the place all day long.

Among these was a Christian from the northern village of Talkeif who sold what was indisputably the best *kubba burghul* in town. He prepared them at home himself and brought them, fresh and hot, at about ten o'clock—and within an hour or so he was gone, his huge pot completely empty and he content and happy with his lot. He never tried to expand the business by making more of the stuff or working in two shifts or hiring an assistant. I loved the *kubba,* the well-shaped ground wheat balls plentifully stuffed with meat, onions, and almonds, and sometimes could even afford to buy one, but my difficulty always was that in a crowded street like that I couldn't possibly buy one myself without being noticed, either by Mr. Cohen or by one of his customers, or my brother or one of his friends, or by some relative or friend of the family—any and all of whom would be profoundly shocked to see me buying or eating not merely nonkosher food but food prepared by a *'arel* (uncircumcised, hence a Christian). Eventually, though, I found a safe way to do it—and here is where Hasan comes in and the story of my friendship with him starts.

Hasan was a craftsman and in his own way a real artist. In his mid-twenties he earned quite a lot of money mending Persian carpets, including especially old and rare ones that used to be brought for repair by what I took to be the cream of Iraqi society and very impressive foreigners, mostly British. He worked very hard, sitting there all day long mending, matching colors, pruning, and in the end performing what seemed to many to be wonders of craftsmanship. An affluent merchant and dealer in carpets hired Hasan. Beside new choice carpets such as those made in Kashan, Qum, and Isfahan, the merchant bought and sold antique carpets of value. I remember how I used to be lost in wonder as to how in the world it was possible that something which to me looked like a threadbare rug could fetch such astronomical sums as fifty, sixty, or even a hundred dinars and more. Hasan tried to explain the mystery to me but I don't think I was really convinced.

Hasan was a Shi'i Muslim from Karbala, which like nearby Najaf was populated exclusively by Persians or Arabized Persians, some naturalized and some still carrying Persian passports. No matter how long they lived in the country, these Shi'i Muslims and their children never managed to speak Arabic without a strong accent—and Hasan was no exception. With his boss, indeed, he spoke hardly a word of Arabic. He read the language, though, and if I am not mistaken he used to speak to the *sahibs* in their own tongue, at least the few words needed to accept an assignment and indicate the prices. He also quite often spoke of the position of his community and of how the Shi'is, although a majority of the Muslim population, were still denied their fair share in the government of the day in favor of the Sunni minority.

It was not at all an easy task procuring my day's portion of *kubba.* The trouble was that as a Shi'i Hasan himself was not supposed to eat something prepared by a Christian—or a Jew—and the purchase itself had to be done surreptitiously lest he be seen by his boss or some other fellow Shiʻi. Soon however another difficulty arose: Hasan would take money from me for the *kubba* no longer. The choice this left me was excruciating—either the *kubba* at Hasan's expense or no *kubba*. Needless to say that, with what I had already learnt about Iraqi males and their ways, Hasan's insistence on buying me one almost every day—at the exorbitant cost of six *fils* each—had to ring a bell with me. But he was so nice and gentle about it, and so damned convincing, that I was able to accept his explanations though with a bit of rationalizing on my part.

Hasan was alone in Baghdad and hardly had any regular contacts with his family in Karbala. He lived in a tastefully furnished room in some residential *khan* not far from where we both worked, and one evening he was able to persuade me to have dinner with him in his room. I must have been a daredevil to go, but I was not disappointed. It seemed a simple, honest-to-God friendship based on some common tastes and interests and also on the merely accidental fact that Hasan earned so much money while I was so poorly paid. The invitation was repeated and became a frequent occurrence—and each time it was exactly the same: conversation, a meal, and more conversation and then it was time for good night and I left. Never in any of those solitary meetings did Hasan ever try so much as to touch me.

This went on for weeks. The food was excellent, mostly kebab and mixed grill, choice fruit fresh or dried, and some other "goodies," and the chats quite pleasant. However, though Hasan never made a movement, certain signs began to appear that gave me cause for concern: The way he looked at me, the manner in which he approached me, and—on second thoughts—the fact that there was in reality no earthly reason for a Shiʻi Muslim in his mid-twenties to befriend a Jewish boy barely fourteen years of age just for the sake of companionship. It began to dawn on me, too, that no one in his senses would spend money to maintain such an innocent relationship.

It was then that I decided to end the relationship, and it remained for poor me to find a decent way out. I was so distraught that I decided to consult my father—the first and last time ever that I had to resort to such a device. Father listened carefully, interrupting my account only when he had a question to ask or a point he wanted me to explain or amplify. In the end, of course, he counseled what was the one and only course to take— stop accepting his invitations and refrain from taking any gifts or tokens but go on being friendly to the man and don't make it seem like a total break.

This I did, as gently and as subtly as I knew how. It didn't work—or it did seem to work but only for a time. The stratagem was too obvious to be veiled and its practical consequences too painful for Hasan to bear or ignore. His many attempts at persuasion and temptation—he knew well my weaknesses—were in vain. I do not know whether it was one of these attempts, but in the meantime he had moved to another, more spacious room on Banks Street itself and began to tell me about his new friend or friends, inviting me to come with them. I persisted. One day, however, he persuaded me to visit him in his room in the early morning hours, when in that busy neighborhood nothing unusual could happen, no shout for help or anything of the kind could escape notice.

It was a nice room, and the table was full of dirty dishes and leftovers from what he said was the previous evening's dinner party. (I never really believed it was anything more than a ruse and I never noticed him talking or going with any likely guests.) He brought a bottle of some white liquid and two glasses. He started on a whole long tearful account of how much he was attached to me and how all of it was quite innocuous and had nothing to do with a physical relationship. Now that I had decided not to see much of him, he said, life had become quite meaningless and was no longer worth living—and he had therefore decided to take his own life. However, having caused him so much pain and unhappiness and being the direct cause of his decision to put an end to his life, he thought it was only fair that I too should drink from the white liquid so that the two of us would perish together.

All this time tears, real bitter tears, were streaming from Hasan's eyes and I was made completely miserable. But I did not desist. On the contrary. Sensing the state he was in and the pain I had caused him I decided then and there that I could not possibly have anything to do with him any more even if it meant participating in his insane suicide plan. Finally, moved by a thousand confusing and contradictory emotions, I acceded, and both of us drank what I took to be an instant killer. But the white liquid was no poison, just pure spirit—and after that ludicrous performance I never saw Hasan again.

PEDDLING SOCKS AND HANDKERCHIEFS

My acquaintance with Hasan, with the tragicomic scenes that led to its termination, all took place during the summer vacation of what was to be my last year at Madrasat Ras el-Qarya. It was obvious after the melodrama in Hasan's room that I could not continue with my work for Eliahu Cohen. It was not difficult to find me a job, now that I had acquired some experience in dealing with haberdashery items. My next job was in fact a better and more "advanced" one, and consisted of assisting the owner of a real posh though small store on Baghdad's main shopping center in those days, Shari' el Shat—River Street. The owner was a middle-aged Jew of quiet, easygoing ways and he soon pronounced me a good worker, quick to learn and to take orders and also nice to the customers.

The store—they were called *maghazat,* from the French *magazines,* in those days—offered quite a variety of things in addition to the goods usually described as haberdashery, such as ladies' stockings, scarves, and underwear; scents and make-up devices; brushes and various pastes and even soap. Every one of these goods was imported from abroad and the clientele was of a certain socioeconomic class, mostly society ladies who, even though they had to put on the *'abaya,* were not strict about unveiling their faces when busy examining the wares offered.

Many of these ladies were Muslim, and for me it was something of an education to see the sharp contrast between their whiteness and the usually dark complexions of their less fortunate co-religionists. It was only later that I learned the reason. Many of these rich or formerly rich but certainly society women were either of local Turkish extraction themselves or the daughters of Turkish mothers and often Turkish fathers. They were in fact relics of the Ottoman period, when Iraqis of standing used to go to Istanbul to study or work or represent their *vilayet* in the Majlis and often came back accompanied by a Turkish wife of pedigree, or a wife from some European part of the empire.

The fact seems to be that, in a country where everyone looked tanned to dark, whiteness was much in demand, especially in women. In addition to those Iraqis who brought wives from their Turkish sojourns, there were of course all those Ottoman officials who came to Iraq to run the affairs of the *vilayet,* established families, married their daughters to local notables, and in many cases stayed on, having been partially Arabized.

My work in the River Street store lasted for a few months. I no longer recall the reason for my leaving that job; it was probably slackness of business or some other factor that had nothing to do with me or with my performance. It was already spring of 1938 when I left—and my brother Eliahu, in consultation with Father, decided that I could make more money if I were to make the rounds of certain parts of the city and their coffee shops peddling a few small wares like socks and handkerchiefs.

It was thus that I became a street vendor at fourteen. My brother Eliahu

took me to a friend of his, a good-hearted Jew who was a wholesaler dealing in these goods, and he agreed not only to sell these items to me on
credit but also to allow me some additional discount so that what I paid
for those socks and handkerchiefs was even less than a retailer paid.

It was a lucrative occupation financially, though tiring and often an-
noying. I don't recall having ever earned so much money in my life. A
pair of socks that I bought at 150 *fils* the dozen I managed to sell at anything between 15 and 20 *fils* the pair. My customers, mostly frequenters of
coffee shops sitting there either playing backgammon or belaboring their
eternal worry beads, did not know much about prices and did not seem
to care—especially during the few first days of the month when something of their salaries had yet been left. They were mostly Muslims, but it
was not a question of their being "dumb *goyim*"—and in the end I doubt
whether they in fact paid more than they would have paid buying the same
goods at a haberdashery store. In those days Japan was already flood-
ing the markets with goods, but their quality was generally so poor that
Japanese-made wares had earned a rather bad reputation. I never peddled
them in my street-vending days and offered only good quality goods—so
much so that I managed to build something of a steady clientele.

It was during this period, peddling my wares one day in Al Mutanabbi
Street, that I happened to enter a large furniture store offering my wares.
Adjoining the store was a small carpentry workshop in which a dozen or
so men hammered, sawed, and glued. The suggestion came from one of
the two owners, themselves working carpenters turned dealers in modern furniture—and the next thing I knew was that I became something of
a clerk-cum-messenger boy-cum-apprentice accountant. The place had
the added advantage of being situated some three or four minutes' walk
from *Beit Yamein,* where we were living at the time. It was there that I
finally finished my elementary schooling, attending night classes at the
Mamouniyya Night School for the purpose.

By now I had built myself a small library, the shelves having been made
for me especially and at cost price at the carpentry shop in which I worked.
As far as my schooling was concerned, I had by then successfully passed
the government's exams, which enabled me to join what was called the
intermediate school, *al-mutawassita.* But I was biding my time, and preferred reading and other intellectual pursuits to the hateful discipline of
the crammed classroom.

At about this time, two years or so after I had left the carpentry store
late in 1939, with Eliahu now again the only breadwinner, a fateful decision was taken by the family after much soul-searching, chest-beating, and

haggling: Hella by now had simply had enough of us—Father, Mother, myself and my youngest sister Simha—and a separation became inevitable. We had to move to another place and leave my brother and his wife and their four children to live their own lives without constant interference from Mother and the rest of us. It was not easy, since among other things Eliahu had to continue to keep us—to pay the rent and a weekly allowance that enabled the four of us to live however frugally. We again became tenants' subtenants, so to speak, but we were at long last through with the endless arguments and fights between the two "factions" of the family.

BUSINESS PARTNER OF SORTS

As far as I was concerned, however, the move did not make much of a difference. Shortly after the move, in the spring of 1940, in what was an attempt to help me earn some sort of living, Eliahu arranged for me to be a minor partner in a small shop on Al-Rashid Street adjoining the gate of the Great Mosque of the Haydarkhana quarter. The other and major partner was none other than Najiyya's husband, my cousin Eliahu, whose wedding I had attended in Kermanshah some eight years previously. It was not long after the couple and their three children decided to return to Baghdad, either for business reasons or just on the spur of the moment. At first Eliahu opened a modest shop in an obscure corner of Suq el-Midan—an overwhelmingly Muslim neighborhood where business was slack most days of the month but pretty brisk the first days of each month. For some reason or other, however, my brother-in-law thought he would make a better living if only he could open a shop on the city's main street, where he planned to sell, besides the haberdashery items he used to sell in the old shop, some foodstuffs such as sugar, tea, rice, and nuts. He was convinced that the best business would be trading in "things for the stomach."

By that time my brother Eliahu had established himself as a broker dealing in the same line of merchandise and was already helping our brother-in-law in small matters of credit and professional advice. It was to Eliahu therefore that Najiyya's husband went for advice and help on his new project—and when his decision to make the shift became final and no amount of persuading on my brother's part availed, Eliahu suggested that he take me as partner, with him providing whatever capital was needed in the form of goods and credit. The deal was made and I—an aspiring intellectual, a dilettante, a book worm, something of a dreamer—suddenly found myself sitting in that tiny shop offering merchandise and bargaining over prices and weighing sugar and rice and tea. All this however would have been tolerable were it not for one unfortunate circumstance: Business proved to be even slacker than it had been in Suq el-Midan, and the sight of the two of us sitting there in that tiny shop eagerly awaiting a customer was just too much for me to bear. Partnership had to be terminated also because the shop could not support even my sister's family.

'ADNAN AL-CHALABI'S MOTHER

It was during those bleak and wearying days that I made 'Adnan al-Chalabi's acquaintance. 'Adnan was a fine lad of sixteen and looked more European than Arab. He had blond hair and blue eyes and was white—no doubt a descendant of some earlier meeting between an Ottoman officer and some young woman from Rumania, Hungary, or another of the countries of Southeast Europe which came under Ottoman rule. It was not really a very rare thing in Baghdad in those days, and it is to be assumed that the breed is still to be seen there. I never managed to know any significant details about 'Adnan's family; all I knew was that his mother was either divorced or deserted by his father, that he lived with his mother and his two teenage sisters.

We became very friendly and I used to take 'Adnan home with me and show him my books and magazine collections. But somehow our friendship never managed to be on that intellectual level. The young man, though he took an interest in current affairs and was something of a budding Marxist, had no real interest in ideas of the kind I had. In a certain sense I was more interested in 'Adnan as a person, and in the story of his life and of that of his family than in his intellectual aspirations or his ideas. I also managed to indulge in some mixture of fantasy regarding the three blonde females living in that house with him. From the things he told me I gathered that his mother was "modern" and liberal socially and wore no veil—and indeed when I visited him in his home the mother actually showed her face to me and even served some sherbet and tea. She was comparatively rather young—thirty-five or thereabouts—and had a shapely figure.

It was really rather foolish of me to think that I could ever reach 'Adnan's mother. If she were some kind of "society prostitute" then she would either be kept by some rich man or her price would bc too high—not to mention the embarrassment of my being a friend of the son. If she were just a liberated woman then she would certainly consider me too young and too inexperienced to take as lover. The whole thing was hopeless as far as the mother was concerned—while the difficulty with the sisters was that they were too young, and a breach of the accepted norms and mores would have been unthinkable—and these mores dictated that a friend of the family, especially a friend of the brother's, was never to touch the sisters unless his intentions were strictly "honorable."

In a sense this untenable situation made of me some sort of "young man about the house" with 'Adnan's family, and I was beginning to feel somewhat protective about the mother and the daughters. One night, all the five of us went to the movies—and when 'Adnan and I spotted some cheeky young men eyeing his mother and even making some gestures and remarks, it was I rather than 'Adnan who all but challenged them—and it was he who tried to calm me down, explaining that this was not an unusual thing to happen to his mother, and that the best thing to do in such cases was to ignore the young men and their antics completely.

Eventually, after we moved out of the neighborhood and I took a job with Eastern Bank, I lost sight of 'Adnan and persuaded myself that no good could come from my seeming infatuation with him and with his unprotected family. One of the strangest things that happened during our months of friendship I must record here, though. One day 'Adnan complained of pain in the throat—a not unusual occurrence what with the sudden changes in the weather. When aspirins and other primitive cures did not help, 'Adnan was forced to see a doctor. The doctor's verdict: 'Adnan had contracted syphilis—in the throat! I had never known—and I dare say I still don't know—of any such cases, nor do I know if the infection is at all possible in any part of the body other than the genitals.

The other problem with that infection was the question as to how, given that it did occur, such a thing would happen to 'Adnan. He swore he had not done anything to explain the mystery and declared himself as puzzled as I was. In the end he said he was receiving the proper treatment; I think antibiotics were just making an appearance in Baghdad and he was getting injections of penicillin. But the whole episode seemed to me so weird and gave me such feelings of revulsion that I gradually disengaged myself from 'Adnan and his family of three lovely and eminently desirable blondes.

| *L*IVING IN SEXUAL DEPRIVATION

*I*n the mid-1950s, observing young men and women in their teens embracing, kissing, and "necking" openly in the streets, buses, and underground stations of London, Paris, Rome, Tel Aviv, and Jerusalem, I could not help thinking of the long years of sexual deprivation of the youth of the Baghdad in which I was born and grew up. And I own that these feelings were not always free of a kind of envy, a nagging awareness of what members of my generation missed in terms of vital human experience.

But it was a life not totally devoid of awards. I don't quite know what youngsters today do for "real" sex—whether, that is, the endless kissing and the very serious-looking necking always leads to actual intercourse. Be that as it may, my own deprivation was not as complete and final as it sounds. Apart from those so-called "nocturnal emissions," in which one had to rely exclusively on the imagination aided by a certain kind of book or picture, there were always some opportunities for physical contact of sorts.

Overcrowded public places and occasional female guests staying with us for a period of time were the main source of such contacts. In the small room in the *diwankhana* we had for ourselves in *Beit Abul Juss,* there were five of us and we had to make do with two beds, one single and the other a rather large double bed. The arrangement was that Father and I used the single bed, while Mother and my two sisters occupied the large one. This was so because of religious and, I suspect, other reasons that made it unthinkable for my parents to share the same bed anyway. But I was supposed to be the spoiled child of the family and I often made use of that piece of fiction to exchange my place with my younger sister, so that I could sleep in the other bed. The temptation to do so became especially strong when we had Hella's younger sister staying with us on her frequent visits from Khanaquin where the family still lived. Sleeping in the same bed with the attractive young woman had naturally its own rewards where my sexual needs were concerned, and it was on one of those winter nights of 1935–1936 that I reached sexual maturity, and I still remember vividly the time I had my first real emission. I cannot say I was frightened or even surprised—I just took it in my stride. I don't know if I already had some knowledge of what it was; but somehow, coming after almost a decade of regular "dry" climaxes, I saw nothing unusual about the phenomenon except the inconvenience of wet underwear and the fear that I would be "discovered."

The reason why Hella's younger sister stayed with us so frequently was that she came to Baghdad to meet a cousin of hers with whom she was having a long and illicit courtship. A senior official at the Ministry of the Interior working directly with the minister's all-powerful British advisor, the young man was rightly considered a great success and his family had very high hopes as to the kind and class of girl they would consider suitable as his future wife. Themselves hailing from the north, they were a hardy, noisy, and querulous lot and quite determined to prevent the betrothal of their son to a cousin who could bring him neither a decent dowry nor social advancement. They kept quite a watch on the poor girl, so that every time she was staying with us two or three of them came—usually the father and the elder brother—and made such a scene that the whole neighborhood could hear. The fights went on uniform lines of argument—the wily and immodest cousin was tempting their innocent darling boy, arranging illicit meetings with him, and trying to snatch him from his family. And they always concluded by swearing that they would never, never let the boy take her hand in marriage. But they failed to keep their word: the two finally did get married and for many years to come there followed a total estrangement between the two sides.

"NOCTURNAL EMISSIONS"

In an essay titled "The Transformation of Puberty," Freud gives this description of nocturnal emission: "In the case of a man living a continent life, the sexual apparatus, at varying intervals . . . discharges the sexual substances during the night, to the accompaniment of pleasurable feelings and in the course of a dream which hallucinates a sexual act." Not only do I feel obliged to take Freud's word for it as a great authority; the fact is that every young man of my generation with whom I dared broach the subject of sex spoke of nocturnal emission as a common and familiar experience.

Speaking for myself, however, I must confess that I never had that experience, not even once in my whole life. Is "nocturnal emission," then, some sort of euphemism for the activity called masturbation? Do young males speak of nocturnal emission because they are loath to admit they masturbate? I have often put this question to myself since, in those days far more than in our own times, masturbation had a frightfully bad name. It was called "the illicit habit," and was said to have such terrible after-effects, such crippling results, that it would not have been in the least surprising had my contemporaries been reluctant to admit the practice even to themselves.

I used to live in terror of the consequences, and when after many years of regular practice I neither went blind nor died of tuberculosis, nor even lost my mind, I was somehow relieved but continued to be afflicted by bouts of self-pity and self-reproach. How, I lamented—how much more alive mentally, how diligent and industrious and healthy and practical and bright, and in a hundred other ways more of a success would I have been had it not been for that accursed habit of mine! Friends with whom I was intimate enough to talk to about these things were usually ready with expressions of sympathy and pity. They were also ready with advice: As soon as you are troubled by sexual thoughts and fantasies, they would say, get busy with something—read a book, do some exercise, take a cold shower, or just drink a glass of cold water, eat a sandwich (preferably with pickles and hot peppers), go out for a walk, think about something else! Needless to say, not a single one of these tricks worked.

There were, too, so many inducements, excitations, and provocations that I never stopped wondering how all those friends of mine who spoke so freely about nocturnal emission could possibly last the day so as to have their hallucinatory sex dreams at night. This is why I kept suspecting my friends of lying, distortion, or at best wishful thinking. One of these days, too, I will have to find out whether the great Freud ever went on record to admit that he had actually experienced nocturnal emission—because only such a direct testimony would go some of the way toward allaying my suspicions that not only my friends but his patients too cheated the doctor shamelessly when they spoke of the phenomenon.

IN THE JURI HOUSEHOLD

Miriam was Mother's favorite sister. My first recollections of her are of a well-dressed, shapely woman a little past her mid-twenties. In fact, by prevailing standards of taste in the human female, Aunt Miriam was something of a beauty—white, round-faced, full without being plump, and with small and well-proportioned features. She was young enough, moreover, not to be expected to wear a *shaqsa,* a loose and rather inadequate headgear that Iraqi Jewish women used to wear for modesty.

To top it all, Aunt Miriam was considered rich. Of all her sisters, she had managed to be married to a well-to-do man. Moshe Juri, a tall man with an imposing figure, was a dealer in tobacco, a partner in one of the first cigarette factories in Baghdad, and the man to operate one of the first cinema theaters in the city—the Royal Cinema. I am convinced that, without the opportunity furnished by this accident, my introduction to movies would have come at a much later stage of life. The arrangement was relatively very simple. I used to loiter there for the hour or so prior to the start of the film and, on the rare occasions when the house was not full, one or another of the employees, almost all relatives of Moshe Juri, let me in.

Royal Cinema was the first to introduce talking movies—and in addition used occasionally to offer actual theater, with a tiny repertoire mostly imported from Egypt and where the star in every case was the indefatigable Yusuf Wahbi.

Aunt Miriam was Juri's second wife. His first, Lulu, both much older than my aunt and totally unattractive, had given birth to a daughter, their first-born, and then stopped bearing children. This was enough justification, both socially and from the point of view of the rabbis, for Moshe to seek another spouse, and the choice fell on young Miriam. The Juris then lived in a spacious house in a good neighborhood, and by the time I was old enough to go there, my aunt had given birth to five sons and everyone was very proud of her.

By the late 1920s, the Juri household included Moshe and his two wives, his daughter from Lulu, his five sons, a widowed sister, Rosa, her two sons, Moshe's own mother Rahel, and one spiv-type youth named Ghali who was a nephew of the master of the house but whose precise relationship to him I never really comprehended and who neither attended school nor appeared to be gainfully employed in any capacity.

The dominant figure in the Juri household was undoubtedly Moshe's mother, Rahel. She had the first and last word in everything and nothing escaped her notice. Of all the matrons I had known, she struck me as being the most domineering and the most awe-inspiring. I vividly remember her sitting, seemingly from time immemorial and till the end of days, in the same spot on the *qanafa* in a strategic corner of the *tarar*— a kind of reception room in the open inner courtyard—watching everybody's movements, making her comments, grumbling disapproval, and giving orders. On Moshe Juri, her only son, she was reputed to have full control, mighty and all-powerful as he himself was. I figure that this influence, which amounted to something of a spell, was a result as much of her worldly wisdom as of the tolerance with which she used to overlook his many naughtinesses.

While still in her mid-twenties and after having borne him five sons, Aunt Miriam rather untypically chose to give birth to a daughter. It was a sad day for everybody in or connected with the household; Moshe Juri did not show up for lunch that day, and the eldest son Haron left the house in anger and disgust. A day or two later, though, the family became reconciled to the new reality, and the baby girl was named Khazna (treasury) after her maternal grandmother. Aunt Miriam then made another try— but this time too the newborn was a daughter. And this one, the last baby to be borne by her, was named after her paternal grandmother Rahel, who had died very shortly before Miriam's second daughter and seventh and last child was to be born, being spared the latest bad news, so to speak.

I don't know much about Moshe Juri's previous "life and loves," but shortly after the birth of the second daughter I became aware of the presence of at least one other woman in his life—a young woman married to a musician-singer from Beirut recently settled in Baghdad. The fact of her marriage did not seem to interfere in any way—neither where the husband was concerned nor where the family, Miriam, or society as a whole were. At one stage of the affair, indeed, the woman and her family lived in the same neighborhood in a house reputedly rented for her by Moshe. Apparently Moshe Juri was a philanderer and a considerable womanizer, and in those days there was nothing, absolutely nothing, a wife could do about a husband's infidelities.

Nor was there any attempt on the man's part to be in the least discreet about it. From older relatives I gathered subsequently that, in addition to the musician's wife, Juri had other mistresses. Sometimes, indeed, on a night on which he had his fill of hard drinks in one of the city's posh nightclubs, he would actually bring home with him some female dancer he had picked and spend the night with her in a room adjoining the master bedroom. Hard though it is to believe, I am also told that at least on one such occasion in summer, he did not hesitate to lay his companion of the night on a bed on the rooftop, where everybody in the household was sleeping and no walls separated the sleepers.

COUSIN EVELYN'S OPEN REBELLION

It was in Moshe Juri's house that I first came to know my long-lost Uncle Menashe, Mother's second eldest brother who had finally come back to Baghdad from Abadan in Persia, where he had spent all his grown-up years and raised his family. Abadan at the time was known as El-Muhammara. It was part of Khuzistan, also known as Arabistan, and shared the Shat-el-Arab river with Basra and the southern parts of Iraq. The province was practically Arab in all respects before the late Shah decided to "Iranize" it by encouraging migration there of ethnic Persians. But these efforts bore little fruit. I remember that as late as the spring of 1967, when there on a study tour, I was surprised to find that despite the Shah's earnest efforts Arabic remained the dominant tongue. In the bazaar, I spoke to the traders and peddlers in colloquial Iraqi Arabic and was answered in the same dialect as if it were the most natural thing in the world. I was even asked if I had come from Basra on a tour and once on an impulse I said, yes, of course.

Uncle Menashe came to Baghdad because his wife was seriously ill and, with three daughters and one little son, he simply could not cope. Only one of the daughters, Evelyn, who must have been fifteen or sixteen, was old enough to be of interest to me physically. She was ravishing and unbearably desirable, a stunning beauty who appeared to have known all about it and did nothing to hide it. I found her breathtakingly attractive — white-skinned, full without being fat, with blue eyes and auburn hair and a lovely little mouth. She was, indeed, everything one could wish for by way of an ideal object for one's youthful sexual fantasies.

I must by then have been ten or coming up to eleven and had become quite nimble at taking care of my sexual needs, modest and quite harmless as they were. What was more to the point, I was also young enough to be considered quite "safe" from the viewpoint of female chastity and decorum. A good deal of physical exposure on the part of a female relative in my presence was not considered taboo and I was indeed having the best of both worlds — being treated as an innocent minor on the one hand and managing to draw all the small satisfactions of touch, sight, and smell, all to be put to good use later in the privacy of the bed.

I was not alone in being impressed by my cousin Evelyn's beauty. All the ladies of the family remarked on her looks and bearing, although there were the usual reservations about the size and exact situation of certain of her features. (I never was to know what the males of the species thought of her since such topics were not supposed to be discussed and each man kept his thoughts to himself; but it was not difficult to guess.)

Now Evelyn was eminently eligible for marriage and Uncle Yuseif, Mother's oldest brother and the father of Yamein and three or four other aspiring sons, had a son who by the standards of those days was long past marriageable age. He was a moody, haughty sort of fellow in his early thirties and was the one in line to be betrothed—and who was supposed to make him a good wife but his cousin Evelyn? But Evelyn, besides being possessed of a rare figure and ravishing looks, had also a mind of her own. All through the short period of their engagement, family gossip had it that she was resisting the marriage—and a number of enlightened elders, including Mother, subtly implied that she was right to be unhappy about the match. After all, the young man was easily more than twice her age, besides being the least successful of his brothers; and yet, these understanding relatives added, it was her lot (*naseeb*), and she had no business actually resisting the marriage.

The marriage duly took place and there was a wedding ceremony in Uncle Yuseif's house where the couple was to reside. I seldom saw Evelyn again. The marriage did not last long, but instead of ending in an orderly divorce or separation—both quite unthinkable in the circumstances—it ended "tragically" with Evelyn's elopement. It transpired that, either shortly before or immediately after the marriage, Evelyn somehow met, was wooed, and seduced by a dark young Muslim lawyer of good family and a great deal of influence. Eventually, he took her for his mistress and then married her. It is said that she converted to Islam on her marriage—although strictly speaking she was not required to do so by Islamic law, which allows Muslims to marry Jewish or Christian women without these having to enter the faith.

THE MARXIST AND THE PROSTITUTE

In Baghdad of the late 1930s and 1940s, relations between the sexes were—to put it mildly—rather problematical; they also depended largely on the community, religion, or class to which a man or a woman belonged.

To be sure, there were a rich enough variety of inducements, excitations, and allurements. In the context of life in Baghdad of those days this may sound strange. What with the strict restraints imposed on women and on their appearances in public, the extremely primitive phase in which makeup was available, the total absence of hair-dos, and the sheer rarity of even a chance of seeing a pretty feminine face in public, such inducements would seem to be pretty rare or nonexistent.

This, of course, is sheer nonsense; it is tantamount to judging one era and one culture by the standards of another era and another culture. There were men and there were women, and their respective instincts and drives were the same as they had been since time immemorial and as they remain today. Even the *'abaya*, the cloaklike black wrap with which all Muslim women and the majority of Jewish and Christian women covered themselves from head to toes, was no guarantee against sexual stimulus. Sometimes, indeed, they were made by their wearers to function in a way that was diametrically opposed to their original objective. If the lady was intent on allurement, she could do it even better with than without the *'abaya*—and if she was homely, middle-aged, or in any number of other ways unattractive in her looks, she could always resort to the *pushi*, which covered her face completely and which was intended to be another and ultimate safeguard for modesty and chastity.

I remember vividly the time I worked as bank clerk when, sitting once in the middle of the day working at figures and trying to balance the accounts, a woman of indeterminate age and a completely covered face stood facing the teller opposite to mine. She was standing there, to cash a check or pay some bill, leaning on the wooden teller; and managing to do it in such a way that her shapely, rounded hips became recognizable in all their crevices and details. She was also shifting her body constantly in ways that I found so provocative and exciting that then and there I had to relieve the tension, using the ever-present and convenient device of my trouser pocket while ostensibly continuing with those figures and columns.

But not all the ladies of Baghdad covered their bodies and faces. For allurement and excitation even more rousing there were the foreign dames euphemistically called artistes, usually imported from the countries of the Balkans and Southeast Europe to work in the newly introduced nightclubs and "cabarets." I don't know how these young and not-so-young women would fare today as sex objects. Snow white, fleshy, and often fat, garishly dressed, and with heavily painted faces and lips, I fancy they wouldn't attract much attention in any Western metropolis today and pretty little of it even in Middle Eastern capitals.

In the Baghdad of those days, however, these foreign artistes were the rage. Of an afternoon, their wily employers would direct them to go out to take the air, and the way they did it was to hire an *'arabana*, a two-horse coach familiar in Baghdad at the time, and to be driven in the main Rashid Street from end to end and at leisure. They sat there in the open coaches, usually two at a go, with their skirts considerably lifted and their thighs on show. Neither the masses of creamy flesh at display nor the blue traces of veins that were there for everyone to see struck me or any of my male compatriots as in any way ugly or repellent. On the contrary, they were easily the best advertisement the owners of those cabarets could have hoped for.

I frequented these cabarets with friends whenever there was enough money to pay for the minimum fare. There was, of course, no question whatever of actually ordering drinks there, and we usually went there after having had a few drinks outside that we could afford. There was no art to speak of, either; the work of the girls consisted of nothing more sophisticated than appearing in a "number" half-naked and displaying their wares, often with the help of a male colleague who would dance with the girl and then, in a moment of mock-fury, would find a way of laying her on the floor flat on her face or in some other way in which the select audience were enabled to see more of her bare thighs. Another way of satisfying the clients' curiosity was for the male dancer to carry the "artiste" and make a bit of circling around so that no one would feel cheated.

We were all chronically half-broke and all we could do was sit and watch the numbers. Luckier men, usually much older than ourselves, managed to get more. A Kurdish classmate of mine at my night school, 'Ali al-Talabani, related to me once an experience his older brother had—and how he actually managed to bed one of these artistes. An army officer of considerable rank, he went to the cabaret on the day he received his salary. He had a few drinks and watched the numbers. There was one artiste to whom he was especially, apparently irresistibly, attracted. Knowing no foreign language well and having no intention of making a fool of himself, he simply took out from his breast pocket the wad of bank notes— the whole lot, something like twenty-four dinars (one hundred dollars) and flourished it before her face. On which she signaled him to follow her to a room upstairs, where it took him only a few minutes to relieve himself both of his physical predicament and his honest month's earnings. There were, to be sure, a few local theaters in which the country's famous singers—Salima Pasha, Zakiyya George, Sadiqa el-Mullaya, and others—stood before the microphone and sang. (There was no dancing involved.) These were cheaper to visit, but the "standard" and, what was far more important, the degree of physical exposure in these places were the thing for us.

MAKING DO WITH THE KALLACHIYYA

Not even one of my acquaintances in those days could afford such extravagances, much as we all dreamed and fantasized about those rare female creatures. Instead, we poor devils had only the natives to go to for consolation. Not that the local girls at the government-licensed red-light compound of narrow alleyways were all of them bad-looking or too old and

unshapely to be quite passable as sex objects. The Kallachiyya, the Turkish word by which the place was known, offered quite a choice of colors,
ages, ethnic origins, and shapes — and prices were convenient enough,
ranging as they did between 50 and 150 *fils* (20 to 60 cents).

But the place had a very bad name, and the policemen stationed at the
entrance were not always convinced or amused by our claim that we were
not under eighteen years of age. Nevertheless we went there, usually myself with one friend who was a little older and more familiar with the tricks
of the trade. There was always the problem of speed: The more attractive
and desirable the girl was, the more clients she attracted — and a gentle
knock at the door in the middle of the act was not an unusual occurrence.
There was not much time to talk, to indulge in love-play, to become sentimental about matters relating to the circumstances in which "a nice girl
like you," so young and so innocent, had been forced to end up in a place
like that. You paid your money, you got your "kicks," and that was that.

Being youngsters, mostly unemployed and with lots of time on our
hands, we used however to try and circumvent this situation by going
to the place late in the afternoon — as soon as the place was officially
opened — rather than at night when the grown-ups and the drunks used
to crowd the alleyways and the houses. It was thus possible for us, as often
as not, to stay considerably more with our chosen girl, to have some fore-
play, to chat with them, and to finish our business in relative peace and
quiet. The one single annoyance we used to experience was that, even if
you stayed long enough, you couldn't have a double orgasm for the same
money and we were far too broke to afford the luxury. In all my experience
only one girl agreed to keep the secret between us and thus her madam
did not demand an additional fee.

As for safeguards against venereal diseases, these were, apart from the
daily examinations the girls at the Kallachiyya were supposed to undergo
as a matter of routine, of two kinds — the "frenchleather" (condom),
which not only prevented direct contact but also entailed additional expense and was thus not always used, and the mandatory large kettle full of
pomegranate water and a basin at the corner where you could wash your
organ after you had finished — and the sooner you used it, it was advised,
the better.

In the streets and alleys adjoining the Kallachiyya, within the disrep-
utable Midan quarter, there were several unlicensed brothels where far
more classy madams operated. In these houses one could get the services of reportedly cleaner and certainly less used young females, at prices
ranging between 250 and 500 *fils,* an exorbitant sum we could afford

but rarely. They were closed, somewhat exclusive establishments run and maintained thanks only to the regular bribes paid to members of the so-called *shurtat al-akhlaq* (morality police) responsible for keeping those neighborhoods free of such goings-on. It was therefore an often-haphazard affair, when on one's next visit one was liable to find the house empty or occupied by respectable folks.

An added advantage of these places was that you could go there quite early in the afternoon. It was in one of them that I made the acquaintance of a young woman answering to the name of Khayriyya—a juicy morsel of a girl hailing from the north, with blue eyes and blond hair and snow-white complexion. I spent more time with her and visited her more often than any other prostitute I had frequented. Shortly after lunch, when the poor thing had a chance to have her siesta, I used to go to the house, where the madam would direct me to the girl's room with the information that I could wake her up, by giving her a kiss if I wished. Her reactions to my attempts at commiseration, which were matched only by the passion of my embraces, never ceased to make me wonder. Without putting it in actual words, her set reaction was a sad and meaningful look of under-standing, pity, and compassion, as though she were saying: What do little naive youngsters like you know about these things? I remember that what used to impress and sadden me most was the apparent absence of hope, the near-despair in those captivating eyes, and my own helplessness and inability to do something gallant and self-denying about what I took to be her terrible plight.

Many years later, a handsomely produced book with an equally inter-esting title came my way—*The Prostitute in Progressive Literature,* pub-lished in Britain by Allison and Busby in 1982. The author, Khalid Kish-tainy, is a fellow Iraqi of my own generation though I never came across him in Baghdad. In the book he devotes extremely little space to "pro-gressive literature" on the prostitute in Arabic but he manages to include a few semi-autobiographical passages that relate closely to the experiences I have just recounted. "It does not surprise me now," Kishtainy writes,

> that the first adventure in writing that I personally made during my university years—the years of student idealism, high-pitched anti-imperialist struggle and dedication to the cause of the socialist revolu-tion in Iraq—was a play about a prostitute who couldn't understand why she was not allowed to dispose of her baby as she wanted. In the early 1950s, the old brothel ghetto of Baghdad, the historic Kallachiyya, became the haunt of the revolutionary intellectuals who frequented the

place almost as a patriotic duty and often without having so much as the money to pay, the confidence to approach a pimp, or the guts to come anywhere near any woman. We used to stroll into the nooks and crannies of the old lanes, reciting passages from the Communist Manifesto and verses by Muhammad Salih Bahr al-Ulum's poem read on the prostitute's grave. There was the painter who paid a black whore only to sit for him. There was the story writer who invited a blind one to a meal of kebab only to hear her story. There was the art critic who went as far as buying himself a rubber sheath only to end up by inflating it into a balloon. There was the real political writer who actually went to bed with Zahra and came out crying . . .

Undoubtedly, my experiences and thoughts were, and are, shared by masses of people in so many places where the struggle against idiotic conditions is at its sharpest. In the concluding chapters of *The Idiot,* Dostoevsky related how the intelligentsia of his time were expected to forego their real love for the women of their hearts and embrace fallen women for no other reason than proving their point vis-a-vis the "woman question," that "a fallen woman was, indeed, superior to a woman who had not fallen." Wherever there is inequality, there is enslavement of women and exploitation and degeneration of sex.

Chapter 10 | *I*DLE DAYS

The years 1937–1939 I spent in almost total idleness as far as work and regular schooling were concerned. The elementary school certificate, marking the successful conclusion of the six forms of primary school, I had finally got in 1938. To be sure, this otherwise indifferent piece of paper entitled me to admittance to an Intermediate School; but what with one thing or other—mainly no doubt the great aversion to schools that I had developed in my years in Madrasat Ras el-Qarya—I did not take that step. It was only toward the end of 1940, when I was coming on to seventeen and soon due to be summoned by the army for a two-year compulsory service, that I finally decided to join a night school, thereby becoming a registered student and thus temporarily exempted from recruitment.

I was thus all of seventeen when I joined Al-Sharqiyya al-Mutawassita evening school—and intellectually fairly well developed as these things went in those days. This was because my years of idleness had not gone completely to waste. Rather, I managed throughout this period to engage in a fairly ambitious though somewhat chaotic private project of self-education. The bookcase that I had especially made for me during my work in the furniture store was being filled to capacity, all nine shelves of it.

It was from quite an early age that I started reading Arabic books and magazines, starting with the numerous historical novels of Jorji Zaydan and the many translations-adaptations of French and English romances and novels produced by the Egyptian Mustafa Lutfi al-Manfaluti and several Syrian and Lebanese literary hacks whose names I don't recall. I was not only an avid reader but also something of a bibliophile. I liked possessing and keeping the books I read, or not read through, and by age fourteen or fifteen I had built myself a sizable home library—collected works of the best and most famous Egyptian writers, among them Taha Hussein, Ahmad Amin, Muhammad Hussein Haykal, Ibrahim Abdel Qadir al-Mazani, Tawfiq al-Hakim, ʿAbbas Mahmoud al-ʿAqqad, and others. I also collected works by classical Arab writers such as *Kitab al-Aghani,*

Rasa'il Ikhwan al-Safa, Ibn al-Atheer's *History,* The *Muqaddima* (Introduction) of Ibn Khaldun, and the collected poems of such classics as Al-Mutanabbi, Al-Ma'arri, Ibn al-Rumi, and others. Also prominent on my shelves were bound volumes of carefully collected and kept weeklies like *Al-Risala* of Muhammad Hasan al-Zayyat, Ahmad Amin's *Al-Thaqafa,* and *Al-Riwaya,* and the two leading monthlies, *Al-Hilal* and *Al-Muqtataf.*

After a relatively short period, however, I became aware of the monotony of the literature produced, most of which consisted either of reprints of Arabic and Islamic classics or contemporary works, the overwhelming majority of which were written in a traditional vein. I felt bored and tired of the monotonous character of most of it and the sheer dearth of really original creative works of literature.

Sometime during the second half of the 1930s, however, a fresh breeze started coming from another cultural capital of the Arab world—Beirut. A weekly with the unusual name *Al-Makshuf*—meaning literally "the bared" but also suggesting candor and exposure—was launched by an enterprising Lebanese Christian and immediately became an outlet for experimental and avant-garde poetry, fiction, and criticism.

It was in the pages of *Al-Makshuf* that some of Lebanon's best writers of the 1940s and 1950s made their debut—and it was there that I first saw the work of these as well as a number of others who already had a limited reputation. These included such names as Khalil Taqiyeddine and Tawfiq Yusuf 'Awwad in fiction; Elias Abu Shabaka in poetry; Maroun 'Abboud and 'Umar Fakhuri in literary criticism; and Costantin Zureiq, Raeef Khuri, and Qadri Qal'achi in ideology and politics. Beside the weekly, its publisher, Dar el-Makshuf, brought out the first works of most of these pioneers of modern poetry and fiction in the Arab world.

In Iraq itself the literary scene was very poor indeed, with the only literary-cultural weekly I can remember appearing in the Shi'i stronghold, Al-Najaf, edited by Ja'far el-Khalili, himself a prolific writer of rather indifferent short stories. This does not mean that there were no writers; but most of these were poets of the classical school and there were very few who took a hand at fiction. Of the poets, easily the most prominent were Muhammad Mahdi el-Jawahiri, Muhammad Salih Bahr el-'Ulum, and Ahmad el-Safi el-Najafi, known widely for his excellent Arabic rendering of Omar Khayyam's *Ruba'iyyat.* These three poets, all Shi'i, were very critical and scathing in their attacks on the system and the regime. Bahr el-'Ulum once wrote, in response to the events of 1936–1937, following Bakr Sidqi's coup d'etat, two lines of verse which I still remember. Translated roughly, they read:

We have a State.
It has grown old and decrepit
When still in its infancy.
It has reached old age before it attained maturity.
(lana dawlatun shakhat wa-in taku tiflatan / waqad
harimat qabla an tablugh-al-rushda.)

The only Iraqi work of fiction I can recall from this period was a collection of short stories entitled *Al-Jamra al-Ula* (The First Ember), written by a young Jewish writer, Ya'qub Bilboul.

Although *Al-Risala* had started publication before I started reading it, I managed to have a complete set of the weekly, bound in volumes of twenty-six issues each, while with both *Al-Thaqafa* and *Al-Riwaya* I was luckier in that I started buying them on their first appearance. I used to conduct forages of secondhand bookshops and buy whole sets of old, usually short-lived periodicals, from which I learned a good deal about literary and cultural developments in Iraq in the preceding few decades.

It was during this interlude of idleness that I also made the acquaintance of Salama Musa's works and his monthly *Al-Majalla al-Jadida,* which, not being on sale in Baghdad, I received through the mail by subscription. Salama Musa, together with a few Egyptian intellectuals such as Isma'il Madhar, Fuad Sarruf, and others, were considered modernists and innovators, their writings having been "scientific," and they having introduced into the Arab cultural scene such new and novel ideas as evolution, socialism, nationalism, and agnosticism.

It was in *Al-Risala* that I first read Homer's *Iliad* and *Odyssey* as well as essays on the Greek and Roman dramatists and summaries of their works —all translated or summarized by Darini Khashaba. From *Al-Thaqafa* I learned about modern philosophy through the writings of Zaki Najib Mahmud, and about Islamic modernism from contributions by Ahmed Amin and others. Some of the finest translations of Shakespeare into Arabic were also published in that weekly, done in free verse by Muhammad Farid Abu Hadid. These two weeklies, together with the monthlies and the books published by the two new publishers mentioned above, opened for me whole new vistas of knowledge and gave me first glimpses of the richness and variety of Western thought and culture.

Another weekly, *Al-Riwaya,* was as its name (The Tale) indicates devoted exclusively to works of fiction, mostly translations but also some original works. It was in *Al-Riwaya* that I first read translations from the works of such giants of the short story as Maupassant, whole novels of Flaubert and others published serially, works by Hardy, Maughm, O. Henry, Melville, and a number of Italian, Spanish and Russian writers.

POLITICAL AWAKENING

It took only a few short years for me to say good-bye to all this, having extracted what was there to be had from it.

Estrangement from my Arabic background in language and literary matters started to show, curiously enough, when I began to be politically aware of the world around me. One important influence on me was the Spanish Civil War, in which the gallant and suffering Republicans were fighting the beastly Fascists supported by the Jews' archenemy of the time — Nazi Germany. Some of the most popular and fashionable British and French intellectuals and men of letters sided with the Republicans, some of them actually taking part in the fighting, the Communists taking the lead, supported by Moscow. In those years of the late 1930s in Baghdad there was very little to go by in the local media, what with their generally extremely poor performance professionally and a growing if as yet unpublicized sympathy with Nazi Germany and Fascist Italy, the main enemies and challengers of the hated "British imperialists" and their lackeys in the governments of the day.

The only way of learning anything authoritative about the world and about its warring ideologies was to know a foreign language, preferably English — and so it was that I launched on my marathon self-tutoring in the language, not resting until I possessed a grip on what was broadcast and written on the wider political-ideological scene. I recall that the first English-language weekly that I ever bought and read was called *World News and Views,* while my favorite monthly was *Labour Monthly.* It may now seem rather strange that such publications were available for sale in Baghdad in those days; the fact is that some Christian tobacconist apparently with Communist leanings made bold to order a few copies for people who bought them regularly. By luck his small shop was not far from where I lived at the time.

Naturally, there was no way of stopping at that point. What with news of the notorious Moscow trials and a restless intellectual quest, I soon turned to the more theoretical and classic works of Marxism — works that began to be made available thanks to Victor Gollancz and the publishing firm which carried his name, and through which books selected by the Left Book Club month in, month out, were sold in at least one bookshop in

Baghdad at fairly cheap prices. These included works by famous "fellow-travelers" like John Strachey, Arthur Koestler, George Orwell, and others, while the firm brought out weighty works on some of these theoretical subjects, one of which, *A Handbook of Marxism,* I read and kept long after my disenchantment with the doctrine and the party. Gradually, however, I found myself turning to works by uncommitted writers on the left, such as Harold Laski, Leonard Woolf, J. P. S. Haldane, and others.

As the 1930s were coming to a close, and with the outbreak of World War II, my library consisted largely of books in English, with a few Arabic novels and works of literary and social criticism as well as poetry, all by avant-garde Arab writers of the time, among them Raeef Khuri, Tawfiq Yusuf 'Awwad, and Elias Abu Shabaka from Lebanon; Edward el-Kharrat, Louis 'Awad, and Ibrahim Naji from Egypt; and Ahmad el-Sayyid, Abdel Fattah Ibrahim, and Mahdi al-Jawahiri from Iraq—to name only a few. It was thus that, almost immediately after my first direct encounter with the West, its politics, its culture, and its literature, and prior to my first meetings with Elie Kedourie and, subsequently, with a number of aspiring intellectuals and dilettantes who later came to be known as "the gang," I gradually sold or otherwise disposed myself of the bulk of my Arabic books and magazine collections. My library now consisted largely of selected Pelicans, Penguins, Penguin Specials—all priced at sixpence each at the time—and the few works of Marxist classics and Left Book Club books that I decided were worth keeping. It was only later, some time in the early 1940s, that I was ready and able to tackle "literature"—general literary works in English, classics, translations of the great Russian novels and short stories, some French classics, basic works of philosophy and literature ancient and modern, and various works by contemporary British novelists—Graham Greene, Aldous Huxley, Evelyn Waugh, the early Orwell.

ZAKI MUHAMMAD BASEEM AND THE MAAMUNIYYA NIGHT SCHOOL

One day in mid-February 1949 the papers carried headlines about the hanging of four prominent Iraqi Communists. They were Yusuf Salman Yusuf (Fahd), Zaki Muhammad Baseem, Husain Muhammad el-Shabibi, and Yahuda Ibrahim Siddiq. Of the four, it was only Yahuda that I hadn't known or met during my short years of flirtation with Marxism. I had met Yusuf, who was nicknamed Fahd and was the uncontested leader of the party, shortly after his arrival in Baghdad during the war years from some place that used to be a well-kept secret. Answers to my casual queries were not consistent. Yusuf was alleged to have returned to Baghdad — now from his hometown in the south, now from "abroad," but finally it was confided to me that he was back from years of "training" in the great Union of Soviet Socialist Republics.

When I first met him, in the house of friends and comrades, one of whom was my would-be political guide and mentor, Abdullah Mas'ud, Yusuf was just beginning to put together the secret organization that was to become the clandestine Communist party of Iraq — as well as trying to get equipment, funds, and people to produce the party's first clandestine periodical — *Al-Sharara* (The Spark). He was a genial, wily fellow and often seemed to me to be just the man for the job. But our ways were soon to part since I was simply not "available" for recruitment or for active political work of any kind.

Somewhat in contrast to Yusuf, Husain al-Shabibi was a true intellectual — serious, always earnest, and often pensive-looking. I did not know him well, and my acquaintance with him was the result of his frequent visits and browsings in Al-Rabita Bookshop, where I started working in 1946. Like Fahd, however, he was not a Baghdadi; he came from a prominent Shi'i family in the holy city of al-Najaf. It is somehow difficult for me to depict him even in my mind as an active Communist who — if one is to believe the public prosecutor at his trial — actually took upon himself the chores of leading the party in Fahd's absence. As a matter of fact, I had the impression — which I seem to remember was shared by others at the time — that the hangings were calculated among other things to show some kind of macabre "evenhandedness" as far as religious affiliations and communal divisions were concerned. And what better proof of this could have been given than to single out for capital punishment two Sunnis, one Shi'i, and a Jew?

I had met Zaki Muhammad Baseem in 1938, when at last I was attending the Sixth Form at the Maamuniyya primary night school. Zaki was also seeking to finish his elementary schooling and take the government *bakalorya* certificate. He had at that time a full-time job as a junior clerk in the Water Department, a government office. A friendship developed, mainly on the basis of shared interest in politics.

Zaki's political development would appear to have been a most curious one, but I think it was not completely untypical of young Iraqi patriots of the time. During the two or three years just preceding the outbreak of World War II, he seemed fired by anti-British sentiments, exactly like so many other politically-conscious members of his generation. He argued endlessly about the evil role the British were supposed to be playing in the country's politics and their share in its perpetually backward state of development. His most fervent wish was to see the last of that influence and Iraq ruled by a genuinely national government minding the country's interests and with no obligations vis-à-vis any foreign power.

I do not quite remember whether he either harbored or showed any sympathies for Fascist Italy and Nazi Germany before the war; but as soon as the war broke out Zaki automatically, and somewhat logically, became an ardent supporter of the Axis powers and a sworn enemy of the Allies. When I reproached him about his attitude, which implied siding with the Fascists and the Nazis, he protested that his sole aim was to see the British defeated and out of Iraq—and that his attitude had nothing whatever to do with the ruling ideology of the Axis, let alone its anti-Semitic ideology and anti-Jewish measures.

Shortly before World War II ended with the defeat of Germany and the Axis powers, Zaki's sympathies became increasingly pro-Soviet, ostensibly partly for ideological reasons but mainly because of the anti-imperialist stance of Soviet policies and pronouncements. I tend to think that Zaki, now in his mid-twenties, finally found a political ideology after his own heart—which also happened to be anti-British and anticolonialist. It was therefore rather natural that, when the war ended, he threw himself wholeheartedly into the Communist cause and, being one of the most hardworking and methodical men I have ever met, he soon found himself joining the ranks of the clandestine Communist party led by Fahd. From then on there seems to have been no limits to his devotion to the cause—and soon enough he was engaging in some most dangerous activities. For the fact is that while the Iraqi authorities during the war years tended to tolerate or ignore pro-Moscow activities, they began to tighten the reins shortly after the fighting ended and the Cold War broke out.

But the Communists went right on with their clandestine activities, and publication of *Al-Sharara* never ceased completely, although its secret premises were often raided and the primitive machine in which it was mimeographed seized and confiscated.

It was sometime during this period of stress and strain that Zaki was called on to take a more active role in party activities—and when things became very bleak for the Communists after the government recovered from the shock of the popular convulsion known as *al wathba* toward the end of 1947, Zaki actually took charge of the organization following the arrest of Fahd and al-Shabibi. Finally, he himself was caught and, after a short trial, was sentenced to death and hanged together with Fahd, al-Shabibi, and Yahuda Siddiq.

Throughout the years 1938–1941, Zaki and I were very good friends, and I would say best friends had he had any other friends. A self-made man with some family responsibilities, Zaki however was too busy improving his lot and being diligent and industrious in his job to partake in the kind of idle pursuits which used to consume all my free time; he was simply far more serious a person than I was—a little too serious perhaps. The result was that, apart from chance meetings and infrequent visits paid by me to him in his office, I saw little of him. When we were still in school and I suddenly lost my job, Zaki offered to help despite the fact that his own financial situation was quite bad. At first I refused, but in the end we came to an arrangement—namely that he "lent" me 250 *fils* a month on the clear understanding that I repay him when I managed to get a job. On the first of each month, for several months, I used to go to the office and collect my loan. On certain occasions, when Zaki worked late and had no time to go home to eat before he came to school, his younger brother used to bring him his main meal of the day to the office, where I often shared it with him when everybody had left.

The sum of 250 *fils* was a considerable amount of money in those far-off days. To be sure, it amounted to no more than five English shillings or a little more than one American dollar all in all; but Zaki's pay for the whole month was probably less than six dinars (thirty dollars) and the money he was willing to lend me made some difference to his budget. However, he used to sound almost apologetic about the whole thing, gently explaining to me that he would be completely penniless anyway as soon as the first day of the month was out, that he himself would start borrowing the very next day to keep things going for the month's duration, and that "it made no difference anyway." On my part, I spent the money on buying a few weeklies, a book or two, and paying my way in the coffee shop for quite a few days. To give one example: One could, and did, spend half a day in the cozy and cool Hasan el-'Ajmi teashop for no more than five *fils*, and if one wanted to read all the morning papers over one's cup of tea, one could do that at the price of two *fils*. Eventually I managed to pay Zaki all my accumulated debts.

In Baghdad in those days the coffee shop was quite an institution. Apart from providing a haven for us idlers, it was the ideal meeting place for friends, and it was there that our endless discussions about politics, literature, and women were conducted. Already at the age of fifteen or sixteen, I started frequenting coffee shops, my favorite being Hasan el-'Ajmi's, which was "classy" and nearby and which served easily the best cup of tea in town. As a matter of fact, the tea was so good and gave such an agreeable aroma that some rivals of 'Ajmi ("the Persian") complained to the municipality that tea served in his teashop contained some sort of drug. Sure enough, a careful investigation revealed that somewhere inside the top of the teapot where the tea was left to "cook" a tiny piece of *tiryaq* (hashish) was inserted, so that what gave the renowned teashop's tea its aroma and special taste was the said drug. No measures were taken against the owner, however, most likely thanks to the few shillings handed the municipal inspector.

El-'Ajmi teashop had another irresistible attraction. The famous Shaftalu, the one who went around offering the clients tiny sips of coffee, was in his own special way a great comedian and entertainer, and he used to go around chanting some of the funniest sayings, which sounded even funnier said in his heavy Persian accent. Among many others, I remember one concerning the difference between squash and eggplant (*shijar* and *badhinjan* respectively): "El-shijar yihub dihin, el-badhinjan ma-yakul dihin" (in frying, squash loves oil, eggplant doesn't consume oil). I also heard somewhere that Shaftalu used to fart on demand; just for the asking.

It was in that coffee shop that I made and cultivated my most lasting friendships in the late 1930s — until, that is, I somehow outgrew it what with my shifting intellectual interests and the steady job I finally got with Eastern Bank.

THE MAKING OF A FANATICAL MODERATE

In the course of a newspaper interview he gave some years ago, the Israeli writer Amos Oz spoke of his preoccupation with the phenomenon of fanaticism. He was spellbound, he said, by "instincts dressing themselves up as ideas or becoming ideas." Asserting that his principal aims were "to fight [fanaticism] as a political being and to decipher it as a storyteller," Oz said he was astonished by how easily, and with what enthusiasm, men discover things they come to consider more important than life itself. He thought there must have been some sort of primal hatred of life at play there — a lack of talent for life.

There is, to be sure, a sense in which anyone who chooses to "fight" fanaticism, or any other sociopolitical phenomenon, is in danger of becoming a fanatic himself, a moderate fanatic or a fanatical moderate but a fanatic just the same. Speaking for myself, I must confess that for a

period extending to nearly five decades I took it on myself to fight—
solely through the written word of course—that brand of Israeli fanaticism which expresses itself now in ethnocentrism and racial-ethnic prejudice, now in culturism, and now in habitually dividing the world into two
seemingly irreconcilable "nations," the Arabs and the Jews and their respective satellites. I wonder sometimes if, ultimately, it is not all a kind
of intellectual game, a play on ideas which can prove dangerous in that it
takes ideas too seriously. However, I like to see this predilection as spring-
ing from a desire to strike some sort of balance through juxtaposition and
confrontation, a kind of curiosity that leads one to put oneself into the
other's shoes—usually those of the assaulted party.

Are we born with such attitudes of mind or do we acquire them through
our own unique life experience? I don't believe there exists a satisfactory
answer to this question. It seems to me, though, that even if a person's temperament and his or her attitudes in these matters are ultimately acquired,
then they must be acquired so early in the course of his or her life that a
useful or meaningful recapitulation of the true causes and circumstances
is rendered well nigh impossible. Here, I propose to deal with a relatively late phase of my intellectual and emotional development—namely
the time when I first discovered in myself a clear political-ideological
inclination.

This occurred sometime in the second half of the 1930s, when the
Spanish Civil War, which had started with a revolt of military command-
ers in Spanish Morocco in the summer of 1936, became an international
issue after Franco proclaimed himself a few months later chief of the Spanish state. At that time I was already engaged in the business of making a
living and was a curious and a highly impressionable lad of thirteen. My
feelings of empathy for the Republican forces that rose to fight Franco's
hordes had less to do with Franco's fascism and alleged anti-Semitism
than with high matters of right and wrong, legitimacy and illegitimacy,
human rights and the treatment of prisoners of war. What seems to have
heightened my involvement in such questions is the fact that that same
year in my adolescence witnessed two more events that were to leave a
permanent impression on me.

The first was Bakr Sidqi's notorious military coup. One mild Thursday morning—October 29, 1936—five planes of the Iraqi Royal Air Force
were seen flying over Baghdad and dropping leaflets containing a proclamation signed by one General Bakr Sidqi appointing himself "Chief
of the National Reform Force." This was to be the first in a long series
of coups d'etat that were to sweep not only Iraq but the Arab world as

a whole in years to come. I don't recall having quite grasped the significance of the move or even its meaning, but I was fairly swayed by the idea of change and by talk about "reform."

The other event occurred on December 11 the same year, when King Edward VIII of Britain, faced with the alternative of giving up his wish to marry Mrs. Simpson or leave the throne, chose to abdicate. The act, which was given a great deal of publicity, left a lasting impression on me, and I found myself lost in admiration for the rebellious monarch boasting the title "His Britannic Majesty."

At the furniture shop in which I was now working, I was at once assistant to the accountant, who came only once a week to make the final entries, secretary of sorts, and errand boy. The owners, two middle-aged Muslims who had made it from hired workers in their profession to independent businessmen who hardly had to work with their own hands, were always either out making purchases or on their feet, serving customers, showing them catalogs, and receiving orders. Most of these orders were made on the strength of colored photographs printed on art paper in catalogs that came from Europe and were accompanied by texts in some European language that no one in the plant was able or even cared to read. The professional eyes of the owners and the wishes of the customers determined the specifications, the sole basis for these judgments being the photographs themselves.

This was the year I started to read the daily newspapers regularly—usually all of the three or four of them. (News vendors used openly to "lend" you the papers to read for half the price of one.) It was also the year in which certain manifestations of nationalist sentiments began to emerge, accompanied sometimes by anti-Jewish acts and pronouncements. I well remember the morning on which Baghdad's leading daily *Al-Bilad* carried a front-page article by Ezra Haddad, a veteran Jewish educator, scholar, translator, and publicist who subsequently brought out a scholarly edition of the *Travels of Benjamin from Tudella*, proclaiming in a large headline: "We Are Arabs Before We Became Jews"—an awkward and inadequate translation of the otherwise smooth-sounding and clear original title, *Nahnu 'arab qabla an nakuna yahuda,* which actually meant something like "We Are Arabs First and Jews Second."

Haddad's plea followed one or two incidents in which Jewish businessmen were shot dead in the streets of Baghdad earlier that year, during Prime Minister Yasin el-Hashimi's "nationalist" rule. It was al-Hashimi who was toppled later by Bakr Sidqi's coup. The writer of the article followed a well-known and fairly well-substantiated argument, to the effect that Jews had lived in the Arabian Peninsula before the rise of Judaism—and certainly before the rise of Islam—and also that the Jews of Iraq had lived there before the Muslim conquest. Its central thesis, however, was one that was universally accepted by the Jews of Iraq at that time—namely that these Jews were loyal citizens who saw in Iraq their only homeland and had no contacts with or sympathy for the Zionists in Palestine.

MENASHE ZA'ROOR'S PREDICAMENT

My first encounters with "politics" and public affairs were also enhanced by the location of the furniture store for which I worked and by the kind of clientele frequenting it. The place, a combination of workshop and furniture showroom, was situated in a prestigious street called al-Mutanabbi Street—also known as the Saray Street because it led from the city's main street, Al-Rashid Street, to the Saray, a huge and imposing complex housing all the ministries and government offices—and also to the law courts. The street was also one of the most sought-after residential areas in downtown Baghdad, with bookshops, offices and newspaper plants. It led directly to the Tigris River—and just before you reached the law courts there, on your left, was the start of the great bazaar, Suq el-Saray, which at that particular end had two lines of bookshops and stationery shops, while midway through it started a chain of shoe and other leather goods stores. That part of the bazaar ended from the other side with Bridge Street—Shari' al-Jisr—of which the bridge was a continuation astride the Tigris and into the Hither Side—*dhak el-saub*—also known as El-Karkh.

On the same side of al-Mutanabbi Street, a few buildings down from the furniture store, there were two newspaper premises—the rather large and imposing *Matba'at al-'Iraq* (Iraq Press) in which the daily *Al-'Iraq* was edited and produced, and the modest, rented editorial offices that housed the weekly *Habazbuz*, Iraq's famed satirical weekly, owned and edited and largely written by a singularly witty and easygoing man by the name of Karim Thabit, who was also known by the name Habazbuz. Since the paper started appearing around this time, I used to have a complete file of it from its first issue—not such a huge collection since it was quite short-lived. The sharpness of its owner's tongue and his scathing criticisms led first to frequent short "suspensions" and then to the paper's closure. One day, when I went to the *Habazbuz* offices seeking old issues for my collection, I had a fairly long chat with the much-feared man who produced it—a modest soft-spoken man in his early forties who answered my questions freely and showed much interest and a certain amount of gratification that someone so young—and a Jew to boot—was so interested in his paper as to want to have a complete collection of its issues.

I doubt whether I ever actually entered the premises of *Al-'Iraq,* but I knew by sight both Razzuq Ghannam—a Christian who owned the paper, the press, and the building but who was known to be virtually illiterate and had no part in the actual editing or production of his paper —and Menashe Za'roor, the man who did all the work. A Jew with a long record in journalism who had spent a lifetime living and working in close association with Muslims, Za'roor produced *Al-'Iraq* every morning single-handedly. He collected the news from the Information Department's handouts and the agencies and radio broadcasts, wrote the headlines, did the proofreading, wrote the leading article, and read and edited articles contributed by outsiders. By observing him from my desk at the carpentry's showroom, I knew that Za'roor used to come to work at about 9:00 A.M. and leave about 5:00 or 6:00 P.M., although he had to produce a morning paper. He was stocky, looked rather stern, relatively young, and always had a cigarette in his mouth. He liked controversy and polemics, a love which accompanied him in his last years in Israel, where he did various odd jobs working for the official and semiofficial Arabic publications put out by the government and the then all-powerful Israel labor federation, the Histadrut, a weird combination of countrywide employer and mighty labor union.

In his years in Israel Za'roor never managed to find his way even to a minimal degree of "integration." His desperate but rather lame efforts in this direction, his wish to find a decent job as a proud and self-respecting Arabic writer and journalist, produced no results. And no wonder. So perfectly at home had he felt in the largely Muslim milieu in which he was born, grew up, educated, and worked, that he simply failed to "fit," much more so than the average Arabic-speaking newcomer trapped in a basically closed, predominantly East European society masquerading as just about the last word in "Westernism" and looking askance at anything Arab or Oriental.

An idea of the foreignness and alienation Za'roor must have felt in these new surroundings can be had from a long interview he gave not long before his death and in which he told of some of his experiences in Baghdad. In that talk he reminisced about the predominantly Muslim neighborhood—Mahallat Bani S'eed—in which he was born—how, when four or five years of age, he was sent to the mullah, the Muslim equivalent of the

East European *cheder* and the Iraqi Jewish *estadh,* and how, after he finished school and started working in *Al-'Iraq,* he attended Koran and Arabic classes in the renowned mosque, Jami' el-Haydarkhana. The teacher, who also was the *imam* of the mosque, Sheikh Rashid el-Dawood, used to go to the paper's offices offering poems for publication. On one of these visits, Za'roor related, the sheikh agreed to the young editor's request and allowed him to attend his classes, which Za'roor said he did for four years.

Another familiar face in Shari' al-Mutanabbi in those days was Khalid el-Rahhal, who worked in the press section of the Ministry of Interior. He too passed by every morning on his way to work. El-Rahhal—the author of the famous laudatory telegram sent to Edward VIII after his abdication—was known for his wide-ranging readings, his knowledge of foreign languages, and his wide cultural interests. For a man with such a reputation, however, he produced very little indeed. The only work of his I was ever to come across was a translation of Maupassant's famous short story "Boule de Suif," which he published as a separate booklet with an introduction hailing the work as perhaps the best short story ever written. But perhaps his most noted peculiarity was his pipe, with which he would never part. And pipes, in those days, were a novelty in Iraq.

Chapter 11 | *D*ISTORTED VISIONS

O ne day early in 1971, making my usual round of the bookshops, I picked up what I would say was almost a personal book—a book which, by virtue of its time, its quality, and its contents amounts to a faithful record of my intellectual and mental development during a crucial decade of my life. The book was *The Collected Essays, Journalism, and Letters of George Orwell,* all in four manageable and now low-priced paperback volumes. Reading the book, or even browsing in it here and there, was quite an experience. Throughout the 1940s in Baghdad I had followed Orwell's writings and the development of his political thinking—all the way from his Left Book Club volumes, his columns in *Tribune,* his contributions to *Horizon, Polemic, Partisan Review,* and other little magazines up to his *Animal Farm* and *1984.*

The fourth and last volume of *Collected Essays* is adorned with a quotation from one of Orwell's essays: "Only by resurrecting our own memories can we realize how incredibly distorted is the child's vision of the world." But can we, really? And is a child's vision of the world so incredibly distorted? How about the other way around? "Only by resurrecting our own memories can we realize how incredibly distorted is our grown-up vision of the world." But perhaps it amounts to saying the same thing—namely that the child's vision of the world is itself a reflection of our own "incredibly distorted" vision of it.

Speaking of my own personal experience, I think I can quite safely say that by all prevailing standards my vision of the world has always tended to be "distorted"—in creeping old age no less than in childhood and adolescence. In this context, by "distorted" I mean unrealistic, impractical, rather naïve, and somewhat romantic. It seems to me, in fact, that there is a certain type of human being who simply refuses to grow up—men and women who just seem to cling to what their whole life experience shows to be a mistaken and at any rate unrealistic view of the world they live in. And they do this, moreover, at great cost to themselves and considerable pain and inconvenience to those who are close to or dependent on them.

If children are as innocent as they are usually depicted by their elders —
which I rather tend to doubt — then I guess I am speaking about innocence — unchanging, persistent innocence and the trust in people that
always comes with it. Until this day, at the ripe age of seventy and over,
I am often chastised by my wife for being so trusting and enthusiastic
about people and for so hastily forming new friendships — not because
she herself is not sufficiently social and sociable but allegedly because I
don't do it with the moderation called for. Where the difficulty starts is
when, usually after a long time of patiently ignoring and tolerating behavior and gestures which to her mind should have been sufficient reason for
avoiding these acquaintances or at least keeping them at arm's length, I
tend to arrive at those conclusions too late and all of a sudden, with all the
embarrassment and the awkwardness that accompany such discoveries.

Nor do I seem to learn from experience — and I often quote with approval a saying in Latin from the diary section of Aldous Huxley's *Eyeless
in Gaza* to the effect that the only thing we learn from experience is that we
do not learn from experience. But I do not in any way regret this character
trait of mine, despite the pain and the disappointments — and my usual
answer to my wife's criticisms is that it is preferable to be innocent or naive
or trusting and often proved wrong than to be suspicious or calculating
or mistrusting and equally often right.

So what is it that shapes a man's outlook, his attitudes, his worldview?
Tolstoy in one of his short stories depicts his hero, Ivan Vasilyevich, as arguing that it is all "a matter of chance." "So you contend," he tells a group
of friends, "that a man cannot judge independently of what is good and
what is bad, that it is all a matter of environment — that man is a creature
of environment. But I contend it is all a matter of chance." The way I see
it, the difficulty with this kind of theory is that even chance happenings
do not happen to one by mere chance. The title of Tolstoy's story is "After
the Ball," and what happens to Ivan Vasilyevich at that point as "a matter
of chance" could not have happened to a less fortunate, nonaristocratic
Russian living in the middle of the nineteenth century and attending no
balls of that kind.

Are we, then, born with the attitudes and the passions we have and
which dominate us all our lives, motivating our actions, determining our
reactions, and in short making us what we really are? In a brief prologue
to his *Autobiography*, Bertrand Russell speaks of three passions which he
said had governed his life — passions he describes as being "simple but
overwhelming" but which, "like great winds, have blown me hither and
thither, in a wayward course, over a deep ocean of anguish, reaching to the

very verge of despair." These passions he lists as "the longing for love, the search for knowledge, and unbearable pity for the suffering of mankind."

It transpires, however, that the third of these passions was in the end to prove to be the most frustrating. Love Russell sought and found, "though it might seem too good for human life." A little knowledge he also achieved, he admits. Love and knowledge, he writes, so far as they were possible, led upward toward the heavens. But always pity brought him back to earth. "Echoes of cries of pain reverberate in my heart. Children in famine, victims tortured by oppressors, helpless old people a hated burden to their sons, and the whole world of loneliness, poverty, and pain make a mockery of what human life should be. I long to alleviate the evil, but I cannot, and I too suffer."

FLIRTATION WITH MARXISM

My flirtation with Marxism, a relatively long one, started roughly during the Spanish Civil War and the era of Leon Blum's *Front Populaire* government in France. The attraction the ideology had for me had to do with a passion and longing I have for knowledge, a pity for the oppressed and the deprived, and an irresistible need to make sense of what happens around me and what had happened in the past. Lewis Namier, who I think was the exact opposite of Russell in his general approach to things, writes in an essay entitled "Basic Factors in Nineteenth Century European History": "Possibly there is no more sense in human history than in the changes of the seasons or the movements of the stars; or if sense there be, it escapes our perception."

But I persisted—and I continue to insist on trying to find some sense! And in those days of dearth, in the late 1930s, Marxism-Leninism seemed to me to make some sense of human history and of human affairs as they appeared to me then. Franco and his Fascist hordes were plainly the villains of the piece, supported as they were by Nazi Germany and Mussolini's Italy and resisted by all the beautiful people then beginning to be known to me.

A budding left-wing movement among Iraqi intellectuals, such as those who rallied around the *al-Ahali* daily, had just begun. Certain books and pamphlets by Abdel Fattah Ibrahim, Qassem Hassan, and other intellectuals of the left, were just appearing in the bookshops. Articles translated from French and English Communist and Socialist newspapers and periodicals were to be found in certain dailies and weeklies—mostly short-lived. One bookshop-cum-stationery store started mysteriously to sell a limited number of copies of *Al Tali'a*, the monthly published in Beirut by the Lebanese Communist party — the only openly functioning Marxist organization in the Arab world.

Al Tali'a was edited by the party's veteran leader Khalid Bagdash, with contributions by such luminaries as Raeef Khuri, Farajallah el-Helu, and Michel 'Aflaq — the same 'Aflaq who was subsequently to found the Arab Socialist Ba'th (Resurgence) party with Akram el-Hourani. With *Al Tali'a* came, occasionally and in very limited numbers, certain pamphlets and books either written or translated by the same group of writers who made the monthly tick — and these together offered me and the likes of me who read no foreign languages the sole intellectual nourishment we had.

ENGLISH SELF-TAUGHT

The fact was that there was little of importance one could learn about Marxism, communism, and the famously socialist paradise called the Soviet Union if one's only reading language was Arabic. This being the case, and my intellectual curiosity seeming all but insatiable, I embarked on my greatest enterprise thus far — to learn to read English come what may. How else would one be able to know more, to find the correct answers, to make sense of things, and ultimately to formulate one's own answers and to decide one's own stands on the burning issues of the day?

Although English was actually taught in every school in Baghdad as a second language, there were at least three kinds of such schools and, needless to say, various categories of pupils — and I hasten to add that, as far as the study of English was concerned, I managed at once to attend the wrong kind of school and to belong to the wrong kind of pupil category. There were, to start with, the government schools in which English was taught beginning with the third form and the standard of instruction was not particularly high. Second, there were two schools in Baghdad in which English was actually the language of instruction — the Shammash School, which was run by the Jewish community with some help from the Board of Deputies of British Jewry, and the so-called American School, which was founded and run by American institutions vaguely and perhaps only distantly connected with some Christian mission or other.

However, to both of these schools only children of the well-to-do could afford to go — although in the case of the Shammash School the gifted among the poor also had a chance of admittance. Those who attended these schools could expect to know the language fairly well by the time they had finished their eleventh year of schooling. These constituted all the three phases of preuniversity education: six years of elementary school, three of intermediate school, and two of secondary schooling.

Finally, there were the two schools, one for boys and one for girls, of the Alliance Israélite Universelle, in which French was the language of instruction but where English (as well as Arabic and probably Hebrew) was taught starting with the first grade. In order to cope with the requirements both of the Ministry of Education's curriculum and the French government *brevé* examinations, pupils at the Alliance schools had to do twelve instead of eleven years before they could take the ministry's final exams. The *brevé* exams were held at the end of ten years of school and many of the pupils then moved directly to the Shammash School, where after two more years of study they usually sat both for the local official preuniversity exams and for London University's matriculation examinations qualifying them for admittance to British universities. Having attended neither the Shammash nor the Alliance school — and thus far failing even to finish the intermediate stage — I was to learn English the hard way.

It was while we lived in *Beit Yamein,* after leaving my job at the carpentry-furniture shop, that I decided to take up English. By then I had registered as an evening student at the Sharqiyya Intermediate School and had there met and become friendly with Dawood el-Sayigh, who taught Arabic grammar and with whom I shared an interest in left-wing ideas and in "progressive" literature. After showing him an article I had published in a local paper on the first collection of short stories to appear by Dhul-Nun Ayyub, a pioneer of the modern Iraqi novel and a Marxist himself, our relations became close and I started to visit him at his home not far from the school. He must then have been in his late twenties, and he lived with his parents, a younger brother, and a sister or two in a modern European-style house in Bustan el-Khas.

Though too preoccupied with other things and rather easily bored with school, I managed somehow with the subjects taught in that first year of intermediate studies — except for English, where I could not muster the minimum mark of 50. I passed the end-of-year exams and was finally allowed to move on to the second year thanks only to a lucky coincidence. In the final exam in English the supervisor — or one of the two supervisors, I forget which — was none other than Dawood el-Sayigh, who helped me by standing at my side and actually dictating to me some of the correct answers, complete with detailed spelling.

It was the last time I needed help with my English. That summer vaca-

tion and for months afterward I devoted up to sixteen hours a day studying English, starting right at the beginning and plowing my way step by
slow step. It was quite an experience. I started with the book we used at
school, *Oxford Reader II* I believe it was, and my only guide was a de-
fective and rather elementary English-Arabic dictionary, the famous Elias
Anton Elias dictionary that was literally the only one of its kind available
to student and general reader alike. I also had an exercise book, and with
a fanatical thoroughness and persistence I looked up every word I didn't
know and jotted it down. The number of words whose meanings I didn't
know was at first infinitely higher than those I did—I would say some 80
percent or more of the total. They included such "words" as *that, for,
about, under, over, up,* and hundreds upon hundreds of others. In the
end I "made it"—and after that I never worried about the marks I would
get at school in English.

But I had other subjects to worry about, among which natural history
was foremost. It was not only a most boring subject—what with the dis-
secting of frogs and, far worse, the drawing of those useless analogies
and contrasts between the anatomies and inside parts of various animals,
sight unseen. What made things worse for me in that second year at al-
Sharqiyya, however, was that the natural history instructor was a rabid
nationalist who had somehow got wind of the fact that I had leftist leanings in addition to being a Jew. At the end of the year I failed in the natural
history exam—deservedly I am sure—and since the rule was that failing
in one subject didn't disqualify one completely from moving on to the
higher class I was given a chance: I had to pass an exam in the same subject at the end of the summer vacation, presumably after having mastered
the material during the summer months.

In the event, what with my many other preoccupations, social and intellectual, I did nothing of the kind and, hoping against hope, I duly sat for
that fateful exam. The examiner was the self-same teacher, Na'im Mum-
taz, who had no conceivable reason to be lenient with me. I was plainly
unprepared and I failed—and consequently duly spent another year in
that class. It was the second time in my school career that I had to suffer
this kind of indignity—and I am absolutely sure that, had it not been for
the conscription orders that kept coming from the army, I would never
have pursued my secondary education.

As far as my English was concerned, by the year 1942 I had taught
myself enough of the language to be able to read political literature in English, and I recall that the first English-language periodical I ever actually
purchased and read was the current issue of a Communist weekly called

World News and Views, which was published in London but seems to have stopped publication some time in the 1940s. It was printed on very thin paper and in tiny typefaces—and it was all text. I ordered a copy from the one news agent who used to sell it and I started to receive it regularly and read it with a gusto that can only come from insatiable curiosity. Shortly afterward I started taking *Labour Monthly,* the late Palme Dutt's brainchild and an orthodox Communist organ. I thought Palme Dutt's editorials were splendid stuff. All in all, in the dearth then prevailing in Baghdad and at my stage of intellectual development, *Labour Monthly* and *World News and Views*—together with the pro-Soviet Penguin Specials written by the fellow-traveler named D. N. Pritt, K. C., and like-minded British publicists—provided me with a whole education, not to mention the immense contribution their reading proved to make to my knowledge of English and the ability actually to read the language.

The person who introduced me to *World News and Views*—and to the Communist doctrine as a whole—was a young man by the name of Abdullah Mas'ud, then a student at the Law College in Baghdad. A Shi'i Muslim, he hailed from Kerbala and he often struck me as being a Shi'i first and a Communist only second. Among other things, he was an amateur poet—and the first line of one of his occasional poems, which was addressed in its entirety to the prominent Iraqi Shi'i leader Ja'far Abul-Timman, said something to the effect that "Lenin occupies no more an exultant position than you do."

I was interested to see, in later years, that of all my former Communist friends and mentors Mas'ud was the only one who survived fairly unharmed. I may be mistaken, but my impression was that his communism was an outcrop of his resentment against the Sunni establishment in Iraq and the way in which his own community, which constituted a majority of the country's Muslims, was discriminated against and deprived of what he fervently believed was its due share in terms of actual power and influence.

FORMATIVE YEARS

Writers of biographies and autobiographies often speak of what they call the "formative years" in the lives of their subjects. A certain period in the life of a writer, thinker, or public figure, they decide, constituted the years in which his style, his thought, and his career were formed. I do not for a moment doubt the validity and usefulness of such an approach, but speaking for myself I cannot think of a single year in my life since I became aware of myself and my surroundings that was not in one way or other "formative." Nor do I find anything in this that can be said to be unique or peculiar to my development.

Nevertheless, if I were to be asked to point to a specific span of years which in retrospect I can call my formative years I would choose the years 1938–1945. During the first three of these years I had my first glimpses of the political, social, and cultural conditions of the world in which I found myself, and in the years 1940–1945 I managed to widen my intellectual horizons to an extent which, considering the conditions in which I grew up and had my schooling, seem to me to be much more than I had the right to expect. The fact that it was during these same years that I finally finished my secondary school—a feat which took me six years to perform rather than the usual five years required—was only a small part of the story, and to my mind an insignificant one.

Glancing the other day at the one detailed school document preserved from those days—a letter addressed by the principal of my secondary school, the Tafayyudh Night School, to the First Recruiting Officer of Al-Risafa District—I noticed that two of the highest marks I mustered in the final Ministry of Education examinations were those I got in English and Arabic, namely 81 and 77 respectively. These results—especially when they are compared to the 53 I got in general mathematics, 58 in the sciences, and 64 in geography—in a very valid sense reflect on the one talent to which I can lay claim, namely a proficiency for language bordering on a true bent.

As a matter of fact, the one subject in which I was to show any distinction throughout my early school years was Arabic, and specifically desinential inflection, grammar, and syntax. I also got good marks in composition, although I tended to be too brief and sparing with words to produce quite the size of piece stipulated and thus to qualify for real excellence.

Both in Arabic and in English, syntax remained my strongest point in school, although in reality I had no patience for grammar. There is a point here that I feel is worth elaborating on. In Arabic, as in other languages, syntax is the essence of grammar. However, whereas in European languages syntax has to do with the grammatical arrangement of words in the sentence, in Arabic it requires the student first to name the part of speech to which each of the words in a sentence belongs, then to define its function and place therein, and finally—most difficult of all—to specify the vowel (*haraka*) with which it ends and ultimately the correct way of reading it.

This peculiarity of Arabic makes it incumbent on the student to learn grammar and even memorize its essentials — a headache I soon discovered was unnecessary with the study of English. For example, though I can write the language fairly well and without any grammatical errors, I cannot until this day name all the five parts of speech in English and cannot say what a preposition is or give an example thereof. (The fact that there are five parts of speech in English is just about the only information I still retain from those long and tedious hours of the grammar class.)

It was only at a later age, when I was eighteen or more, that I started to try my hand at writing something for publication. If my memory does not fail me, the first thing I ever had published was an Arabic translation of a wartime pamphlet by Professor Harold Laski, one in a series published by Oxford University Press and whose title was *Liberty in the Modern World*. It was one of the few works in English that I could read with relative ease and I decided, partly because I liked its contents and partly as an exercise in my ongoing effort to master the language, to sit down and translate it.

I had an acquaintance, Sadeq al Uzdi, who was managing editor of a leading Baghdad daily, *Al-Akhbar*, and I took my courage in my hand and submitted the manuscript to him. I was delighted by the swiftness with which the paper made a positive decision — and for the coming four or five days the pamphlet was printed serially on the front page, with the translator's name side by side with that of the author's.

I think the publication of the pamphlet, in those years of World War II when anti-British sentiment in Iraq was rampant, did not pass unnoticed by the still very powerful British Embassy staff, and I was soon to be approached for more translations. However, since the paper — owned by Jabran Malkon, a stingy Christian gentleman from the northern town of Talkeif — did not pay me a penny for my effort, I never offered them anything else. (Nor, to be quite honest, had I expected them to pay; but considering their enthusiasm I thought they should have made a gesture however small.)

The only other work I clearly recall writing and being published was a review of a collection of local short stories. The author of the collection was Dhul-Nun Ayyub, and that was his first appearance in book form. Dhul-Nun (which is the Koranic rendering of Jonah) was indisputably a pioneer of what can be termed the fiction of social criticism in Iraq.

Essentially a radical and socialist, Dhul-Nun was no great craftsman of the short story, and his attempts at a later stage in novel-writing proved to be no more successful when judged by literary criteria then prevalent in the West. But he was something of a sensation when he made his debut, and I decided that his first collection of short stories was worth the effort.

It was a critical review and it appeared in one of those literary weeklies which used to make brief appearances and then get closed by the authorities for some naughtiness or other they committed, or simply disappear with or without a word of explanation.

In those days I was in my second form (or should I say the first of the two years which I had to spend in the second form) of my intermediate schooling, and Dhul-Nun was our Arabic teacher. I must say he took my criticism quite amicably when I proudly showed him the review, in which I praised his courage as a social and political critic while expressing regret that the stories did not stand up to standard, stylistically and technically.

I think the reason for my writing so little in Arabic was that, by the time I am writing about, I had already been immersed in my English readings and was becoming rather hard to please—and also that I was taking less and less interest in what was produced in Arabic whether locally or in the Arab world as a whole. By that time, indeed, I had dispensed with all but what I judged to be the worthiest of the books and periodical collections that had constituted my library, and was fast building my English-language library of books and periodicals. Although I was then still in the middle of what I will call my Marxist years, my intellectual interests had already begun to widen to embrace non-Marxist or just radical-liberal writings.

I AND "THE PENGUIN GENERATION"

I have somewhere seen the phrase "the Penguin generation" used by some historians of the British literary-cultural scene during the 1930s and early 1940s. In many ways I was a member of that generation; at half a shilling a title, even hard-up me could afford to buy a Pelican book now and then. The first titles I purchased, read, and kept were—if I remember correctly—Leonard Woolf's *After the Deluge* (never to be reprinted and now completely forgotten); J. B. S. Haldane's volumes on science and scientific topics, with his welcome Marxist leanings and his various eccentricities; R. H. Tawney's *Religion and the Rise of Capitalism*, which

I never managed to finish reading; Eileen Power's *Mediaeval People;* and books by Laski, Waddington, and others whose names I forget.

But it was really with hard-core Marxist literature that I was most pre-occupied at the time. I remember the appeal which certain books published by Victor Gollancz made to me, and the regret that I couldn't afford them (these were the days before the Left Book Club was launched). There were a few Gollancz titles that I could not possibly miss and for which I think I was willing to borrow or steal money. One of these was a tome with the title *A Handbook of Marxism,* edited by a plainly card-carrying British Communist writer by the name of Burns. That volume was something of a bible to me for a year or two; but I also managed to procure enough money to buy a few Gollancz novels, all translations and of which I remember Sholem Asch's epic story called *Three Cities* and one or two modern Russian works of fiction whose titles I cannot remember.

But it was Pelican and later Penguin titles on which my literary and cultural education was to depend for some years since those first days of reading English. In those days, Penguins—and probably Pelicans too—used to come out in batches of ten at a time, and I remember spending hours browsing and weighing and agonizing before I was to decide which was to be the first of the batch to spend 30 *fils* on—or the first two or three if I happened to have such incredible sums on me. And it was not only the books, properly so called, which Allen Lane's new venture produced, that had to be bought.

Already in the early 1940s Penguin Books started publication of such indispensable occasional publications as *Penguin New Writing, Penguin Film Review, Penguin Parade,* and even a periodical specializing in Russian studies. Of all these, however, *New Writing* was the most eagerly awaited and read; it was in this periodical, edited by John Lehmann and printed on cheap newsprint because of wartime shortages—that I first read something by George Orwell (it happened to be his classic piece "Shooting an Elephant"); Stephen Spender ("In Memoriam" and "A Trance"); W. H. Auden ("Lay Your Sleeping Head"); and such lasting favorites as Louis MacNeice, Cecil Day Lewis, and Henry Reed.

Not that these paperbacks, and English and American books in general, were easy to get in those years. We had to do quite a good number of regular, almost daily visits to all bookshops and all the stores where books were sold, so that we could catch the consignments as they arrived—and sometimes it was a matter of two or three months before a ship arrived with the precious packages.

MAKING ELIE'S ACQUAINTANCE

I say "we" because at one point during this period I met Elie Kedourie and he was to have quite a role in my literary education. It must have been in the last days of the summer of 1941, shortly after I had moved from Marxist literature on to reading more general books and especially works of fiction, poetry, and literary criticism. I had read about the appearance of a new monthly, *Horizon*, edited by Cyril Connolly, and lay in wait for it so to speak — until one day I spotted a copy in the magazine section of MacKenzie Bookshop.

I asked the manager if they received enough copies of it so I could buy it regularly there and he said no, that was the only copy they had, and if they kept receiving it regularly, they would get only one copy of each issue because that was the best their London suppliers could do. Thereupon I promptly placed an order for the magazine and kept getting it regularly through them.

In those days there were in Baghdad several places where English books could be purchased. But the only establishment dealing solely with English books and periodicals was the MacKenzie Bookshop. The other shops — all owned by Jews — either started as bookshops and eventually found they had to sell other goods as well because books and magazines did not bring them enough income, or were planned that way right from the start.

There were two or three such stores, but none of them would have heard of *Horizon* or similar periodicals, let alone ordering and offering them for sale. *Time, Look, The Saturday Evening Post,* various glossy American monthlies, and a few "girlie" magazines were all they offered in the periodicals line, while in the field of books they tried to get as many Penguins and Pelicans as they could. (Apart from these there was at that time no paperback series, except a line of reprints of British and American novels produced in Germany and which stopped coming as soon as the war started.)

Mackenzie Bookshop was an exception and the reasons were obvious. Founded by a Mr. Mackenzie shortly after British troops entered Baghdad toward the end of World War I, the store at first catered mainly to members of the sizable British colony in the city. When the British presence dwindled and Iraq became an independent monarchy, Mackenzie continued with the good work, probably with the encouragement and help of the British Embassy.

The bookshop also had another, safer source of income: It had an absolute monopoly as importer of English books chosen and recommended by the Ministry of Education for its schools. (In later years I was to be instrumental in breaking this monopoly, when as manager of Al-Rabita Bookshop I persuaded my boss, Abdel Fattah Ibrahim, to use his connections at the ministry with a view to securing for our bookshop a share in the annual bonanza.)

I had seen Mackenzie himself a few times before but there was never any communication between us other than strict business. By 1940, however, the old man retired and his chief assistant, a local Christian named Iskandar, took over. I never managed to learn about the precise arrangement — whether, that is, Iskandar became sole proprietor of the bookshop or continued to work for a wage. But it was essential to be on good terms with him in those days of shortages, as the case with *Horizon* showed.

One day, Iskandar told me that some young man was desperately trying to get hold of the periodical and that, having been told that the only copy they got was being kept for somebody else, had asked that he be given a chance to meet me and speak to me about the matter personally.

Secretly, of course, I was somewhat flattered and felt proud of myself — and also became very curious about the young man in question. Having arranged a meeting between us in the shop itself, I came one afternoon to find a young lad in shorts waiting for me. It was my first sight of Elie — a boy of sixteen or seventeen about to finish his penultimate year of secondary education. Naturally I agreed to lend him the issues of *Horizon* as they came immediately after I had finished reading them. But over and above this shared interest in a literary periodical, something bigger and far more significant happened: We had discovered each other and started a lifelong friendship.

THE HOUSES WE LIVED IN

One of the curses of being poor in Baghdad of the 1930s and 1940s was to be a subtenant and share the same house and the same single kitchen, toilet, and washing place with one or sometimes two other families. If I were to give a list of the houses in which I lived during my last eleven years in Baghdad, I would certainly lose count. There was always a reason to make me decide to move out — usually too much noise, little opportunity for sleeping at night or resting in the afternoon, lack of privacy, or just dislike of fellow-tenants.

After *Beit Yamein* we took residence — without Eliahu's family — in the

'Aquliyya quarter, in a house in which two brothers and their respective families lived with an ageing mother and an unmarried sister. I no longer remember what went wrong there, but after six months or a year we moved to another house nearby, *Beit Abu Ya'qoub,* where we shared the house with a smaller family and where finally I could do my reading and get my sleep in relative quiet. We were living there when the traumatic events of May–June 1941 took place—and the reason for our leaving the place this time had nothing to do with my whims or needs.

What happened was that my sister, Simha, now sixteen and a beauty in her own way, was actually seen walking with the youngest of the brothers living in the adjoining house. Even had the young man been Jewish, the thing would have been terrible enough; but he was a Muslim, and Simha was allegedly seen with him while hiding behind the convenient and accepted garb of *'abaya* and *pushi,* which between them provided total protection, covering the wearer as they did from head to foot. I don't know precisely how our move into another house was deemed then to provide any sort of security against Simha's continuing to see the young Muslim, but in the end it did help.

The next house to which we moved was situated in the Haydarkhana quarter, even deeper into Muslim neighborhoods. For some reason it was called *Beit Abul 'Aghaq,* after our landlord Dawood, who either made the said alcoholic drink or sold it or both, and with whom we shared the place. With a very large internal courtyard and rather generously sized internal balconies, the house seemed to offer what I needed most—some measure of quiet and the opportunity to have my few hours of sleep at night without disturbance.

In the event, it proved to be even worse than the previous houses. Dawood Abul 'Aghaq, it turned out, suffered from some rare kind of chest ailment which made him cough almost uninterruptedly—and cough loud and clear. The attacks usually came at the worst possible time—just before dawn—and the poor man seemed to cough his lungs out continuously until well into the morning. There was no respite—and apparently no cure or an attempt to seek a cure. I never imagined a human being could cough so hard and so long and stay alive. And there was no escaping the maddening noise; whether the man was in his room, on one of the balconies or—worst of all—sleeping on the roof nights as everybody else did in summer, the noise was loud and monotonous enough to drive one crazy.

But there were two advantages in living in *Beit Abul 'Aghaq,* and I made good use of them during the six months we lived there. Practically next door to us there lived a rich Muslim family who employed a young dark beauty as a maid—a beguiling creature with a finely built and well-proportioned figure and features. Often enough on passing by that house she would stand there at the half-open door, with her various charms in evidence even behind the long skirt but with her face uncovered. I had the impression she did this especially to catch my eye and I took courage to smile at her admiringly—and once or twice she actually reciprocated.

Only once, however, did I have an opportunity of actually necking with her—and "to climax" as the expression goes nowadays. The great event took place when the girl's employers went on a day's trip to some nearby village or small town, and for some reason failed to take her with them. On my way back for lunch that noon I saw her standing there—and was a little taken by surprise because that was the time when she should normally be busy inside serving her master and mistress and helping with the lunch.

I felt that something out of the ordinary happened and deepened my customary smile and almost invisible wink. Soon I was inside and we were in a passionate embrace. But it was obvious that the girl was a virgin and in mortal fear of being "discovered." It was as usual in such circumstances a rather clumsy affair and I remember thinking that, if that was all that there was to it, the whole ungainly episode should better stop there.

The other advantage was more substantial—and more lasting. By some coincidence Dhul-Nun Ayyub rented rooms a few steps from where we lived and established there the office of his new monthly, *Al-Majalla*. What with my knowing him from school and my friendship with Abdul-lah Mas'ud, I used to visit him quite often to chat and meet people of like minds since Dhul-Nun always had some visitors in the afternoons.

| ℛ ASHID ʿALIʾS COUP AND
ITS AFTERMATH

𝒯he one and only productive thing I remember doing during the whole month of May 1941 was read-
ing the bulky William Collins's edition of *The Complete Works of Oscar
Wilde*. I was then out of a job anyway and in the second form of my intermediate school; I don't quite remember whether there was school during
that month of war, but our stay in *Beit Abu Yaʿqoub* enabled me to have
my own quiet corner to read.

Although the trouble had started early in April and had resulted in the
escape from his palace of the Regent Abdul Ilah, actual hostilities between
Iraq and Britain started only at dawn on May 2. Twenty-eight days after,
on May 29, a Committee of Internal Security was formed by the mayor of
Baghdad, Arshad al ʿUmari, with a view to negotiating an armistice following Rashid ʿAli's escape across the border to Persia together with his
chief lieutenants. On May 30, al ʿUmari went to see the British ambassador, Sir Kinahan Cornwallis, and there signed an armistice agreement
whose terms were dictated by the British.

Throughout the war, which some have called the Thirty-Day War, the
populace in Iraq's major cities was in a state of euphoria, which alternated
with attacks of fear and xenophobia. There were some cases of minor mo-
lesting against the Jews, whose every movement tended to be interpreted
as some satanic pro-British device. Jews engaging in completely innocuous activities in the course of their daily lives were accused of making
signals to British airplanes flying over Baghdad, and in some cases were
taken to police stations and then released after the absurdity of the accu-
sations became clear.

A number of Jewish merchants and traders took home valuable goods
and items from their shops and places of business for safekeeping. It was
not quite safe or wise for a Jew to be out at night and, if he or she were
really careful and sensible, not even during the day. Not only did this state
of affairs fail to interfere with my life: I actually used it to advantage. At
long last I was able to stay home and do my reading in peace, without any

nagging from my parents about "finding something to do besides lazying around."

But there was trouble still to come. On May 31, after the facts became known and the regent announced he would return to Baghdad the following day, the Jews started to relax. The day was a Saturday and life for them seemed to return to normal. The following day, however, happened to be the first day of the Feast of the Pentecost. It was a habit with the Jews of Baghdad on such holidays to go out for a walk after prayers and breakfast—and on that particular Sunday many Jews felt it was safe enough to go out for a stroll, dressed up in their Sabbath clothes and usually with pockets full of watermelon seeds and an assortment of nuts to while away the time.

That day being also in some way a day of deliverance from the dangers posed by the pro-Nazi regime of Rashid 'Ali, however, many Jews thought the occasion worthy of a double celebration, and what with reports of the crown regent's impending arrival some of them saw fit to go out for the specific purpose of participating in what was intended to be a mass welcome for him and for his entourage. Little did they know the nature of the surprises that were awaiting them.

Various versions have been told of what actually happened that Sunday and the following day. According to official figures, the riots and murders that took place on those two days claimed a total of 110 dead, among them 28 women, and 204 injured—and that the victims were from both sides, Jews and Muslims.

The number of homes and shops assaulted and broken into was not given by the authorities, but according to statistics prepared by Jewish community officials the figure for shops and stores alone was 586, while the total value of goods, valuables, and money looted was 271,402 Iraqi dinars. As to homes, the community gave the figure as 911, with a total of 3,395 families and 12,311 inhabitants—and that the total material loss sustained by them was 383,878 dinars. Unlike the official version, again, which mentioned no cases of rape, the community gave an estimate of three or four such cases.

The Jews of Baghdad were caught completely unaware. To be sure, they had very good reason to celebrate: Here at last was an end to the month-old molestation and harassments to which Rashid 'Ali's regime subjected them in so many petty and unpredictable ways. The British, who were fighting Hitler's hordes, were victorious. Thus when they went out to watch the crown regent's triumphal march back that fateful Sunday, they thought they could afford to appear a little defiant, feeling secure in the knowledge that the army and the security forces were now fully in control.

What actually happened, however, was that not only did the British forces fail to enter the capital but the defeated Iraqi soldiers and officers were disbanded and allowed to enter Baghdad singly rather than in formation—and these could not help noticing the small groups of Jews heading in the opposite direction, dressed in their best clothes to welcome the regent and his entourage. What must have made things worse was that the day was a Sunday, and as far as these soldiers knew the Jews had no apparent reason to dress so festively and loiter in the streets other than the day's special occasion—namely the return of the regent under open armed protection from the hated British.

The trouble started late Sunday morning, when a group of soldiers crossing the Khir Bridge to the western side of the city met a group of Jews on their way to share in greeting the crown prince. The Jews were attacked, first with blows and then with knives—and of those who couldn't run for their lives a total of sixteen were injured and one died of his wounds. As the morning progressed and the attacks became more savage, some of the civilians, passersby, and bystanders took part in the fracas—while the policemen on duty at the bridge acted as mere onlookers and did not lift a finger.

Word quickly spread to the other side of the bridge, where the Jews were concentrated—and when it reached the slum areas adjoining King Ghazi Street groups began to gather. Rumors spread that the police were not interfering, although on several occasions they fired warning shots into the air when houses were forced open and their contents looted.

Taking heart at this obvious encouragement and seeing that not only the soldiery but some of the policemen were taking part in the forages, the mobs in such destitute neighborhoods as Abu Sifain and Ras el-Tchol— where Muslims and Jews lived in close proximity—became more systematic, and by early afternoon large trucks were seen moving furniture and other household goods from one side of the city to the other. According to an official commission later appointed to investigate the events and report on them, soldiers accompanying these lorries told enquiring police officers that they were merely moving the office furniture of the Iraqi Air Force headquarters, which had moved to another address!

These forages, often accompanied by physical violence resulting in deaths and injuries, and provoking no effective reaction on the part of the police, led the governor (*mutasarrif*) of the Baghdad Province to try to take charge himself. But when he asked the police officers on the spot why they were refraining from shooting at the attacking mobs, the reply was that "there were no orders." He got the same reply when he approached the chief of police.

It was only when he brought an order, signed by the regent himself, that orders were issued to fire at looters and murderers. It took just over an hour to scatter the mobs and empty the streets. By that time, however, the *farhud* (the untranslatable Arabic word which best describes the events of those two days) had spread throughout the poor neighborhoods in and around Ghazi Street as well as to some far districts like Al-A'dhamiyya and el-Karrada al-Sharqiyya. In this latter neighborhood, where the attacks took place only on the second day, six Jews were injured and one Muslim who tried to defend his Jewish neighbors was killed.

It is interesting to note here that Karrada and some of the more fashionable suburbs of Baghdad, where Jews constituted a majority of the inhabitants, witnessed the least trouble, some of them none at all. In many cases, armed Muslim neighbors stood guard and managed to chase away mobs intending to attack and loot.

THE *FARHUD* AND I

Totally unaware of what was going on in other parts of the city, I left the house just a little after 4:00 P.M. that same Sunday and took the bus to Bab el-Sharqi, where the open-air cafes and snack bars were. As usual, my friends and I had a meal of kebab, chips, and salad and sat there chatting and discussing the month's events for the nth time. Although a true patriot himself, my Muslim friend Salman was pleased with the outcome of Rashid 'Ali's rebellion since the British and their allies were fighting the Nazis and Fascists. Anti-British he certainly was, but like many moderate Iraqis with left-wing leanings he was content with leaving his anti-imperialist sentiments in abeyance.

But, of course, our preoccupations were not solely or even mainly political, and Salman and I discussed literature and my latest readings and "discoveries," while he related his endless jokes and anecdotes both from Arab literary and social history and from his experiences in Al-Zubeir, a townlet in the south of Iraq from which he hailed and which was known mainly for two phenomena—the exceptional quality of its dates and the disproportionate number of active homosexuals in its population. Salman

himself, I suspected, was a homosexual; he never had a good word to say
about a woman's looks and throughout our time together I never could
persuade him to accompany me on my way to see a prostitute.

There was no indication whatever of what was going on not far from
where we sat and chatted—and when it was time to leave—about 10:00
or 11:00 P.M.—we decided that the weather was too good to take a bus
and walked the whole length of Al-Rashid Street on the way to our homes.
During that long stroll, I began to feel that something was not quite as it
should be. There was, for instance, a small group of Jewish young men
who were carefully following in our footsteps, trying not to lose sight of
us. There were also fewer buses going.

But it was only when we approached Suq el-Shorja and the adjoining
way that led to the Taht el-Takya quarter that I began to feel something was
definitely wrong. Besides Salman and myself, there was with us a young
Jewish friend whose home happened to be in an alley leading from Taht
el-Takya to a parallel alley also leading to Al-Rashid Street. Seeing that
something was wrong, we decided to walk him to the door of his home
and thus took the turn to the way leading to the Jewish quarter. As soon as
we took that turn, a group of about ten or twelve young men felt encouraged to do the same—but they decided to make a run of it. They knew
no doubt what was going on at the other side of the city.

We duly saw our friend safely home, refusing to leave him until he was
inside the house. Then Salman decided, and I did not object, that he
should see me home as well. I will never forget the way in which I was let
in. I had a key to the door, but the door was bolted and I could not go in.
When I knocked I was asked who it was and only after assuring the people
inside that it was me did they agree to come down from the roof—where
Baghdadis slept in summer—and opened the door. It transpired that my
people, and the family that was sharing the house with us, had got wind
of what was happening and, seeing that I was so late (it was nearing mid-
night by the time I was home) simply gave me up for dead, killed by one of
those murdering bands of agitated Muslims roaming the streets and the
alleyways.

They wanted me to tell them what was happening and the terrible
scenes I had presumably witnessed—and they were visibly baffled to
learn that I was not even aware of the looting, killing, and raping that were
taking place. I kept my cool, told them not to panic, and went to bed. But
even I could not help hearing the shots fired at a distance and even some
of the shouts for help.

The next morning things worsened considerably as word spread among slum dwellers and members of displaced tribes that there was a lot to be gained by joining in the fracas. I remember watching from a window groups of men clearly from out of town and hardly knowing their way about carrying bundles of loot and streaming up and down that section of our alley that led to another alleyway. Where we lived was just two or three houses before the end of a blind alley, and ours was the only Jewish household there.

I do not remember the idea having crossed the mind of any inhabitant of our house that our Muslim neighbors would so much as touch us. The most skeptical and hysterical among us expressed fears that our neighbors would not interfere and just let the ferocious mobs do what they like with us.

They were wrong. Without even being approached, the three older sons of our aging neighbor — one of them a government official and one a student at some college or other — assured us we could rely on their protection. They were of good and well-established Baghdad family and as such they usually had some firearms. They kept watch but I don't think there was any attempt that day on the part of the mobs to attack our house, most probably because they were not even aware of the fact that Jews inhabited it.

WHAT ACTUALLY HAPPENED

What exactly happened on that fateful summer day in 1941 is now fairly well-known and documented. But the chain of events that had led to it, the motives, the blunders, the machinations, the failures, and the foibles that made the event possible and probably inevitable are not and will perhaps never become conclusively clear. Baghdad had fallen to the British and the government of Rashid 'Ali was put to flight. Yet the British troops did not enter the city — and the results were disastrous for the Jews and greatly embarrassing both to Britain and to the pro-British regime that succeeded the rebel government.

Somerset de Chair, the British intelligence officer who was on the spot at the time, told the full story — or something approaching the full story — in his book *The Golden Carpet*. There he records that one of the officers with the troops asked him: "Why do our troops not go into Baghdad? They may already be looting. I know. There will be many people killed if our troops do not enter."

"This," de Chair writes, "was my own view and the ways of the Foreign

Office are beyond my comprehension. From the hour of the ceasefire their word had prevailed. Having fought our way, step by step, to the outskirts of the city, we must now cool our heels outside. It would apparently be lowering the dignity of our ally, the Regent, if he were seen to be supported on arrival by British bayonets."

Another interpretation was that Regent Abdul Ilah, acting on information from his friends and agents in the city, decided that the time was not quite propitious for his entry, in view of the strength of anti-British feeling and popular resentment against his own regime. According to this theory, the regent and his entourage, including strongman Nuri el-Sai'd, were hoping for — and indirectly encouraging — just the developments which took place.

The advantages of this tactic were seen as self-evident. In the first place, the mob would vent its anger and resentment on a ready scapegoat, the Jews. Second, the new regime could make good use of the resulting general confusion in order to settle old accounts with the prorebel elements.

The psychological consequences that the *farhud* had on the Jews of Iraq, and its effects on their morale, were far-reaching. The Jews of Baghdad, the most influential and well-established single element in the city, were shocked, terrorized, and demoralized. In the long history of this community, indeed, no other event had been so traumatic. It could well be said that the mass exodus of 1950–1951, when almost all the Jews of Iraq were hurriedly transferred to Israel, was the end result of a process that had started on those two fateful days of June.

It was those events that made the Jews of Iraq receptive to Zionist teachings and ideology, an ideology that had failed to take root because most of them could not reconcile it with their seemingly complete integration into Baghdad life. For though the Zionist movement had made modest beginnings as early as the 1920s, and though it was known in Iraq even earlier than that, it was only after Rashid 'Ali's revolt and the anti-Jewish riots of 1941 that Zionism began to make real headway in Baghdad, especially in the ranks of the young.

There were, of course, other factors and pressures — notably the situation created by Iraq's participation in the Palestine conflict in 1948 and the defeat the Arabs suffered at the hands of the new state of Israel. But the events of 1941 were what really started off the cataclysmic process.

Following the entry of British troops, the majority of them Urdu-speaking Indians, residents of respectable neighborhoods became so annoyed with the harassments of these sex-hungry young males that many of them found it necessary to take some sort of action. They decided to put a huge sign at the entrance of each side street or alley reading *Aki Jana Man'a Yi,* Urdu for "No Prostitutes Here!"

BANK CLERK

After several years of what seems to have been total idleness, in which all I did was teach myself English, read books, and attend evening classes, I finally landed a job — the first regular job I was ever to have. Someone suggested that I should apply for a job as an apprentice clerk at Eastern Bank Ltd., a British overseas banking institution whose Baghdad branch was one of the two largest banks in the city, the other being Ottoman Bank. I duly applied, and to my surprise I was accepted and immediately given the job of a "ledger keeper," with a monthly salary of the equivalent of eleven pounds sterling.

According to the certificate I was given on leaving the job, my work for Eastern Bank lasted for the incredible period of over three years — April 10, 1942, to May 30, 1945. During that period I managed to finish my intermediate school and the two years of secondary school as well as continue my various pursuits — socializing, reading, and a perfunctory interest in politics.

Like all other banking and business institutions in the Baghdad of those days, Eastern Bank was an overwhelmingly Jewish affair. Apart from two or three Britons, who held the senior positions, and a few Christians, all the employees were Jews. The head of the current accounts department in which I worked was a Scot of a rather nervous and excitable temperament, but the "head clerk" was a relatively young Jew by the name of Ephraim. He was gentle and soft-spoken and I don't remember any serious clashes with him; but I didn't like the tone of the head of the department and I don't think Ephraim liked it either.

Apparently, and somewhat surprisingly, the job I did was just about good enough to keep me out of harm's reach and I enjoyed the unexpected prosperity of earning the kind of money I was earning. Although in absolute terms the conditions were pretty bad, they were better than those prevailing elsewhere and certainly better than anything I had known. There was no annual leave, no social benefits whatsoever, no pension fund, and no severance payments — and when after three years of working for the bank I decided to leave in protest against their failure to grant me a raise in salary all I got was the salary of the last month, while on my part I had to give the bank a month's notice.

One tragic episode that I will never forget—and which also provides a good example of the sort of world ours was—occurred one summer day toward the end of my work for the bank. On the morning of that day Ephraim failed to show up for work and everyone was set wondering what had happened. Toward noon, however, word came that Ephraim had died that very morning: On his way to the bank, while passing a construction site, a brick fell directly on his head and he died on the spot.

As far as I can remember, there was not even talk about such an elementary gesture as taking part in his funeral, and if there were colleagues of his who paid condolence visits to his family then I did not know of them. There was no talk either of the bank's paying the widow and children compensation—nor was any case made against the construction company or whoever it was that was responsible for dropping the stray brick.

What gave me the measure of self-confidence needed for threatening to leave Eastern Bank was that I had already found a job with a small banking firm—a better and more responsible job and with a considerably higher salary. Bank Zilkha was a private Jewish bank, much smaller than the two large banks but doing a lot of business for its size. They were in need of someone to take charge of the so-called "credit department," which dealt mostly with importers.

But my work for that bank was rather short-lived—just over two months. Having been accustomed to the strict rules and the fixed charges and commissions at Eastern Bank, I failed to adjust to the rather shifting, easygoing manner in which business in a small private banking institution was conducted. Often, when a customer came to me and I told him about the terms and the charges, he would go to the manager and obtain better terms—and then I was overruled. By the end of the second month I thought I had had enough.

My work for Bank Zilkha gave me a better insight into the workings of the world of business than all the three years I spent at Eastern Bank. I also had a glimpse into Jewish business society—and I was even able to make a piece of small mischief of my own. One day the manager gave me a letter he had received that day from somebody in London. The letter was short—a request for information about a man he called Mr. Richmond who used to teach at the Shammash School in Baghdad and who, back in London now, was apparently seeking the hand of some Jewish young lady. Now Elie used to talk incessantly of Richmond, now praising him, now condemning him for "airs" and snobbishness.

I thought I would be giving Elie a chance to settle accounts with Richmond and I took the letter to him that same day seeking his advice. Together we sat then and there and penned a reply, which, though not down-right damning, was vicious in tone and insinuation. The next day I had the letter typed and mailed—but when the manager finally read it he was visibly unhappy and the incident contributed to the tension that was building up and which finally resulted in my resignation.

KHADDURI KHADDURI MAKES A DISCOVERY

However, as in the case with Eastern Bank, I now see from the certificates in my possession that I left Bank Zilkha only after securing my next place of work—Al-Rabita Bookshop. What actually happened was that, while waiting for a place to house the planned bookshop and ordering stocks, I held a temporary position as a translator in the Directorate of Supply and Rationing. Curiously, I got the job thanks to my new free-lance occupation as roving bookseller specializing in avant-garde literary works and books and periodicals of the left and the far left. I had heard of Khadduri Khadduri and his leftist leanings some time before he introduced me to my future boss Abdel Fattah Ibrahim. As Khadduri was now working—on loan from the Ministry of Interior—as virtual boss of the directorate, I decided to go to him with a batch of Left Book Club books and kindred publications. The first thing I knew he was offering me a job as translator into English, in the department dealing with the thousands of applications coming in daily concerning the work of the directorate. The translations were made for the benefit of the British "adviser" who was then heading the whole outfit temporarily for the war's duration and its aftermath.

I accepted Khadduri's offer, my work consisting of rendering into English whatever my direct boss, a congenial Assyrian, decided was fit for the big boss to see. It was during my work there that I first met Sasson Dallal, who also worked as translator. Dallal by then had finished his secondary schooling and passed the prestigious London University matriculation exams.

Already in those early stages of his Communist experience Sasson Dallal was a fanatic and a true believer. Eager, quick-witted, a legendary controversialist, and habitually red in the face, he was always arguing and preaching his Communist gospel. I had the feeling that were it not for Khadduri's backing he wouldn't have survived the job for one more day.

Dallal was to become a leading member of the clandestine Communist party and, with all its leaders in prison, the sole leader and decider. He ended up being sentenced to death by hanging, which took place in the summer of 1949, a few months following the public hanging of four of his comrades. It was widely reported that he ascended the scaffold shouting "Long Live the Union of Soviet Socialist Republics," "Long Live Comrade Joseph Stalin!"

BRIEF ENCOUNTERS

After a brief spell at the Directorate of Supply and Rationing, I met Khadduri's friend Abdel Fattah Ibrahim, the initiator and leading light of Jam'iyyat al-Rabita (Al-Rabita Association). Abdel Fattah was then busy planning to open a bookshop carrying the same name, and he offered me a job there. In the course of the four years I spent with the bookshop, working closely with the politically deeply committed Abdel Fattah, I naturally met and got to know a good number of political activists, journalists, and foreign reporters who came seeking to interview the leader of the newly licensed political party. Some of these I was to see and exchange reminiscences with in other parts of the world years later. One of them was Jon Kimche, with whom I worked and established a lifelong friendship starting in 1962.

I had seen Kimche's byline in the London weekly *Tribune,* which was styled roughly after the *New Statesman* but represented a viewpoint considerably to the left of the latter—and was widely considered a mouthpiece of the supporters of Aneurin Bevan, a leading figure in the Labor Party. Kimche actually was executive editor of *Tribune,* in which George Orwell wrote regularly under the title "I Write as I Please."

One day, shortly after the outbreak of the first Arab-Israeli war following the establishment of the new state in May 1948, Jon Kimche appeared in the bookshop, asking for Abdel Fattah, with whom he had an appointment for an interview. Kimche was then working as a roving correspondent for one of the leading London dailies—and very possibly for the Jewish Agency too through the Zionist Federation of Great Britain—but he chose to present himself as a "Swiss journalist." However, while letting Abdel Fattah know that I was familiar with the man's byline in a left-wing British weekly I did not suspect a thing; I did not even know that Jon was Jewish.

Nevertheless, thinking about it later it did strike me as strange that the man should take on a Swiss identity. It was only later, however, that I learned that Jon was indeed a Swiss national, having been born there but refraining from naturalizing as a British citizen throughout his long career in British and in Anglo-Jewish journalism.

For, beside his editorship of *Tribune,* he later became editor of the Zionist Federation's *Jewish Observer and Middle East Review,* with which I became closely associated and from which he was summarily ousted in March 1967 at the proddings of Eshkol's associates, as Kimche was known to have been a great admirer and consistent supporter of Moshe Dayan and of his friends in the dissident Rafi group. Kimche also subsequently founded and edited the short-lived monthly *New Middle East.*

Apart from "sympathizers" — better known these days as "fellow-travelers" — and two or three journalists who worked for Abdel Fattah's new party organ *Al-Ittihad Al-Watani,* only one active member of the Al-Rabita Association was Jewish. Ibrahim (Abraham) Naji was among the scores of people I came to know during my work for the bookshop. Partner in a major wholesale business specializing in medical equipment and medications, Naji was fairly well off economically, and he generously aided both the association and the party. I was in a position to know this in my capacity as accountant of the former though I had nothing whatever to do either with the party or with its short-lived paper.

Unlike Abdel Fattah and his band of moderate socialists, however, Naji was eventually discovered to have been an undercover Communist and deeply involved in the work of the clandestine Communist party. During the early 1950s, when the persecution of the Communists resulted in many of their leaders either executed or jailed, the police somehow got wind of Naji's clandestine activities and, when the police apprehended him and searched his home, they seized no less an incriminating piece of evidence than the equipment used for typing, printing, and producing the Communist party's clandestine broadsheet *Al-Sharara.*

Naji was detained, together with his young wife, who was then in an advanced phase of pregnancy. They were sentenced to life imprisonment. Also, as a result of the shock, the couple's would-be firstborn baby was miscarried and the wife rendered infertile, apparently for life.

Eventually, some time in the late 1950s following Abdel Karim Kassem's revolt of July 14, 1958, an amnesty was granted to imprisoned Communists and other leftists, and Ibrahim Naji and his wife found their way to Israel, where, they thought, they would be able to work for the cause undisturbed. After all, there was already a Communist movement with an honorable record, with its Knesset members, its daily organ, its own printing plant, with Arab and Jew working closely together to establish a truly socialist society.

They were to be sorely disappointed, however, and because of the state of her health, the wife died only a year or two after their arrival. Work with the local Communists was not at all easy, largely because of a creeping rift between Jew and Arab within the movement. Finally, Naji one day made the rounds of his close friends and former associates — unceremonious brief visits which eventually turned out to be his way of bidding farewell. At the end of his round of visits Ibrahim Naji took his own life.

Chapter 13 | ℬOOKSHOP DAYS

𝒜t some point my mind began to wander — I cannot say exactly when. I was sitting there in this university auditorium attending a very special and exclusive seminar given by Professor Bernard Lewis, one of the most distinguished historians of the modern Middle East. The subject was Arab-Jewish relations, Jews in Medieval Islam, and "anti-Semitism in Islam." The lecturer was speaking about what he called "the myth" of Spanish Islamic tolerance toward Jews and how it had been fostered precisely by Jewish scholars in Europe in this century, allegedly using it as a stick with which to beat their Christian neighbors. Muslim-Arab scholars in our own day, he was saying, particularly delighted in ascribing the virtue of tolerance to Spanish Islam.

And so on. It was round about this time that the lecturer all but "lost" me, and I began to think of a more recent period and a more personal recollection — Baghdad of the mid-1940s and my own experience within the largely Muslim-Arab milieu in which I grew up and found the nearest thing to emotional and intellectual maturity and fulfillment. What with the difficulty of organizing one's thoughts in such circumstances, I caught myself hopping from scene to scene, person to person, and place to place — and I finally managed to concentrate on those formative years of the second half of the 1940s, some of my peers and elders at the time, and the general atmosphere of "tolerance" in which we moved, read, loved, and just plain lived.

The lecturer was still splitting hairs about tolerance, and how "the myth of Spanish Islamic tolerance" furnished an interesting example of the pitfalls and ambiguities of history and the writing of history. He was talking of two kinds, at least, of tolerance — tolerance as the absence of discrimination and tolerance as the absence of persecution. It was when he began to elaborate and allocate marks that I ceased to listen altogether and started reconstructing the faces and scenes involved in the launching, thirty-five years previously almost to the day, of my career as an assistant bookseller.

Some of my fondest memories of Baghdad, in fact, have to do with my work in Al-Rabita Bookshop, an offshoot of a cultural association of the same name that was founded by a group of intellectuals with leftist political leanings who stopped short of being card-carrying Communists. The association's secretary and honorary treasurer, Khadduri Khadduri, had asked me to help with the establishment of the store, which was to deal almost exclusively in English-language books.

I then had a short interview with the association's chairman, Abdel Fattah Ibrahim — and in what seems to be no time at all a place was found, books were ordered directly from individual publishers, shelves and desks were set, and the shop opened. Except for the more specialized works on sociology, economics, and history, which were chosen by Abdel Fattah himself, I had a completely free hand in making the orders, and my various literary predilections and inclinations played a decisive role in establishing the character of the bookshop and the type of clients who frequented it.

I recall clearly that on opening day and during the week that followed a large ad was placed in a local paper listing what purported to be "Ten Books that Changed the World" — all of which were available at the new store at fairly low prices. The books included Plato's *Complete Works* and Darwin's *The Origin of Species,* Marx's *Capital* and Freud's *Basic Works* — in the Modern Library Giants series; but it also included Tolstoy's *War and Peace* and James Joyce's *Ulysses.*

The bookshop, which was opened in the spring of 1946, soon became a meeting place for intellectuals and bookworms of all kinds — and although I already had my own circle of friends and fellow-literati, some of my best and most lasting intellectual friendships and associations had their origin there. Baghdad of the mid-1940s was a comparatively provincial little place with a rather limited number of people who actually read foreign languages with ease or for pleasure. Even among the Jewish community, foreign languages — mostly English and French — were the languages of commerce and trade, and rather useful if you wanted to get a job in one of the foreign banks or firms.

There were, to be sure, three or four bookshops before Al-Rabita, all specializing in English and French publications. However, although they offered works of the classics and some topical political books, contemporary works of literature — the novel, poetry, and criticism of the 1930s and 1940s — were practically unknown. As Elie used to say rather disdainfully of certain members of our generation, "English literature, for them, ends with Oscar Wilde."

The novelty of Al-Rabita Bookshop, and of the circle of literary aspirants which it helped to create, was the introduction of what was considered the last word in literary fashion—in poetry the works of T. S. Eliot, Ezra Pound, Auden, MacNeice, Spender, Barker, Edwin Muir; in fiction the works of Joyce, Kafka, Mann, Koestler, Orwell, Greene, Warren, Trilling, and Bellow—not to speak of the host of little magazines fashionable at the time—*Partisan Review, Sewanee Review, Kenyon Review, Hudson Review,* and *Politics* from the United States; *Horizon, Scrutiny, Cornhill, Life and Letters,* and *Polemic* from Britain.

THE COMPANY I KEPT

Among the young men whose acquaintance I made through the bookshop was Buland al-Haidari, a true bohemian and an as yet immature poet who was to become one of Iraq's leading pioneers of "the new poetry."

Buland was born in the Kurdish province of Arbil in 1926 and came to Baghdad when a little boy. At the age of about fifteen, under the influence of Hussein Mardan, a fellow bohemian who taught him that the family was "the great killer," he left high school in midcourse and lived the life of a real tramp, roaming the streets during the day and sleeping in public parks and under the bridges of the Tigris at night.

Feeling the gap in his education, he used to go into the Public Library and read anything that came his way. At one point he "specialized" in psychology—so much so that he became a laughing stock among his friends as "Mr. Psycho."

Eventually, Buland published his first collection of poems, entitled, typically enough, *Heart-throb of the Mud (Khafqat al-teen)*. The book came out in 1946, when the poet was just turning twenty. It is impossible to say now whether he preceded everyone else in pioneering the practice of free verse in Arabic, but one thing is clear: Of the young Iraqi poets who started the fashion—and it was undoubtedly in Iraq that the fashion started—al-Haidari was in the forefront, together with Badr Shakir el-Sayyab, Rashid Yasin, Akram el-Witri, and others.

It must be pointed out here that the introduction of free verse into Arabic would have been unthinkable had these young men not come under the influence of modern and contemporary European poetry. To appreciate the significance of Buland's contribution, one must remember that the modernist movement in Arabic poetry was ushered in when he and his contemporaries shifted to free verse. For reasons too academic to go into here, this shift to *vers libre* represented a radical movement in Arabic letters, ending as it did a tradition of rhymed, rhythmic poetry of some fifteen centuries' standing.

Buland himself has related how he and his friends used to gather together and read aloud some of the works of contemporary British and American poets. In the Beirut weekly *Al-Usbu' al-'Arabi* of June 23, 1975, he confesses in an interview that, with their English being what it was, he and the others read these works usually in the presence, and with the help, of one whose knowledge of the language made it possible for them "to grasp the poetic dimensions of those experiments." He mentions the names of two of these early mentors: Jabra Ibrahim Jabra and Najib al-Mani'. His account, as printed in the Lebanese weekly, includes these remarks:

> During this period I came to know Jabra, who played a leading role in transferring the poetic experience to us. Also, my relations became closer with Najib el-Mani', Hussein Hadawi, and Salman Mahmoud Hilmi. We used to frequent Al-Rabita Bookshop, where we met a Jewish intellectual by name of Nissim Rejwan, who used to make typed copies of any book of poetry that reached the store and sell it to us at a cheap price. Among those books I remember T. S. Eliot's *Four Quartets*.

I regret to say that here the poet's memory simply fails him. No one had the time to make typewritten copies of books or even of individual poems. What happened was that the books were sold at full price, and Buland and his friends were apparently willing to forgo a meal, a movie ticket, or even a visit to a brothel to purchase them.

Buland was one member of an intimate circle of young men whose friendship was based mainly on a shared interest in things of the mind. During endless hours spent in Cafe Suisse on Baghdad's main street in winter evenings and in open-air coffee houses and restaurants on the banks of the Tigris in summer, some of the latest literary "discoveries" were endlessly discussed and analyzed: Orwell's *1984* and *Animal Farm*, Kafka's various works in their recent English rendering, the latest issues of *Polemic* from London or Dwight Macdonald's short-lived *Politics*, Ezra Pound's *Cantos*, Eliot's poetry and plays — and of course the mysteries of James Joyce's *Finnegan's Wake*. We also discussed and debated local literary and political developments. Essentially, however, we tended to be apolitical.

When, late in 1947, following the adoption by the United Nations of the Partition Plan for Palestine and the mass convulsion in Baghdad in reaction to the Portsmouth Treaty between Iraq and Britain, Palestine again became the main subject of agitation, Buland composed two lines of traditional verse which fairly reflected the mood then prevailing in our circle — both among the Jews and the Muslims. (As far as I can recall, there were no Christians in that circle — except for Jabra Ibrahim Jabra who came to Baghdad later as a refugee from Jerusalem). It is difficult to render Buland's lines into English, partly because they are interspersed with colloquial idioms and expressions. But this is a fairly faithful rendering:

> Do let the Jews have it, and good riddance!
> Our patience it has sorely tried,
> Depriving us of faith and all guidance.
> For far too long we have been plied
> With its troublesome palaver.
> Will this stranglehold go on forever?
> For how much longer will it hold us in thrall?
> By God we are sick and tired of it all!

POLITICS OUT OF BOUNDS

During these troublesome days, just following the Arabs' defeat in the war of 1948 with Israel, a young Briton made his appearance in Baghdad. His name was Desmond Stewart, and as a kind of identity card he brought with him an English rendering of one of Plato's *Dialogues.* He worked in the English section of the local radio station and taught English. When the authorities discovered that he broadcast talks that no one had authorized he was given the sack but managed to keep his teaching job and stayed on in Baghdad for some time.

Stewart, who in the meantime has written a number of books on the Middle East as well as a study of Theodor Herzl, was an anti-Semite in the classical Western sense of the term. Out to capitalize on recent events in Palestine and what he judged to be growing Arab resentment against Jews, he started discreetly to circulate a little pamphlet he had brought with him from England. It consisted of eight or so pages and contained the text of a long poem of his that seemed to contain all the conceivable anti-Jewish sentiments and allegations constituting the main gist of the anti-Semitic doctrine current in Western Europe in the nineteenth and early twentieth centuries. The poem, composed in an old-style epic vein, included crass statements such as "And Jews are the descendants of the Devil."

Stewart meant to address his poem precisely to the kind of young, educated, English-speaking Arabs who were part of, or frequented, our small circle, or "gang" (*shulla*) as Buland used to call it. But he had a little unforeseen problem on his hands: The circle included two or three Jews who somehow seemed to be quite at home in it and shared a high spirit of friendship and camaraderie with the Muslims. Finally he found a solution. He gave copies of the pamphlet to the Muslim members of the circle beseeching them not to show it to me and extracting a promise from them accordingly.

But the ploy didn't work. After reading the broadsheet in verse, at least one of my Muslim friends, Najib, told me all about it and gave me the pamphlet to read. I never confronted Stewart with this; it just seemed of so little significance especially since the poem had no impact whatever on the people around us.

As a matter of fact, all the seemingly world-shaking events of the time — the Partition Plan for Palestine, the Portsmouth Treaty and the popular convulsion in the streets of Baghdad which came in its wake (better known as *Al-Wathba*), the dispatch of an army unit to Palestine and its defeat there at the hands of the "Zionist bandits," and the wave of persecution and harassments to which the Jews of Iraq were subjected subsequently — all these and many more developments occurred without relations between Jews and Muslims in our circle being in the least affected.

Not that there was an attempt to ignore these events or gloss over them. Quite the contrary. Sometimes, indeed, there developed some fairly heated arguments over the rights and wrongs of the Arab-Zionist conflict in Palestine. These debates were conducted only because two of our members held what was taken then to be the Pan-Arab and Arab nationalist position and were really perturbed by what was happening in Palestine.

Khaldun Sati' al-Husri, oldest son of the man who is considered the founder and leading ideologist of modern Arab nationalism, was then teaching at some high school or college in Baghdad and was endlessly preoccupied with the problem of Palestine, following events in the Holy Land day by day. I myself was not really interested in "politics," although when it came to the subject of Jews and Palestine I had my own, admittedly amateurish opinions.

I remember one quite fierce argument with Khaldun, who was discoursing in his quiet, soft-spoken way on the injustice done to the Palestinian Arabs by the decision to partition their land and establish a Jewish state there. When he spoke of the role of the Jews or the Zionists and how they had managed to "take" the land from its rightful owners, I remember arguing in reply—not very profoundly I am afraid—that, strictly speaking, it was not the Arabs of Palestine that the Jews fought and took the land from but the British.

Now, with the advantage of hindsight and the experience of fifty years, I consider that argument to be shaky and the remark positively vicious. But I recall very distinctly that no one among my listeners, not even Khaldun, took it amiss, and we habitually turned to the other, more interesting topics of our usual discussions. The last I heard of Khaldun Sati' al-Husri was that he was working as lecturer at the Arab University of Beirut and wrote a number of books—one of them, in English, about the fathers of the modernist movement in Islam.

REUNION

The other Pan-Arab nationalist in the group was 'Adnan Raouf, with whom I shared far too many interests—literature, time-out, and just plain companionship—for him to allow his political views to interfere in our friendship. To be sure, there were the usual differences of opinion about the subject of Palestine and the Jews. I remember giving him John Hersey's *The Wall* to read and that he was deeply touched by it. (It had then just come out.) But we were definitely more interested in exchanging pleasantries and jokes than in engaging in futile discussions about the topics of the day.

It was only in the late 1960s that I heard of 'Adnan's whereabouts— when he worked for his government in New York as deputy ambassador at the United Nations. Knowing of this from the papers, I decided to establish some sort of contact with him, however indirectly. I found an occasion in the winter of 1969. Ronald Sanders of *Midstream*—which was then edited by Shlomo Katz—had asked me to write an article for them depicting a composite profile of an East Jerusalem intellectual, and as the subject appealed to me greatly I did this promptly and the piece was printed in the February 1969 issue of the magazine.

Knowing 'Adnan was in New York and out of harm's reach (for how would I have a Jewish Agency publication sent to him at the Foreign Ministry in Baghdad?), I asked Sanders to send a copy of the issue to him at the U.N. Headquarters. He did—and in a letter dated February 20 and addressed to me, Sanders wrote: "I sent a copy of the February issue, as you requested, to 'Adnan Raouf, and today we received from him the following letter, which I quote in full: 'Thank you for your letter of 13 February 1969, and for the February issue of *Midstream*. I should like to thank Mr. Rejwan directly for his kind attention, and I would welcome your advice as to how this could be done.' I, of course, sent him your address, and I presume you'll hear from him soon."

Interestingly enough, Sanders added the following story: "The next day after sending out the 'marked copy' to him, Shlomo [Katz] had begun having second thoughts. He feared that we were perhaps getting somebody in trouble (we had sent it, of course, in care of the Iraqi U.N. delegation—now we have his home address, which I will give you below), and I was inclined to agree. Everything seems OK now, however, and Shlomo has suddenly become very excited about being in touch with a real live Arab diplomat this way." Giving me the home address, Sanders added he thought I should use it rather than the U.N. one—and concluded: "Let me know what happens."

Well, nothing happened! For one thing, owing to reasons which I cannot go into here and which had to do with the "record" I had with the so-called Shin Bet (Security Services), I refrained from writing to 'Adnan, much as I wanted to do so. So there was no communication. For another— and here lies the real reason why he never came around to writing to me personally to "thank me"—I had asked Sanders to continue sending 'Adnan new issues of *Midstream* as they came out—and as luck would have it the very next issue of the magazine, the March one, carried an article of mine on the notorious hangings in Baghdad involving a number of plainly innocent Jews who chose to stay and work in Iraq after the mass exodus of the early 1950s. Among those hanged was an old friend of mine and in my article I condemned the massacre.

It so happened, too, that precisely at that juncture 'Adnan was finally appointed acting ambassador at the U.N., succeeding 'Adnan al-Pachachi, who was said to have resigned his post in disgust or despair at his government's behavior in general. It was therefore quite out of the question to expect 'Adnan to write a letter to an Israeli address, and I respected his reticence and did not want to embarrass him in any way.

I explained this in a letter to Sanders dated March 17, adding: "Incidentally, he has accused Israel of organizing a world-wide campaign against his country—so I am afraid that when he reads my article in the March *Midstream* he may see it as part of that campaign. He should know better though."

ABDEL FATTAH'S REMONSTRATIONS

Khaldun and 'Adnan were really exceptional in holding Pan-Arab convictions, at least in the circles in which I mixed. My nominal boss at the bookshop, Abdel Fattah Ibrahim, was a social democrat by conviction and had little respect for the kind of xenophobia that then went by the name of Arab nationalism. George Orwell used to call the ideology he believed in "democratic Socialism," and (as Bernard Crick relates in his excellent biography) used to insist on writing it with a small "d" and a capital "S." This is exactly how I would today describe the political position of Abdel Fattah.

Some time before I began working at the bookshop, Abdel Fattah had resigned from a very senior government position (as director-general of the Ministry of Education) because of differences of opinion with the minister and also because he was dissatisfied with the whole system generally. Shortly after opening the store, he initiated the formation of a political party and started a daily—both leading the party and editing its newspaper. Neither lasted for very long, and when the party was banned the paper had already been ordered to stop publication.

I remember, with some embarrassment I must admit, that when Abdel Fattah made an appearance in the bookshop the day he learned about the ban on his party, I said something to the effect that perhaps one should congratulate him on the occasion. Seeing he was not in the least amused, I asked seriously whether he was sad—and why? "You don't seem to understand," he said with real sadness. "How should I put it? It's like the death of a baby you've begotten, tended, and cared for for a certain period of time."

I was, of course, extremely touched and left it at that. Not that there had not been differences of opinion and heated discussions between us. I recall one occasion on which I debated with him the whole subject of democracy and whether it was "practicable" in Iraq in the circumstances. Again I am afraid it was basically a half-baked idea of mine, but I remember clearly arguing for hours with Abdel Fattah about it. My "stand" was that, although I wholeheartedly agreed with his views about the desirability both of democracy and socialism, I was not sure Iraq and the Iraqi people were "mature enough for democracy." Endlessly he reasoned with me on this point, explaining with exemplary patience that there was no such thing as a people unfit for a democratic system of government.

Now, in retrospect, having seen how democracy and parliamentarianism can be manipulated and bowdlerized in the best and most "advanced" of societies, I tend to agree with this viewpoint. Indeed I have come to believe that, whether illiterate or educated, wild or civilized, the so-called man-in-the-street tends to have a healthy instinct about regimes and rulers that is not always displayed by the politically sophisticated members of the society.

There was certainly not a trace of anti-Jewish feeling or prejudice in Abdel Fattah Ibrahim. Shortly after the rout of the Arab armies in Palestine in 1948, however, I thought I began to detect in his talks with me a feeling of sadness—which bordered on resentment sometimes—about the turn things were taking. "The Arabs have a very long memory," he said to me one day when news from the front finally indicated that the Arab armies were not making any headway. "They are not likely ever to forget this humiliation." He always spoke of "them" when referring to the Arabs, never of "us." I am certain this was by no means an attempt on his part to dissociate himself from fellow Arabs and coreligionists. It was simply that detachment one usually finds in the true intellectual. And he said what he said neither in anger nor in bitterness—nor even with a sense of real involvement. It was, rather, a kind of warning, a grim prophecy concerning the shape of things to come. It must also have been a subtle comment on the way in which I myself reacted to those happenings, making no attempt whatsoever to hide my satisfaction at the course events were taking.

I don't think Abdel Fattah was an anti-Zionist either. (Nor, of course, was he a Zionist.) But he had a great deal of empathy for the Jews and the Jewish problem. "You Jews," he said to me on another occasion, "are the salt of the earth. How do you think you are going to manage to live in a state of your own—all cooped up together in one place and having solely yourselves to deal with, depend on each other, earn your livelihood one from the other!"

Then, no doubt reflecting on the trouble he himself was having with his own government and his own people, he said in a gesture of mock-desperation mingled with his typical good humor: "All right! Have it your way! Have a bloody state of your own! Come to think of it, why should we be the only sufferers? You will soon discover what burden it entails!"

Abdel Fattah was especially eager that I personally should know what I was doing when I took the decision to leave Iraq permanently and go to Israel. "If," he said to me on one occasion, "you imagine for a moment that you are nearer, in outlook and temperament, to a Jew, say, from Germany, Russia, or Poland than you are to me or to Iraqis in general then you are quite simply mistaken. You just don't know what you will be in for!" But I remained coolly unconvinced—and after that he quietly gave up trying.

A SOCIETY IN TRANSITION

Iraq of the years of World War II can justly be described as a society in intellectual and political turmoil. The influx of foreign troops, the relative relaxation of press censorship on most subjects unrelated to the war effort, the increasing toleration of activities by covert Communists and fellow-travelers following Moscow's entry into the war against the Axis powers—these and other factors all coincided with the emergence of what appeared to be a new generation of politically and socially conscious educated young men and women eager to have their say and to take part in what seemed to be a fast-approaching era of social, cultural, and political change.

It is thus possible to say that Iraq of the years immediately following the end of the war, in May 1945, was ready for a veritable upheaval, something that can justly be viewed as a renaissance. What came to be called a "new force" in politics, and which in reality consisted largely of intellectuals, educators, lawyers, poets, and men of letters, was making itself felt, and the authorities themselves began to realize, and often publicly acknowledged, that unless this new force was permitted to play its role through constitutional channels it could prove disruptive if not positively destructive. Following this line of reasoning, the government allowed new political parties to be organized.

Three leading parties were formed—two on the moderate left and one with a Pan-Arab nationalist agenda. Abdel Fattah Ibrahim, who was to establish the Al-Rabita Association and the bookshop which became a meeting place for left-leaning intellectuals and a rising class of young men interested mainly in cultural and literary matters, led one of the first two leftist parties, while Kamil Al-Chadirchi, a former associate from the famous *Ahali* group, headed the other party. The difference between the two parties was hard to locate, but it was generally accepted that Al-Chadirchi's group placed their emphasis more on democracy, while Abdel Fattah's stressed socialism—and Jam'iyyat al-Rabita and the bookshop that was given the same name, was one of the results, another being a daily newspaper.

| 𝒜 DEEPENING FRIENDSHIP

T he first poem that I was to read and appreciate in English was Eliot's "The Love Song of J. Alfred Prufrock." It seems like a strange start—almost as if you began a book with the last sentence. But in my case it was rather natural—a result of the circumstance that, on the one hand, I had no formal education of any kind in English and in English literature and, on the other, my enthusiasm for the new coupled with my budding friendship with Elie. At first, Elie used to come to me in the bank to return the last copy of *Horizon* he had finished and take the next one after I had finished with it.

The truth, however, was that I could read and appreciate only parts of the magazine—some political-cultural essay, a short story, some of the literary criticism and most of the book reviews. Poetry was my weakest point—until one night, after our usual gathering at Cafe Brazil, I accompanied Elie home and he insisted on reading Eliot's poem aloud to me. Elie was a great admirer of Eliot and had just been reading Ezra Pound's *Cantos* and the poems of Auden, George Baker, Louis MacNeice, and Dylan Thomas, and his enthusiasms proved infectious.

In those last years of World War II getting books was a difficult and rather haphazard affair, and it was a matter of hit or miss to get Eliot's *Collected Poems* or the Faber selection containing "The Wasteland" as well as "J. Alfred Prufrock." But there were some new anthologies of recent verse and certain British publishers were putting out books of poetry by younger poets. Above all, we had the benefit of following the various little magazines where the new poetry was published. Later, a year or so after the war ended and shortly after I started working for Al-Rabita Bookshop, things in this respect became far easier and the difficulty now was to find enough money to purchase all the books we wanted to have.

Our interests were not confined to poetry. With his good knowledge of French, Elie was already reading Proust in the original and I followed by grappling with the Modern Library edition of *Swann's Way* and subsequently with the complete two-volume translation, also published by

Random House. Somehow Elie had also read James Joyce's *Dubliners,*
his *Ulysses* — and was actually reading the selection from *Finnegan's Wake*
in the Faber edition. He liked to read to me aloud the famous Anna Bella
Plurable and parts of Mrs. Bloom's unforgettable internal monologue
toward the end of *Ulysses.* But the list is too long — Kafka, Mann, Gide,
Paul Eluard, and of course, Sartre and Camus. Elie one day actually produced a letter written and signed by André Gide and addressed to him!

The story of that famous letter started when Elie read some remarks
made by Gide in a lecture or essay to the effect that the younger generation suffered from anxiety and too many worries and such — and Elie, ever
eager to make a point (and an impression) took pen in hand and wrote
Gide saying something like: Why, but no! On the contrary, anxiety and
worries were the very thing that was conducive to creativity and inspira-
tion; in fact, what would we do or be without anxiety!

And poor Gide, no doubt taken completely by surprise, wrote Elie
telling him how right he was — and how foolish and/or negligent of him,
Gide, to have made such a silly remark! It was a great day for Elie, who
came to the cafe armed with the letter and showing it to those of us
who read French while translating it for me and his other disadvantaged
friends.

For all his real merits, his brilliance, and his genuine appreciation of
modern literary works, Elie was a wee little too artful and too fond of
"airs." He was also — not unlike me, I must confess — a self-confessed
"cultural snob" and in fact very near to being a snob without the qualifica-
tion although he would have liked to be known as a "reverse snob." There
were certain traditional dishes he would not touch: On Saturdays, instead
of sharing in the usual overnight chicken and rice dish known as *t'beet,* he
would eat out of a tin of sardines or some other cold, Europeanlike lunch.
He was rather hard on people who had no pretensions in the spheres of
culture and literature and was very rebellious where social customs were
concerned. One day Elie read a poem by D. H. Lawrence with the lines,
"How beastly the bourgeois is / Especially the male of the species," which
he kept repeating to me and to himself. Not that the females of the species
had much more appeal for him — and my impression was that the feeling
was mutual.

But Elie was fun — and a great help where my literary education in its
first stages was concerned. When time finally came for his departure to
London in 1947 I felt so desolate and alone that Abdel Fattah once caught
me in the bookshop shedding real tears. His first thought was that the reason had to do with some insult or indignity I might have suffered at the

hand of a customer or colleague. I assured him that was not the reason—and had to tell him the truth. He said he understood. For weeks on end I was all but inconsolable.

As for Elie himself, there was some silence before he could find the time to sit down and pen his first letters from London. He had, it seemed, wanted to study medicine and to specialize in mental health. But there was nothing doing in that direction and he joined the London School of Economics and Political Science. In one of his early letters he confessed that his experiences in London made him realize the extent to which he was "made in Baghdad."

Totally alienated as we might have seemed to be—from the society and the polity not less than from the culture—Elie and I nonetheless had our deeper roots dug firmly in the soil of Iraq. We were not only unaware of this but vehemently denied it, before ourselves even more than before others. It was only when he finally managed to leave Iraq for study in London that Elie was to realize how "different" he was and how different the English were from what he had imagined them to be.

As far as the "literary bent" which Elie and I shared—a phrase that was to become something of a joke we used to crack at our own expense—there was a significant difference between our respective entries into the field, at least as far as the first steps were concerned. Having had the formal education I managed to get, for what it was worth, in government schools, I naturally grew up with Arabic as my one means of communication with the outside world and the only channel through which I could receive my literary apprenticeship.

Elie, in contrast, had his schooling first at the Alliance school where French was taught from the very start, then in the Shammash Secondary School where English predominated, the result being that even before finishing his preuniversity education he was able to satisfy his literary predilections by reading English and French works of literature in the original.

It was really only with Elie that I began to become familiar with what was then considered the best, latest, and most avant-garde of English and other Western literary products. It was what I would call the golden age of "the little magazines," and to publications like *The New Statesman, Tribune,* and *The Spectator* were now added John Lehmann's *Penguin New Writing,* Cyril Connolly's *Horizon,* and *Life and Letters* from England; the American *Partisan Review* and later Dwight Macdonald's *Politics, Kenyon Review, Sewanee Review,* and others.

Many of these publications were available either for sale to specific clients placing standing orders for them at the two or three local foreign-language bookshops or in the modest premises of the British Council and the U.S. Cultural Center's reading rooms. It was in the latter, in fact, that I first made my acquaintance with *The New Yorker*, which used then to come there in a funny Armed Forces Edition printed in tiny type on thin paper exactly half the size of the original and thankfully with no advertisements whatsoever.

Elie had a room of his own, and usually, after we had had our coffee and cakes at the Cafe Suisse or Cafe Brazil and said good night to whomever of "the gang" happened to join us there, we retired to his room later in the evening and together read from the latest arrivals, especially works of poetry by Eliot, Auden, George Barker, Stephen Spender, Louis MacNeice, Herbert Read, and Edwin Muir (whom we first encountered as a cotranslator with his wife of Kafka's works).

My own favorites, some of whom were to become my "culture heroes" for decades to come, were all in those "little mags." The first I ever saw of Simone Weil's work was her remarkable essay, "*The Iliad*, a Poem of Force," which had its first appearance in 1945 in *Politics;* I encountered Koestler, Orwell, Saul Bellow, James Agee, Delmore Schwartz, Hannah Arendt, Sidney Hook, and scores of others in *Horizon, Polemic, Partisan Review,* the early *Commentary, The New Yorker, The New Statesman,* and other quarterlies, monthlies, and weeklies, some of them rather short-lived.

THE GIRL FROM CAIRO

She said her name was Helen. She must have been in her mid-twenties and was not particularly bad-looking. She sent a messenger boy to call me from the second floor where I was busy balancing my accounts, waiting downstairs herself. And she said she brought me greetings from "friends" in Cairo. She seemed very careful not to be spotted or overheard.

In those days of World War II, two or three years after Hitler's invasion of the Soviet Union in June 1941, the Iraqi authorities and their British mentors had relented a little as far as pro-Soviet or even openly Communist activities were concerned. In Baghdad itself, one monthly was launched with clear left-wing leanings and sympathies — *Al-Majalla,* edited by Dhul-Nun Ayyub — while certain daily newspapers employed a number of known leftists and fellow-travelers as news editors and editorial secretaries.

But real, hard-core Communist literature and publications continued to come solely from abroad—mainly from Beirut where a number of periodicals were controlled and edited by card-carrying Communists or committed left-wing intellectuals like Raeef Khuri, Qadri Qal'achi, and others, who between them edited and wrote an extremely readable and intelligently written monthly called *Al-Tareeq*.

Nothing comparable came from Cairo, which then was the uncontested cultural capital of the Arab world. There was, however, one exception—*Al-Majalla al-Jadida*. Now a monthly by that name had been founded and edited in the mid-1930s by the veteran socialist-evolutionist-agnostic Egyptian Copt intellectual Salama Musa. Eventually Musa found he was unable to continue to bear the financial burden and the monthly stopped publication. In the early 1940s, a group of young progressive intellectuals took over the name of the magazine and started producing a new version of it, livelier and far more coherent intellectually.

The new monthly was edited, and much of its contents written, by Ramsis Yunan and George Henein, aided by a number of other left-leaning intellectuals, poets, and short story writers. With the magazine the new team inherited the old one's list of subscribers—and it was thus that I received the first few issues, with the usual offer to renew my subscription. I did this with enthusiasm.

In the first year or so of its appearance, the new *Al-Majalla al-Jadida* appeared to follow a line fairly identical to that of orthodox Marxism-Leninism and was pro-Soviet in its general tone. Then, suddenly, following some particular development or just because of a change of heart among its editors, the editorial line became distinctly anti-Stalinist and the name of Trotsky started to appear in articles, together with favorable expositions of his theory of the permanent revolution and his polemics against Stalin's doctrine of socialism in one country.

This change of ideological line happened to coincide with my own growing disillusionment with Stalinism, now that I had become better acquainted with some historical facts such as the notorious Moscow Trials and the Great Purge. I felt growing empathy with the magazine and its editors, and since *Al-Majalla al-Jadida* was nowhere on sale in Baghdad I decided to take the unusual step of ordering a number of copies—ten I think it was—and undertake their sale myself through one newsagent of my acquaintance. And so it came to pass that I became a sort of agent for the monthly.

It was shortly after this, a few months at the most, that "Helen" made her appearance at the premises of Eastern Bank. She said she brought greetings and expressions of gratitude from the editors — I think she used the words "the group" — with whom she said she was associated, linked by an identity of views. She even implied she was actively working with "them," and that she was asked to find out about "your circle," how active we were here in Baghdad, the nature of our activity, and whether we needed any help or assistance.

I believed every word she said, and eventually invited her home to my room for a private chat. She came late one afternoon, and was visibly disappointed to discover that there was no "circle" or activity of any kind, and that the whole thing was no more than intellectual curiosity run wild. She examined my library very closely, and must have been astonished to find the works of almost every "degenerate" poet, novelist, and intellectual that she could think of, not to mention copies of *Horizon, Penguin New Writing,* and other totally noncommitted periodicals.

She could not hide her astonishment, and somewhat reluctantly obviously came to the conclusion that here she had business with a one-man rather than some mass Trotskyite movement actively engaged in a plot to overthrow the regime. I remember her saying, at one point after finishing her tea: "So it's just a kind of intellectual pursuit on your part personally." I said yes and she left.

I must say I felt somewhat disappointed. Secretly — as it was the case in most such encounters with young women — I must have hoped that a kind of "relationship" would develop between me and Helen, and then who knows! However, I had no inkling of just how lucky I was in not having been an active Trotskyite leading some clandestine movement.

It was like this: I had told Elie all about the girl from Cairo and even managed to point her out to him one day when walking on Rashid Street; I may even have made the introduction. Be that as it may, Elie, who I had thought sounded somewhat skeptical about the story, made no comment though he made it clear he wanted to have nothing to do with the girl. After all, he was completely apolitical in temperament and I myself by then was more interested in the literature and arts section of *Al-Majalla al-Jadida* than in its politics.

After our private talk in my place, Helen never contacted me again, and since I had no idea where she lived and what her phone number was I similarly let the whole matter rest where it had at the end of our meeting. One day, however, Elie came to the bank to break a piece of sensational news: He had spotted Helen in the street, in full British Army uniform and accompanied by a British officer! Now apart from the outrage of her being a British soldier and going out with an officer too, what made the scandal even greater was that the two belonged to none other than the intelligence branch of the army!

As usual, it was the all-knowing Elie who discovered it. Elie had a number of friends and acquaintances who were serving with the British Army at the time—cultural officers with whom he shared literary interests and by whom he was often invited to watch an improvised stage performance or attend a lecture, and Palestinian Jews who were serving in that army and at the same time acting in some capacity or other to help organize and promote the clandestine Zionist movement in Iraq. It was from these contacts that he had learned how to distinguish between the various insignias and emblems worn by British soldiers—and he promptly identified those worn by Helen and her companion as belonging to Intelligence.

LETTERS TO ELIE

Did you know that foolish old man Eastwood? Fancy he came here the other day and asked for *The Battle of the Books*. Before knowing my name he said that the *Times* review was "bloody awful." "It was alright for a boy in a secondary school to have written it. But to be given the authority of the Leading Newspaper in the Country! However, if he can write such things and get the editor to publish them and gets away with it—well and good . . ." And fancy I was on the verge of regarding this as about the only sensible comment on my pieces! But then Mr. Eastwood did not know or care for Gubbins, or for any other material published in the *Times*. After this I introduced myself as Mr. Rejwan, offered the old buffoon a chair and had an hour's talk with him. He was pleased, he said, that I received his comment "in the right spirit." I still think that his remarks were not devoid of all sense, but I suppose one must start somewhere!

(Baghdad, October 17, 1947)

Someone whom I'm proud to have met recently is Yusuf el-Kabeer. He called at the bookshop—to see me! He asked, in the most casual of ways and without any introduction "where are those books you were writing about yesterday?" They were Crankshaw's *Russia and the*

Russians and his *Russian Review*. I think Crankshaw an
extraordinary fellow (have you, by the way, read his review of Trotsky's *Stalin* in the N.S.?). His book is really
good, one of the sanest about Russia. Andy must have
had a hell of a time deciding to publish my review, which
pleased a lot of commies and fellow-travellers. Strange?
Not at all, I think. What advantages have our Anglo-
Saxons on Russia? Molotov is behaving like Bevin, and
this in turn talking Truman, whose proper place should,
I fancy, be in the accountancy department of some big
company. At the very least, Russia is offering the only
real alternative to chaos! Anyway, Andy was publishing
a series of 7–8 articles by Middleton Drew on Russia
(propaganda). This was not entirely unconnected with
my decision to write on those two books, I must admit.
A little embarrassment for the chap, I thought! Surely
enough, on the day on which my article appeared, the
series was broken. There was no M.D. on Wednesday the
7th. And next day Andy told me he thought from my review that the book was "too biased in favour of Russia."
Told him I didn't think so. Like it? Tell me.

(Baghdad, April 16, 1948)

It is now almost exactly a year since you left for London.
You can laugh at me, but I never for one moment ceased
to feel having had lost something irreplaceable. During
the first weeks after you left I almost felt that it was not
entirely reasonable to be so sentimental about it, but I
have since learnt, to my cost, that it was both reasonable
and unsentimental at all; your departure was evidently
a personal catastrophe no less. Need I add that I've not
succeeded in finding a substitute? Ridiculous to imagine
I could!

(Baghdad, May 22, 1948)

You probably remember what I once told you—namely
that I was "speaking strictly as an onlooker." You thought
I was kidding. I wasn't. And there exactly the danger
lay—and lies. The horror of it has just lately struck me.
An attitude of complete non-identification is impossible,

or it requires super-human powers. But one of identification with one side is equally impossible because it needs too high a measure of narrowness. Perhaps the best role would be one of interpretation and reconciliation—in action. Some such thing I think would be the best solution. After all there is such a thing as a duty, duty toward oneself and duty toward others, certain others . . .

Someone has said of Matthew Arnold, not quite without a note of disparagement, that he deliberately conceived himself to be a corrective. "He prided himself not upon telling the truth but upon telling the unpopular half-truth. He blamed his contemporaries not for telling falsehoods but for telling popular truths." He goes on to say: "Arnold suffered from thus consenting merely to correct; from thus consenting to tell the half-truth that was neglected. He reached at times a fanaticism that was all the more extraordinary because it was fanaticism of moderation, an intemperance of temperance." Fanaticism of moderation? Intemperance of temperance? I rather like the sound of it!

(Jerusalem, November 1, 1952)

Chapter 15 | THE START:

MOVIES, BOOK REVIEWS

One of the few personal papers I managed to take with me to Israel, where I arrived as a new immigrant in February of 1951, was this:

January 31, 1951

To Whom It May Concern:

Mr. Nessim Rejwan contributed film criticisms to this paper from June 1946 to August 1948 and book reviews from May 1947 to August 1948. These were a regular and popular feature of the paper. Mr. Rejwan also contributed occasional articles on a variety of topics and his work was of a very high standard.

G. Reid Anderson, Editor, The *Iraq Times*

The circumstances which had led me, seemingly so arbitrarily, to stop contributing my "regular and popular" reviews to the *Iraq Times* precisely in August 1948 had to do with the first Arab-Israeli war and the debacle of the Iraqi army in that war, and I don't intend to go into them. Here I will try and recapitulate the circumstances in which I started writing regularly for that English-language, British-controlled Baghdad daily.

Those in fact were my first steps in "journalism." With the exception of a few pieces which I had contributed to the local Arabic press—all on nonpolitical subjects—and an Arabic rendering of a wartime pamphlet by the political science professor Harold J. Laski, my contributions to the *Iraq Times* represented my very first efforts in the business of writing.

It was Elie, with whom I shared most of my intellectual interests, who, one day in what seemed to be out of the blue, told me he decided to approach Anderson, offering to contribute a weekly book column to the paper. I said *What?* The explanation was simple. The editor, an old man who was also a typical sample of the colonial British sahib, had just retired and Anderson, about thirty years of age, was the new editor; he must be more open to such an offer. Sure enough, Anderson accepted the offer, and Elie's first reviews were extremely well written, highly sophisticated, and rather biting. A few weeks after he started his contributions, Elie one day again took me completely by surprise when he suggested that I offer the *Times* my services as a film critic, undertaking to speak to Anderson about it himself. I hesitated—partly out of stage fright but really because I did not think my English was good enough. After some agonizing and a good deal of prodding, I gave in and took the plunge.

In the years 1946–1948 I wrote regularly on movies, three and some-times four short reviews a week, under the pen name which Elie sug-gested—The Nightwatchman—while Elie himself continued to contrib-ute book reviews. Shortly after Elie left for London to study, in the summer of 1947, I was asked by Anderson to take up the book column as well as the movies. Since my intellectual interests had, by that time, become almost purely literary—and since, too, "politics" was not a safe subject for any-body in Iraq to write about anyway—the books I selected for reviewing were mostly novels and works of belles-lettres, with only a few that dealt with general social, philosophical, and political subjects. In those days, my knowledge of Iraq itself, and my interest in its affairs and in those of the Arab world, amounted to very little indeed. In fact, I became used to seeing myself as a kind of amateur literary-cultural critic, an observer and connoisseur of British, American, and European literatures—roughly in that order.

As far as my views and attitudes on these matters were concerned, I was fiercely and overly avant-garde and rather rash with my judgments. It was in those days that Elie and I stumbled on Virginia Woolf's essay "Middle-brow," in which she coined that word to indicate all that she found ob-noxious and objectionable in culture. She herself, she wrote, was a "high-brow" and rather proud of it. As such, she was able to appreciate, respect, and even enjoy "lowbrow" culture and literary works. "Middlebrow," however, was something else again. Judging it "neither here nor there," neither fish nor fowl, she held everything she found "middlebrow" in contempt. What is more, she was outspoken enough to name names, rele-gating the works of Arnold Bennett, H. G. Wells, and Somerset Maugham to the middlebrow variety—and into the dustbin.

As far as Elie and I were concerned, we perceived ourselves as being militantly highbrow, and as such we gladly and enthusiastically tolerated what we chose—mostly arbitrarily—to call lowbrow. Anything that even remotely smacked of the "middlebrow" was rejected by us out of hand and made an object for the most merciless of assaults.

JAMES AGATE AND I

In those days the *Iraq Times* subscribed to the feature service of the *Daily Express* of London, a mass-circulation daily known for its sensationalism and a preoccupation with sports and what was then considered "sex." One of the *Express* features used by the *Times* was James Agate's weekly column of book reviews. Now if anyone was for us a middlebrow it was Agate—whom we also considered a philistine to boot. He seemed to us in those days to be the nearest thing to a personal challenge—always dismissive and scornful of the new and the avant-garde and letting no opportunity slip of savaging such of our idols as T. S. Eliot, James Joyce, and Virginia Woolf, while openly admiring and praising everything that was traditional and "middlebrow" in literature and the theater.

On one occasion, Agate was brash enough to attack Eliot really viciously. Reviewing a critical evaluation of T. S. Eliot's work by Helen Gardner, he wrote among other things that Gardner made a frantic attempt to persuade him that Eliot was a poet. He went on to say that for him a poet was somebody who writes something that's going to make him, Agate, happier for the rest of his life—and that Eliot, having failed to accomplish that feat, was therefore no poet. This finally provoked me into writing a long, sharp and, I can now see, rather humorless letter to the editor, which he printed under the title, "Mr. Agate—'The Cultural Fascist.'"

A joint effort of Elie and myself, the letter tried to be a ridiculing, tongue-in-cheek affair. With reference to Agate's complaint that Eliot failed to make him happy for the rest of his life, we wrote: "Having read both Miss Gardner's essay and Eliot's poetry, and in fairness to these two despicable 'highbrows,' permit me, Sir, to point out that neither of them had ever tried to do anything of the kind, and to express my firm conviction that, had they tried it, they would certainly have failed."

Reading that letter now—it was printed in the March 15, 1947, issue of the paper—I cannot help being both impressed by and shocked at the tone of it—the intensity of feeling, the depth of involvement, the sheer rashness. It seems that not the least irritating feature of Agate's onslaught then was the fact that excerpts from Gardner's essay had first appeared in John Lehmann's *Penguin New Writing*, which along with *Horizon* and a number of other "little magazines" from Britain and the United States provided the only intellectual nourishment available to us at the time.

Be that as it may, after having what fun we could with Agate, we wrote in our letter (which we decided that I alone should sign):

The trouble with James Agate and his like (Lord Elton, Alfred Noyce, and F. L. Lucas, to name only the touchiest) is that they simply refuse to recognize the fact that no modern poet or artist worth the name is interested either in pleasing their important little selves or in persuading them of anything whatsoever. They accordingly dismiss anything they are too narrow-minded to understand as unworthy, even ridiculous. (Mr. Agate says in his piece that the book he is reviewing is well worth buying "if only for the laughs.")

These gentlemen's sole interest is vested in the dead and the established; in fact they live off the dead and half-dead. Time and again, for instance, I find Mr. Agate boasting of being able to spell correctly the names of Dickens's characters—as if that mattered. If they had their way, nothing short of burning all modern books of poetry and destroying the "modernist horrors" in painting would have pleased these spinsterish middlebrows. They are, in short, cultural fascists.

And then, seemingly in an attempt to say something positive, the letter concludes with this paragraph:

I did not, however, write this simply to make the above remarks, but to enter a protest with you, Sir, for allowing such misleading nonsense to be introduced to readers of your paper. My point, put simply, is this, that whereas readers in England can, either by taking them very lightly or by ignoring them completely (which I know many of them do) afford Mr. Agate's reviews, here, where a small public for English books is growing steadily, and where at least some of your readers are uninformed enough to take these reviews seriously, they are bound to produce more harm than good.

"NIGHTWATCHMAN" AND THE PHILISTINES

This was shortly before Elie's departure to London and my taking up the book column. About this time, my uncompromising "highbrow" tone was nearing a point where not only readers but the editor himself found my film criticism unsettling. The immediate postwar period in the movie industry was notorious for the number of spectacular historical films produced, especially by the then thriving London Films. There were some six movie houses in Baghdad, and a few more in summer when open-air cinemas offered their wares. It was thus quite often a chore to cover all the new films, especially since very few of these were shown for more than one week. And so, week in and week out I had to undergo the drudgery of watching these movies, mostly two a night—and what with the quality of most of them, the reviews became consistently scathing.

Looking back on those days I cannot help being impressed by the good humor and the patience shown by my editor, a congenial Scot. I remember with a shudder that the very first review, a matter of 150 words, took me the best part of one summer night to write!

I was then twenty-three and full of burning convictions and high-sounding ideas (boys then used to grow up at a much quicker pace than they seem to do these days). There was also a good deal of defiance and a little mischief—and I remember reflecting that had Anderson known what trouble he was courting he would have looked elsewhere for a film critic. But he was a fair-minded and straightforward man and, once the deal was made, he went on with the arrangement through thick and thin. The most shocking "incident" occurred not long after the reviews were launched. The week following the appearance of an especially nasty review of an immensely popular British production called *The Wicked Lady,* as I was making my way into the King Ghazi Cinema hall with the usual announcement that I was from the *Iraq Times,* I was curtly though politely refused admission. I didn't argue and proceeded to purchase two tickets (it was a two-seat invitation and I had a friend with me)—not so much to see the movie but to prove a point. And the point was that I duly wrote the review and it duly appeared in the paper—just to show the philistines that there was no escaping the vigilant watch of The Nightwatchman!

The next day Anderson, on hearing the story, immediately instructed the advertising department that, unless the proprietors promptly apologized and renewed their invitation, the paper would stop carrying their ads. The move was a shrewd one. The *Times* being the only English-language daily in the country and its readership being the natural patrons of English films, there was simply no other way than through these ads of knowing what was showing in the movie houses. And so the apology duly came, and the invitation was renewed—and the infuriatingly pointed, demonstratively highbrow reviews continued, to the vexation of cinema owners though not, alas, always to the satisfaction or edification of the moviegoers themselves.

Which brings me to the second major "incident" of my movie-reviewing days. This occurred over a Universal Pictures film starring Abbott and Costello, *Here Come the Co-Eds.* This time the editor himself had some difficulty with the review, in which I attacked Universal for the trash I claimed they had been producing and called the film "third-rate entertainment."

Abbott and Costello, the review complained, repeat their tricks all over again. "They contrive to make messes of whatever jobs they are given to do. The little, and apparently more important of the two (what's his name?) is put in the most awkward of positions, so that he is given opportunities to give more and more of his usual yells which seem to be the thing that his devoted fans like most. The thought just crosses one's mind that these two have far more possibilities as comedians than they have been given till now; but, after all, movies are not made by actors only — they are chiefly the work of the directors who, though the only creative workers in the field, are dominated, in Hollywood, by those good-for-nothing businessmen who like to call themselves producers and who in actual fact 'produce' absolutely nothing."

I handed in the review one morning, and to my utter surprise I found it in the paper the next day printed under the title "Can You Write Film Reviews?" and with this introductory note:

> The editor of the *Iraq Times,* having himself seen this film, and having heard various opinions of it, asked both the Nightwatchman and a friend to write reviews of it. The friend was shown the Nightwatchman's criticisms of this type of film. As the editor has a great deal of sympathy with both points of view, and is also greatly irritated by both, he would be interested to know what YOU thought of the film. Write briefly. If you write long letters they will be cut down, so save your energy. All criticisms which have something to say will be published. The original critics will be allowed to hit back and the editor will sum up.

The editor's "friend," signing his comment "R. B. M.," opened with a question: "Is there any reason why a film should be hit at just because it is neither intellectual or a masterpiece of production?" His reply was that the film under review "is a slapstick comedy and never pretends to be anything else," and that as such it was pretty well up in its class and gave him "several hearty laughs and the patrons of the cinema — doubtless there were very few analysts among them — very many." His conclusion: "If the patron gets what he pays his money to see, who is the critic to complain? He may record his own views, but surely he should say, at the same time, for the guidance of the public, that very probably such and such a film is one which they would want to see."

I don't know how many "reviews" the editor's appeal produced. What was actually printed was a group of six responses — three for the film and against the Nightwatchman, two against the film and one wavering. One of my critics, trying to be funny, wrote that my review would have been more justifiable had I called myself "Morning Watchman." As a matter of fact, he added, "We need such comedy films to be seen sometimes during the night, at least to give us a relief from business troubles we experience during the day." Another recommended the comedy to "those in need of mental relaxation," while a third wondered, "How can one apply the same criteria of criticisms to films such as *Great Expectations* and *Here Come the Co-eds?*"

My reply to this challenge, which seemed all the more ominous because of the editor's obvious involvement in it, was lengthy and typically unsparing. The cinema critic, I complained in my opening paragraph, was in a rather tricky position. "He is expected to judge films by the same aesthetic standards with which an art critic or a literary critic judges pictures and books, and at the same time he must, somehow, play the high priest to the popular mystery which is now the cinema. For the cinema is an art-form, but at the same time it is much more and much less than that. In the drabness and boredom of the modern world cinema, apart from the races and the football pools, is the only place which provides the immense majority of people with the excitement and the glamour which they cannot find in their waking, everyday lives."

And so on. The gist of the argument was that all this made the job of a film critic "determined to preserve certain obvious standards" a tough and rather thankless one. This was followed by responses to specific points made in the letters solicited by the editor. At one point I declared I was glad "that I am useless as a guide to tired businessmen seeking sweet forgetfulness from drafts, ledgers and bills of lading." In reply to one of my critics I wrote: "He seems to imply that a critic, if one should be there at all, must not condemn a film popular with the public, or, better still, that he should be a mirror reflecting public taste. If this is accepted, then I suggest that the critic's proper place is not inside the theater at all but in the box-office where, having counted the tickets sold on the first night, he may forthwith go home and prepare his report."

"To my mind," I concluded after a few more forays at my assailants, "a critic's true function is to weigh and consider, in the light of past master-pieces and helped by his 'critical instinct,' what a piece of work is worth when compared with other pieces of work in the same category. This, I submit, is the only service that can reasonably be asked of him and that he could properly render."

This incident, I must add, caused no interruption whatever either in the flow of the reviews or in the stringency and aggressive militancy of their tone. Now, however, after all those years, I am not quite sure what measure of good the reviews managed to accomplish. Indeed I myself began to feel that even the cinema owners ceased to be vexed, while a joke made the round as to the usefulness as a guide to cinemagoers this par-ticular critic was. The Nightwatchman, this went, had indeed become a good guide — only it was important to remember one small detail: When he praises a movie you should avoid it like the plague, while the worse the review the better you are advised to see the film!

BOOK REVIEWER

In retrospect, and after nearly six decades in the business of reviewing books, I find myself still marveling at the sheer range of interests, and the ready willingness of the editors of the *Iraq Times* both to order the review copies and to print all the reviews I chose to write, week in and week out with minimal editing on their part.

In June 1947, after fourteen months of regular moviegoing and film re-viewing, I suddenly found myself enthusiastically accepting the added burden of churning out a weekly book column for the *Iraq Times,* so that now I became its regular book reviewer in addition to the chore of the movie reviews. Apart from a life-long attachment to books and the printed word, I was mentally and ideologically ready for the job, which I real-ized would naturally involve expressing opinion and revealing personal predilections and prejudices on a great variety of subjects, persons, and places.

For the truth was that by the time I left Eastern Bank, where I worked as a ledger keeper in the years 1942-1945, I had become completely es-tranged from all Marxist schools of thought — Stalinist, Trotskyite, Lenin-ist, and even pristine "Marxist." My interests now were mainly literary and also cultural in the wider sense. Lacking a regular education in English and its literature, however, I was "spared" the labor and what I thought was the tediousness of studying English literature in any kind of chronological order, and instead of plowing through Middle English, Chaucer, Milton, Shakespeare, and the rest of the classics, I was able to start with T. S. Eliot and Ezra Pound. In fact, one of the first English poems I read and appreciated was "The Wasteland." At the time I found nothing unusual in this, although with the passage of the years I began to wonder if a good grounding in the classics would not have been a better way to begin.

It was in such a mood and with such a background that I joined the *Iraq Times* as a regular book reviewer. The first review I wrote for the paper was of two new short books dealing with the state of the film industry in Britain— *Tendencies to Monopoly in the Cinematograph Film Industry,* prepared for the president of the Board of Trade by the Films Council and published by His Majesty's Stationery Office, and *Films: An Alternative to Rank,* by Frederick Mullaly, published by the Socialist Book Centre, London. The thrust of the review was an attack on the "monopolistic nature of the film business," and the villain of the piece was, of course, the Rank Organization, which at the time was producing what I thought was in the main "third-rate entertainment."

In the case of this first book review, I had made my choice very carefully. On the one hand, here was an official report whose authors expressed opinions I could cite with approval. To give one example, referring to the view, "held by some quarters," that the British cinematograph business is to be regarded merely as one business among others, and that it is out of place for Parliament to show special concern for its conduct and future development, the authors of *Tendencies to Monopoly in the Cinematograph Film Industry* say:

> We do not share that view, and we are confident that Parliament will continue in its endeavor to safeguard the industry's future by means of special legislation not applicable to industry in general. A cinematograph film represents something more than a mere commodity to be bartered against others. Already the screen has great influence both politically and culturally over the minds of people. Its potentialities are vast, as a vehicle for expression of national life, ideals and tradition, as a dramatic and artistic medium, and as an instrument of propaganda.

Another aspect of the report with which the review dealt and which is worth mentioning here as an indication of the type of concerns that I had in my mid-twenties was the subject of "marketing British films abroad." "Until now," I pontificated,

British films have been made chiefly for the local market. Mr. Rank maintains that there is no hope for the British film industry if it does not fight for overseas, and especially across-the-Atlantic market. Now, the American public being completely "sold" on Hollywood films, the only chance for this "invasion" being successful, the argument goes, is to produce films which, to appeal to that public, must in one way or another be no more than imitations of Hollywood.

To accomplish this the Rank Organization is now engaging American "stars" and ace-producers and directors at fantastic expense. Apart from this, a group of pictures must be made with an eye on the overseas screen. Hence *Love Story, Madonna of the Seven Moons, The Wicked Lady*, and *Caravan*. Hence technicolor musical colossal productions like *Caesar and Cleopatra*, and even Betty Grable. In short, British films, in the sense that French films are French and Russian films are Russian—and in the sense also that American films are never American—will be no more or very rarely available even to the British public, unless they are produced by independent groups and enthusiasts who, as we have already seen, are in a very precarious position.

Although I have not been successful in preserving cuttings of all my book reviews, I have always kept in my files a piece of paper listing the dates and headings of those reviews. One early review dealt with a book by Aldous Huxley called *Science, Liberty and Peace*, published by Chatto and Windus at 3s. 6d. Huxley was one of my culture heroes at the time, and a review of one of his works of nonfiction afforded a very good opportunity for me to make a point or two that I felt had to be made.

As a matter of fact, looking at the list now and reading some of the stuff, I realize how in almost all the reviews I wrote I bared some of my prejudices and ground some of my many axes. The appearance of a new book by Henry Miller, for instance, was deemed by me to be a rare opportunity for giving America and its culture a sound beating. A review of three British Council pamphlets on poetry, the novel, and prose literature in Britain since 1939 was made an occasion for offering overenthusiastic appraisals of the works of one's favorite British contemporary writers and poets. A combined review of new books about the newspaper industry in Britain was used as a vehicle for a savage attack on the popular London press and the preoccupation with sports, sex, and crime (and was rejected on the ground that it was too opinionated—which it plainly was!).

A selection of these reviews is given in an appendix.

Chapter 16 | OUT IN THE COLD

O ne Sunday noon in the summer of 1948, while in the bookshop giving the finishing touches to the week's book column, a messenger came in with an envelope bearing my name and bookshop address. It read:

Dear Rejwan,

Owing to the prevailing depression of business I find it necessary to cut down our expenditure on editorial contributions. It is with regret therefore that I have to inform you that as from the end of this month we will be unable to publish book reviews and we will also have to stop film criticism. You will appreciate that I did not wish to take this step but am forced into it by the fact that business is so bad. With kind regards.

Yours sincerely,
G. Reid Anderson, Editor

The date of the editor's letter was July 24, a Saturday, so that my last book review was to appear on Wednesday the 28th of the month — a notice of barely four days. Also, while it was true that the paper paid me for the reviews and the columns (the total came roughly to about twenty pounds a month, a handsome enough pay by the standards then prevailing), Anderson's allegation about the depression of business did not quite convince me. I was so attached to the work I was doing, and the habit by then had become so deeply rooted, that I honestly offered the editor to continue my contributions for half the pay or even for no pay at all. His response was brief and enigmatic — a dismissive smile and some polite mumbling about his not dreaming of making me do unpaid jobs. Eventually, with the help of his secretary, I was to learn that Anderson had dictated the letter by telephone from "the Embassy," where he was in the habit of going for meetings and consultations every Saturday after that day's paper had been laid to bed.

I never managed to discover the whole truth about this affair but I think the reason for Anderson's hasty decision is not far to seek. In those days, the *Iraq Times* was something of an institution and enjoyed a great deal of independence and influence. Apart from considerations of prestige and the quality of its readership, it was also virtually the country's only newspaper that was immune to the shifting fortunes of its contemporaries, which on any day of the week could receive a government order to suspend publication because of some irregularity real or imaginary.

There seemed, thus, to be no reason why, at a time in which Jews were being systematically dismissed from government posts and certainly from all positions connected with information and the media, the one English-language paper with obvious connections with His Majesty's Government should continue to employ Jews in its various departments, with one Jew working as sole book and film reviewer.

Be that as it may, my very last contribution to the *Iraq Times* was a special assignment made by Anderson a few months after my services were terminated—a full-page survey of the year in contemporary Iraqi literature which appeared in the special Christmas–New Year issue toward the end of December 1948. The piece was well-received, both by members of our circle, many of whom figured in the article, and by outsiders including the notorious Desmond Stewart and the young Englishman who was then director of the British Council in Baghdad.

Apart from being Jewish, however, there were a number of factors which I cannot help thinking had some bearing on Anderson's abrupt decision to stop publishing my reviews. In the first place, the decision came only a few weeks after the search conducted by the police of the house where we lived as tenants (which I describe below). Three years before that, there was the surprise visit by Helen, the girl from Cairo who turned out to be a soldier in British Intelligence.

More significantly, perhaps, there was also that invitation to the Criminal Investigation Department (CID) back in the early 1940s. Inefficient and often quite inept though they were, the Iraqi security authorities had at least one professional virtue: They kept ample records of the personal details and other "specifics" of all those who ever had anything to do with them, whether guilty or innocent. On at least one occasion—the one in which I was questioned by the CID man about the multitude and variety of books and publications reaching me by mail—I had politely been asked to furnish detailed information and particulars about myself before I was "set free."

The circumstances leading to my summons by the CID had to do with the fact that I used to get all my mail through Eastern Bank Ltd., where I worked in the years 1942–45. Now if I were asked to list the places in which I lived since the four of us — Father, Mother, Simha, and myself — left *Beit Yamein* in 1939 and until 1946, I think it would emerge that we moved houses at the rate of at least one every nine months. This was why during those years I always received my mail in care of the bank and the other places in which I worked. The mail consisted mainly of printed matter, and postal services during the war years being what they were, the books and the periodicals I used to subscribe to and order came in batches and heaps.

One day, when everything seemed to have arrived at the same time, the dispatch clerk at Eastern Bank was shocked to find that practically all the packages and large envelopes were addressed to me — two or three Left Book Club selections and a similar number of issues of *Horizon, Readers Digest, Life and Letters, Partisan Review, Left News,* and *International Literature* (sent direct from Moscow although the subscription had been made through a London agency). Fortunately, it was only the Left Book Club packages that caught the clerk's attention — and when he asked me what they were and what "left" meant, I lied promptly, claiming it was a firm dealing with "left" in the sense of left-over or remaindered books. The ruse worked on the clerk but apparently not on the Iraqi Censor's Office, then full of literate British soldiers and men and women of all nationalities and linguistic backgrounds who had joined the British Army (including, incidentally, many Jewish recruits from Palestine).

In the course of my interview with the CID man, I was given to understand that the one saving grace about my "conduct" — and naturally the circumstance that made the powers-that-be overlook the uncommon interest I was showing in dangerous and subversive ideas — was that my interests were so wide and eclectic that such "safe" reading as to be found in *Readers Digest* interested me side by side with the Soviet literary monthly *International Literature.*

SEARCH WARRANT

My second, and last, encounter with the secret police occurred five or six years later. One day in June 1948, in the sweltering heat of Baghdad at high noon, I made my way by bus from the bookshop in Ras el-Qarya where I worked to the house in Bustan el-Khas. It was my lunch break, which I always managed to exploit for a shower and the day's main meal — and also the inevitable siesta. We were then living in two rooms — Mother, my sister Simha, and myself — in a house owned by a Jewish family just arrived in the metropolis from the far province of Hilla. It was a noisy, self-asserting, almost exhibitionist lot, with four or five unmarried sons and daughters all trying to make it in the big city. Sharing the house with them was something of an ordeal, especially what with the eagerness of each of them to find favor and with the parents having more than an eye on what they considered a highly eligible young man so near at hand.

One of the sons, Ghazi, attended an evening intermediate school nearby. One night in the winter of 1947–48, on his way back from school, he somehow became involved in one of those antigovernment student demonstrations, was detained briefly and then released, unharmed and with no further questions asked. The snag, however, was that his "particulars" — name, address, occupation, and so on — were duly taken by the police and tucked away somewhere. This was normal procedure with the police in those days. The government of the day was neither in the mood nor popular or strong enough to take action against organizers and participants in hostile demonstrations, and it was deemed to be enough just to keep a record of the names and whereabouts of those disturbers of the peace.

The device was to prove its usefulness very shortly afterward — at least where the Jews among the lot were concerned. In their systematic, indiscriminate campaign of harassment against the Jews, which they launched immediately after the establishment of Israel and the official outbreak of the war in Palestine, the authorities chose to open those records of names and addresses. Search warrants were issued against all Jews who took part or in some other way became involved in antigovernment demonstrations — and there were many such demonstrations since the U.N. approved the Partition Plan for Palestine. Ghazi was one of these, and the police search of the house was carried out on that same day in June.

And so, arriving home some time after 1:00 P.M., looking forward to some rest and quite famished, I was greeted by Simha at the door who whispered to me that "they" were searching the house — and indeed that they were now in my own room upstairs. It transpired that, having come looking for Ghazi and armed with a search warrant, they happened to look through one of the windows looking out on the inner courtyard — and, lo and behold, they spotted *books*, indeed a hell of a lot of books and other printed and handwritten matter. Protestations by my own family and the parents of the "suspect"—who were even more eager not to have their son's name associated with such fearfully mysterious things as books —were to prove futile. Granted, they were told by the two policemen, that the books did indeed belong to someone else and not to their son, they were in duty bound to examine them lest they included "subversive literature."

There was no one in the house—or anywhere for that matter—to stand up and answer this argument. The search went on—and when I arrived I found the two cops plowing through the piles of periodicals, the shelves full of books, and what folders there were containing personal papers, letters, and cuttings of articles. They were in something of a quandary. They greeted me, incredulously somewhat, with the question: "Is this all yours?" I hastened to say yes, and that I was willing to sign a statement to that effect. I added that their "suspect" Ghazi (whose parents and brothers were in the meantime bewailing their son's misfortune in being associated with the books) had nothing whatever to do with the collection. It was to no avail. The policemen continued with their search, unable sometimes to suppress their awe at what they considered the sheer variety of the subjects and trends they located in the books and the periodicals. At one point one of them could not help expressing his wonderment that the library contained the Koran as well as the Old and New Testaments.

I was fortunate on that occasion. Not because the two policemen were actually looking for someone else to victimize but because their knowledge of English was hopelessly inadequate for the job at hand. Because of an almost incredible combination of reasons, they failed to locate any of the books that the authorities then considered subversive and therefore incriminating. They could identify words like *Russia* and *Russian,* but failed to comprehend the meaning of terms like *communism, socialism, anarchism,* and even *Marxism* and their derivations. They knew what *Israel* and *Palestine, Zionism* and *Zionists* meant, but they overlooked books and periodicals with the words *Jew, Jewish,* or *Jewish people* in their titles. They knew who Lenin and Stalin were, but not Marx, Engels, Trotsky, or Plekhanov. They finally could identify as Russian—and therefore dangerous and subversive—authors like Tolstoy, Dostoevsky, and Simonov, but none of the names of left-wing authors from Britain, the United States, Spain, or France.

The result was amazing—and would have been quite funny were we living through normal circumstances and times. The two policemen took with them, as possibly incriminating material, the Modern Library collection of *Russian Short Stories* and Tolstoy's *Anna Karenina,* but not *The Communist Manifesto* or Burns's *Handbook of Marxism;* Lowdermilk's *Palestine: Land of Promise* but not Herzl's *The Jewish State* or a tome titled *History of the Jewish People* whose author's name I forget.

As far as periodicals were concerned, the omissions were even more surprising—and rather decisive. They did not so much as touch *Commentary,* of which by then I had a pile, although its cover announced in fairly large letters that it was published by the American Jewish Committee. They did not bother to have a second look at *International Literature,* a monthly published in the Soviet Union and to which I had taken a year's subscription. Nor did they find anything suspect in the piles of Left Book Club publications—or even an official Communist periodical like *Labour Monthly,* of which I had kept a number of back issues. I was also rather lucky in that the two policemen—one of them with the rank of officer— could not identify the Arabic periodicals they found there: collections of old issues of Khalid Bagdash's monthly *Al Tali'a,* an openly Communist publication; recent issues of the pro-Communist *Al-Tariq,* the Beirut monthly; and the Trotskyite Cairo monthly *Al-Majalla al-Jadida* of George Henein and Ramsis Yunan.

However, while being so negligent in their choice of books, the two policemen took with them every piece of paper, hand- or typewritten, on the ground that they didn't have the time to examine them on the spot. This was the most grievous loss of all, since the loot included all letters received from Elie and Sylvia, his friend and future wife, in addition to other letters, notebooks and jottings of which I was never to see a trace.

In the days to come it became something of a joke among family and friends—and a standing testimonial to my eccentricity and sheer "cheek" —that before they left with their trophy the two policemen were stopped by me and told in a clear and perfectly formal tone: "And please don't omit to return the books and the papers to me after you have finished the investigation. Also please remember they belong to me and not to Ghazi whom you've come to arrest."

The two or three weeks that followed, with Ghazi detained pending his trial, were naturally full of tension in our shared residence, what with Ghazi's parents and family feeling that the materials the police seized were to be used as incriminating evidence against their innocent son. We all awaited the day with impatience and forebodings, with me offering to appear in court to testify that the books and the letters belonged to me and to me alone—all the time knowing full well that it would be a sham affair and that all that was involved was money.

Sure enough, when the so-called trial was finally held, there was no trace of my books and papers — and naturally no mention of my name, let alone my alleged involvement. The whole masquerade took only a few minutes, at the end of which Ghazi was pronounced guilty of taking part in "anti-government rioting" and sentenced to two years in prison or, alternatively, a fine of two thousand Iraqi dinars. Needless to say, Ghazi's family managed somehow to mobilize the cash, their son going back home safe and sound.

LOVE UNDECLARED, UNREQUITED

Nadi Khirrijiy al-Alyans (the Alliance Graduates Club) in Karradat Maryam was something of an exclusive affair and I figured that, not being a graduate of the school, I could not have become a member even had I wanted to. I didn't, and even Elie who was a graduate and did frequent the place was by no means enthusiastic or happy since he found nothing of interest that he could share with any of the members. Highbrow, sophisticated, and rather avant-garde in his tastes, he was really not at home in the club and often voiced his reservations and pithy criticisms. The trouble was that even those of the members who had intellectual and literary pretensions were not nearly good enough for either of us. For the one — so we used to say — English literature ended with Oscar Wilde; for the other, Somerset Maugham's novels were the limit of comprehension; and for the third, the names of Kafka, Mann, Joyce, Eliot, and our other culture heroes meant nothing whatsoever.

For me, however, "the club" had its attractions — or rather one single attraction: It was a mixed one and membership consisted wholly of unmarried young men and women. In a society in which mixing between the sexes was almost unknown and took place only in the framework of families and relatives, this was something of a novelty. Consistently deprived of female company as I was, and having unlike Elie attended only schools for boys, I was bound to be attracted to a place like the Alliance Club, and the fact that I seldom went there was something of a disappointment for me.

But the club had an added, and decisive attraction to me personally — a young woman named Marcelle. Marcelle, a graduate of the Shammash School who also had passed the London matriculation exams, worked as secretary to the editor of the *Iraq Times*. In those early days of writing, although I had purchased a portable typewriter and had one in the bookshop as well, I used to submit my reviews in handwritten form and Marcelle was entrusted with the task of typing them. It was thus and through other day-to-day contacts that I came to have a very special liking for the girl—a liking that grew into what I took to be everlasting love. There was, of course, no question of an actual declaration. To start with, these things were just not done, and I was not quite the type. I wanted, and planned, for things to happen almost naturally and of themselves — through looks and gestures and tones of voice and such subtleties. But it did not work—and until today I don't think I know where the trouble lay. Was I not forward enough? Was I not good enough in her eyes? Did she have some block somewhere? Or could it be that she simply didn't get the messages?

I don't know—and I don't think I will ever know. One thing is clear and may conceivably provide a clue: Marcelle's mother had for some time been estranged from her father and probably even separated from him — something almost unheard of in the Jewish community. Did Marcelle have something against "men"? Be that as it may, she was always cheerful and polite and smiling and generally with an optimistic approach to life. I don't quite know how it came about, but I still have in my papers a cutting of an article Marcelle wrote for the Christmas 1947 number of the paper—the only appearance in print she was ever to make in the *Times* or anywhere else. The piece, with the title "What I Want from My Life," starts with this startling statement: "I am the greatest optimist alive. No evil will ever happen to me. All my hopes will be realized and ambitions come true. I am confident that I can make a success of whatever I put my hands to, and that failure will not come near me as long as I live."

A rare, rather special kind of optimism! Does it come from lack of self-confidence, some nudging uncertainty about the future? "This optimism requires some really hard work and I realize that," the writer continues. "But then I am glad that it should be so. Success in life cannot be attained easily, and the toil and sweat that lie on the long road to it make it only more desirable and more of a challenge to our capacities."

But what did Marcelle want from her life? First of all she wanted to be given an opportunity "to beat the achievements of others," an opportunity "to prove myself equally efficient, if not more efficient, than my friends in my studies, my work, my sport or indeed at anything that young men think young women are not good at." Then she wanted "to be entrusted with responsibility"—for although she liked to feel carefree and light, "it boosts up my spirits when difficult undertakings, entailing great responsibility, are put in my charge."

Other things Marcelle wanted from her life were "the opportunity and ability to help others"; "to be able to continue into higher studies and improve my general knowledge" and, above all, "to attend a college or a university abroad and bathe in the noble literature of ancient and modern civilizations"; "an opportunity to see the world," since "one cannot say that one is fully educated just because of reading books and attending schools."

I don't know what my reaction to this article was at the time. I know what it ought to have been. But, then, the heart has its reasons which Reason does not know.

Sometime in the summer of 1952, in Israel, seeking to renew an old acquaintance and—who knows?—an old flame, I wrote to Marcelle briefly, referring to what she had written in that *Iraq Times* article about "ambition." Here is her brief reply, dated August 15, 1952 (Tel Aviv):

> Dear Nissim,
>
> Thanks. The idea is excellent. I'll be glad to come to Jerusalem on a Friday evening and stay till Saturday evening. Only the feasts intervene and I would rather wait until the latter days of the Feast of Tabernacles. I will write you again in this respect.
>
> Do you think that ambition is unthinkable here? I can only say that the ambitious find better opportunities here for the fulfillment of their dreams than they ever had in Iraq. Only our dreams tend to change with the passage of time. Old ones die and new ones take their place. The important thing is to take our dreams seriously and try to snatch some good out of this mad/wise world.
>
> To my next letter. Shalom.
> Marcelle

Hard as I try, however, I don't seem either to remember or to find any trace of a "next letter," let alone an actual weekend in Jerusalem. As far as "ambition" and the ambitious are concerned, I am reminded of a remark made by an old friend of mine who had known me well in Baghdad, who told a mutual friend—when the going was getting rather rough for me and my very livelihood was being threatened—that my case made him ruminate on a flip that was making the rounds at the time in Israel: "You want to make a small fortune? Make *aliya* with a large one!"

ABDEL FATTAH DECIDES TO CLOSE THE BOOKSHOP

For almost two years following the termination of my work for the *Times* I continued working with Abdel Fattah and the Al-Rabita Association. In addition to the bookshop, Abdel Fattah had planned to establish a printing plant and a publishing firm, and we were then busy ordering the machinery and building the plant. I did all the correspondence and the bookkeeping involved in these operations as well as running the bookshop, ordering books and periodicals, keeping the accounts, and acting as sole salesman.

With the onset of 1950, with the machines at hand and the plant finally erected, Abdel Fattah started having second thoughts about the bookshop. He thought, rightly, that the business was no longer paying its way — or just about doing that and nothing more. The fact was that, with a completely free hand and little thought about the business side, I was ordering almost any book that caught my fancy and there was simply no market for such books, either for lack of interest or lack of money. To confound the situation, Abdel Fattah himself ordered books rather indiscriminately — weighty, expensive books whose only merit was that they were "good" or "important" or "essential," regardless of whether they were saleable.

The result was that by the end of 1949 we had on our hands a rich and variegated stock of books of history, philosophy, sociology, science, literature, and poetry that few individuals could afford and whose only potential purchasers were libraries and academic institutions. Abdel Fattah therefore considered and then decided that the books should be transferred to the new building, where they could be offered for sale to such libraries and institutions with no difficulty. He decided to transfer his office there so that he could manage the printing and publishing part of the enterprise and also deal with the books when the need arose. This meant, in effect, that I was left with little to do — and since by that time I had already been toying with the idea of emigration, I declined an offer to work on a part-time basis and left Al-Rabita at the end of March 1950.

It was during my years with the bookshop that Father died. One day in the summer of 1947, while enjoying the early morning breeze on the roof of the flat off the Al-Sinak junction that we shared with my sister Najiyya and her family, I woke to the sound of Father complaining of pains in his left leg. It was the morning of a night I spent watching two movies and struggling with the reviews to be submitted to the paper, and it was hard for me to be fully awakened. On inspection, however, it turned out that the leg was swollen and Father, being his typical experienced and no-nonsense self, was murmuring that this was to be "the end." I remember reflecting that, being such an experienced observer of human affairs in so many spheres, Father would in the end be proved right.

Now Father then was barely sixty-seven, and in those days was considered old, although his age hardly marked the end of a fairly healthy man or woman. But Father was right, as he so often was, and before we went through the complicated business of calling for a doctor—with no telephone anywhere near at hand and nothing by way of a family or any other kind of doctor—Father died peacefully after less than an hour.

The seven days of mourning and prayer were conducted in our flat, with brother Eliahu and sister Na'ima spending them with us, mourners being barred from going out except for prayer and for visits to the cemetery. It was an occasion for renewing contact with members of the family with whom I had lost touch ever since I became involved in work of my own and became the family's sole breadwinner.

It was not long after my departure from Al-Rabita that I and Mother went to the Mas'uda Shemtob Synagogue in Bustan el-Khas—which was volunteered by the Jewish community temporarily to house offices and officials dealing with Jews who wanted to surrender their Iraqi nationality and emigrate to Israel. Simha, my sister, had by then arrived safely in Israel and more than eight thousand Jews had registered for emigration. It was shortly before the stampede that was caused by some bombs thrown or planted in Jewish institutions and resulting in some injuries—bombs, the masterminds of which to this day are unknown and which some people continue to claim were the work of Zionists—in an attempt to cause panic and accelerate the exodus.

The synagogue was fairly quiet that morning, with no long lines and with a few Jewish activists of "the movement" offering counsel and guidance to those who came to register for emigration. It took us but a few minutes to sign the relevant documents and get the tatty certificates allowing us to leave the country for good. I still have the two documents and I often wonder at the ease and speed with which the whole fateful "transaction" was finalized.

| 𝒟ISPOSING OF A LIBRARY

𝐵y early 1950, what with me being out of a job and members of our circle studying to be lawyers or employed in various minor government positions, the fact of my decision to emigrate was known to all my friends, so that the act of bidding good-bye to them spread out over a period of a few months. The material aspect of the move was easy enough to tackle—no real estate to sell, no furniture to speak of, a mere $750 in savings to transfer illegally. The only worldly goods I could have claimed to possess were my private library—hundreds of books and magazines in literature and the humanities. There were three ways of disposing of them—offering them for sale, sending part by mail abroad for safekeeping, and giving some away as gifts.

The largest and most substantial sale of my books I ever made was the deal I had with the librarian of the College of Arts and the Humanities in Baghdad, whose dean, Abdul 'Aziz al-Douri, and a number of whose teachers and lecturers used to frequent the bookshop. It was a relatively new college and al-Douri was one of a new generation of Arab scholars whose works on Arab history in general and on the Abbassid period in particular earned him praise from no less a pedant than Abdel Fattah Ibrahim himself, who once told me that al-Douri was in the forefront of what in those days one could, with great difficulty, call the New Arab Historians. I still keep a copy of his very first work, *An Introduction to the History of Islam,* a daring fresh critical look at the teaching of Arab history and an analysis of the birth and growth of early Islam.

I had made detailed lists of all the books I wanted to sell, mostly in English but also including the relatively few selected Arabic books I had kept, and passed them to the college librarian, who in turn passed them on to the dean and faculty. On the day the selection was made and the prices fixed, the dean himself was present.

I had indicated the reason why I was liquidating my library and not one of those present made any comment, it having been fairly generally understood why an aspiring Jewish young man or woman would want to leave the country. Expressing admiration verging on awe at the quality and the sheer variety of the books offered, al-Douri made a very generous selection, paying the full prices specified. The variety of the subjects taught at the college and the wide interests of the academic staff allowed for the purchase of books in almost all the fields in which I was interested—history, philosophy, politics, travel, literary history and literary criticism, anthologies, and works of the classics ancient and modern. In its own modest way and considering the current economic conditions, it was a remarkable deal in more senses than one—and it helped enhance the few dinars I had till then managed to save for what I knew were the difficult days to come.

Disposing of the remaining books was relatively easy. Those I had decided I would want anywhere I was destined to land, including an almost complete set of *Horizon* (which happened to have stopped publication at the end of 1949), a complete set of *Penguin New Writing*, numerous early editions of works by the younger generation of British and American poets, as well as some of the works of Joyce, Kafka, Thomas Mann, Elias Canetti, Connolly, Bowra, and many others, I packed carefully into thirty or forty parcels of two to three kilograms each to be mailed to Elie, then at St. Antony's College, Oxford. The rest of the library, especially works of younger Arab poets from Lebanon, Egypt, Iraq, and Syria as well as works of literary criticism and some novels, I gave away or sold at very cheap prices to members of the gang, some of whom never paid, chronically penniless as most of them were.

Almost a year passed between my leaving my work at Al-Rabita and my departure to Israel. It was a year of idleness, during which I think Mother and I had again had to turn to brother Eliahu for help with the rent and the grocery bills. During those long months, virtually all I needed was pocket money. Spending so much time at home reading, I only left the house in the late afternoons, heading to wherever it was that members of our circle were to meet that day. Usually it was a cafe or teashop either on the River Bank, or River Drive, promenade, or on the city's main street, depending on the time of year and the weather.

What with everybody being aware of my plans for leaving, there were many expressions of regret, genuine or otherwise. With some, indeed, it bordered on the sentimental. Three of the circle I was particularly sad to leave, and then not to be able to see for no one knew how long, were Najib, 'Adnan, and Buland.

NAJIB AL-MANI' AND F. SCOTT FITZGERALD

Of Buland al-Haidari and 'Adnan Raouf I wrote in a previous section. But it was really in Najib that I found the most intimate and satisfying intellectual and emotional match. Gentle, somewhat shy, wise for his age, and extremely receptive of ideas, Najib was an insatiable reader and had somehow picked up a knowledge of English by no means common among our group. Najib and I could talk about Kafka, whose books we read concurrently, for hours on end — or about Sartre's *Nausea*, which had just come out in English, making analogies between the situation described there and our own situation as some sort of caged intellectuals. It was a period of time in which some landmarks in contemporary literature were just coming out — Orwell's *1984* and *Animal Farm*, the English translations of *The Stranger* and other works by Albert Camus, renderings of Rilke's works, some of Lorca's plays and poetry, and Thomas Mann's *Doctor Faustus*. Cyril Connolly's *Horizon* was still coming out and *Partisan Review* was in its heyday. In all these and many other literary and intellectual treasures Najib and I shared; we pondered on them, discussed and analyzed them for hours on end sitting mostly in an open-air cafe on the Tigris not far from where I lived. I have no idea how Najib in the end found the time to prepare his lessons and how he managed to graduate from the law college where he was then studying. Shortly before I left Baghdad, he wrote me a long letter in English, full of sweet sentiments and very appreciative and sad — a sort of farewell letter, which I took with me to Israel, where it somehow disappeared from where I knew I had put it. I believe that some dumb man from the Shin Beth (Israel's secret services) took it after searching our tin hut in the Talpiyot *ma'bara* (transition camp) as evidence of my alleged Communist affiliations — or worse.

It was only in the late 1960s that I heard from Najib. An Iraqi Jew who came to Israel shortly after the Six-Day War, a journalist, brought me regards from my old friend, who was then working for the Ministry of Foreign Affairs. From time to time I had seen Najib's name in certain periodicals published in Beirut, sometimes as the author of a short story and at others a book review or critical essay — and on the rare occasions when I was abroad I always had the urge to place a telephone call to Baghdad and ask if they could connect me with him at his place of work or home. But the situation then being what it was, I always resisted the urge.

One day in the summer of 1971, while chatting with Mahmoud Abu Zalaf in his editor's room at the office of the East Jerusalem daily *Al Quds*, I caught sight of a slim paperback volume lying on a side desk. It was one of the famous Egyptian fiction series published monthly by *Dar el Hilal* in Cairo—but the book in question struck me as something that one would not expect that particular series to care much about. The Arabic title was *Gatsbi el-'Azeem* and it took me a few seconds to link it with the original work—Scott Fitzgerald's masterpiece *The Great Gatsby*. My curiosity was great as to who took the trouble of translating it and how a series such as *Riwayat el Hilal* decided to publish it. Picking up the volume and examining the title page I read the words: "translated by Najib el Mani' and edited by Jabra Ibrahim Jabra," whereupon I asked Abu Zalaf if I could take the book, and he said, "Why of course."

I was curious about the quality of the translation and on going over some passages I found it quite good—something of a feat in fact considering the original. There were also two biographical notes about the translator and the editor. I had known that Najib was born in a small town near Basra but I did not know he was almost exactly two years my junior. The information given on the back cover included the bit that he was a graduate of the law college, had a special interest in English and French, wrote "a number of short stories and articles in Iraqi and Arab periodicals," was a foreign ministry official, and was now working on translating a selection from Abraham Lincoln's letters and speeches. That meant that during an interval of some twenty years and more Najib did not find his way to publishing a work of his own, not even a collection of short stories.

I was not surprised, knowing how fastidious Najib would be about anything he wrote. Some eight years later, however, I finally stumbled on a book of his at the Muhtasib Bookshop in East Jerusalem—a novel with the striking title *Tamas el Mudun,* a fairly untranslatable phrase that I would render as *A Proximity of Cities* or *Cities Chafe*. I thought it was artfully done and written with taste and economy. It dealt with a period not known to me—the 1950s and 1960s—but I thought I detected some of the characters and identified the places. It is an obviously autobiographical novel and deals with two themes that no doubt represented a later development in Najib—love, marriage, and women being one and Arabism and Arabs the other.

Sometime in the late 1980s, having seen his byline on articles in the literary pages of the London-based Saudi daily *Al-Sharq al-Awsat* and learning that he was working for the paper as a freelancer, I made bold to write Najib al-Mani' a brief note saying hello and seeking to establish contact with him. The letter, sent care of the paper, was not answered, either because it never reached Najib, reached him with the inevitable office gossip that he was getting mail from Israel, found him bewildered

and possibly a little frightened that such contact could be established—
or for all these causes put together.

SAMIRA AL-MANA

After nearly ten more years during which I heard nothing either from
or about Najib, a friend sent me photocopies of parts of *Al-Ightirab al-
Adabi,* a literary quarterly published in London and devoted to the work
of writers and poets living in exile, mainly Iraqis who found they couldn't
do their work in the suffocating atmosphere of Ba'th-dominated Iraq. To
my shock and grief, the first several articles were tributes by friends and
fellow émigré writers and intellectuals to the work and the personality of
Najib al-Mani', who had died suddenly of heart failure one night in his flat
in London, alone amongst his thousands of books and records of classical
music.

Feeling the urge to know more about my unfortunate friend and seeing
that Najib's sister Samira was *Al-Ightirab*'s assistant editor, I wrote her a
long letter of condolences and asked her to give me additional information about her brother's years in exile. Did he die a happy man? Was he
married? Lived with someone? Any children? And so on. All I learned
from the tributes was that his room was scattered with books and records
and papers. Damn the books, I murmured to myself, being then in the
midst of a colossal operation aimed at getting rid of some two-thirds of
my private library.

Samira's reply was as prompt as it was touching and detailed. "Dear
Nissim Rejwan," it read in part, "the name that I heard Najib mention
so often. I also saw the photograph in which you appear with him in a
coffeeshop on the banks of the Tigris in Baghdad in those distant days . . ."

The story she had to tell about Najib's fortunes and his end seems to
have been typical of those of other Iraqi writers and intellectuals in exile.
After spending most of the 1950s and 1960s in relative comfort, occupying high official positions — among which were director-general of the
ministry for foreign affairs, a director of the Iraq Petroleum Company,
and others — Najib came to London in 1979 "for some fresh air," leaving
behind a wife, three sons, and a daughter. Shortly afterward, with the outbreak of the Iran-Iraq war, two of the sons were sent to the front, the result
being that Najib's wife was unable to leave for London to join her husband. To complicate matters even further, the daughter married while he
was abroad and her husband left her shortly afterward; he stayed in Hol-

land to evade army service, and it was discovered later that he had taken another wife and continued living in Holland. About Najib's last years in London, this is how Samira described it: "He lived alone with his lame cat in a flat in London . . . He died in the company of someone he loved, his open book was on Najib's chest. Is there anyone better than Proust in situations like these!"

So it was Proust that he was reading in his last night — Proust to whose work we had all been introduced as early as the late 1940s and whose *Remembrance of Things Past* in its English rendering was made available for the first time in Iraq by Al-Rabita Bookshop. Truth to tell, I found myself regretting the scant part I myself had played in Najib's incessant preoccupation with works of literature — apparently to the exclusion of much else by way of real life.

Reading the words of appreciation written about Najib — two of which by close friends of ours who evoked their youthful memories of the man — I found myself mourning not only Najib but that whole world of our youth which seems to have been lost forever. I caught myself pondering the question as to how many young men and women in Baghdad today — forty-five whole years after those days — are even aware of the kind of literary figures and their works that were so to preoccupy our thoughts and consume our spare time.

JABRA AND "RUBEIN THE ARMY OFFICER'S" DAUGHTER

Jabra Ibrahim Jabra was the last to join our circle — if "join" is the right way to put it. Being almost the only "gainfully employed" person among us, with degrees from British and American universities, a steady job, and boasting a few translations from Shakespeare, he was not a regular presence in our idle gatherings and endless discussions. But, like most members of the cultural elite of Baghdad at the time, he frequented the Al-Rabita Bookshop.

Jabra died suddenly toward the end of 1994. The numerous obituaries and appreciations published all over the Arab world on the occasion had nothing of note to add to what was known to us. Born a Christian Orthodox in Bethlehem in 1920, he attended the Arab College in Jerusalem and pursued his studies in England, where he got his master's degree in English literature from Cambridge University in 1948. In the years 1944–1948 he taught English language and literature at the Rashidiyya College in Jerusalem, and shortly after the outbreak of the first Arab-Israeli war in

May 1948, he came to Baghdad, where he lectured at the Higher Teachers College and the College of the Arts till 1952. It was there that he met, and befriended, his first girlfriend in Baghdad — Evelyn, "Rubein the army officer's" daughter, a bright, vivacious, modern, stylish, and attractive young woman in her early twenties.

Jabra's interests and skills were numerous. He published nearly sixty books — novels, criticism, translations and two volumes of autobiography. He also dabbled in painting and was a lover of music. Though he was quite friendly with members of our group — especially with Buland al-Haidari who was his next-door neighbor in the Baghdad suburb of Al-A'damiyya — he did not spend much time with us loitering or whiling away the days in coffee shops and bars and bookshops.

He was a thrifty, hard-working man by nature. He also no doubt realized that as a refugee he had to work harder and show doubly better results — and indeed between the year 1954 and his death he did eminently well, occupying various official positions always connected with some cultural activity. Shortly before I left Baghdad for Israel, Najib, Buland, and I used to visit him — always unannounced — in his room at the Al-'Asima Hotel on Al-Rashid Street, and I remember him often politely protesting that he had too much on his hand either to entertain us for as long as we would have wished or to accompany us out. He was then working on a translation of Shakespeare's *Sonnets,* but if I am not grossly mistaken he never managed to finish the task. Apart from several novels which he wrote subsequently — almost wholly about Baghdad, one of them in English — his published works included translations of *King Lear* and *Hamlet,* while some of the sonnets which he translated seem to have appeared in periodicals. His other translations include James Fraser's *Adonis* (a chapter from *The Golden Bough*) and Frankfurter's *Before Philosophy.*

Concerning his private life, all I could learn from acquaintances was that he married a Muslim girl from a good Baghdad family and that he was on several occasions in the United States teaching at universities during his sabbatical years. Shortly before I left for Israel, I asked Jabra if he wanted me to convey anything to his friends or family or if he had anybody to recommend for me to see in Jerusalem. With Jerusalem divided, however, there was not much to do in that direction. But he insisted that I convey his very special regards to two persons in Jerusalem — Evelyn, who in the meantime had emigrated to Israel and was working as a receptionist at a leading Jerusalem hotel, and a bosom friend of his who was then chief librarian of the YMCA in Jerusalem and one of the very few Arabs who were to stay in the city after the disturbances of 1947 and the ensuing first Arab-Israeli war. I had met Evelyn in Baghdad—a shapely young woman and a fine specimen of her generation of well-educated, modern Iraqi Jewish women—and when I finally found her and spoke to her I thought I detected a tone of resignation in her voice—a feeling that there was no way to retrieve that part of her past and that she would have to rebuild her life again. Eventually she did, and was doing fine when last I saw her.

The YMCA librarian was delighted to hear about his friend, but I thought he was a little surprised and even suspicious and apprehensive— as though he were murmuring to himself inwardly: how in the world could his friend Jabra, a fugitive from the Jews, have had this Jew for a friend? But he was nice and polite, and in the coming weeks and months he was friendly and helpful to me when I started my studies at the university and had to spend days on end in the library, the lobby, and the swimming pool and showers in that splendid building.

Sometime during the 1950s, as he relates in the second volume of his autobiography, Jabra met Lamee'a Al-'Askari, fell in love with her, and de- cided to take her for wife. In order to do this he had to convert to Islam— which he did, and the two raised a prosperous and proper Iraqi family. In all these years, the turmoil and the suppression and persecution suffered by his many Iraqi friends notwithstanding, Jabra kept quiet and sought— and duly gained—the support and approval of the powers-that-be, as Bu- land made abundantly clear in a brief article he wrote shortly after the death of his erstwhile friend.

Chapter 18 | $\mathcal{E}$ND OF A COMMUNITY

*I*t is all but impossible to pinpoint a date or an event with which the position of the Jews of Iraq began to deteriorate and take the course leading finally, and inevitably, to the destruction of the community. Some observers link it with the *farhud*. Others maintain that the whole process started only with the adoption by the U.N. General Assembly of the Partition Plan for Palestine late in 1947.

I do not pretend to offer anything like a satisfactory answer—which in any case I think doesn't exist. However, in a book published in the mid-1990s on Iraq's involvement in the Palestine question throughout the years, I came across what I believe is a singular document. The author of that document, C. J. Edmonds, worked for several years as senior adviser to the Iraqi government, and the report he wrote was addressed to the British Foreign Office.

In his report, dated as early as August 29, 1938, Edmonds wrote that the position of the Jews of Iraq was being threatened by growing Iraqi opposition to Britain's policy in Palestine and by the example of the perse-cution of the Jews by Nazi Germany. He concluded his report with these words: "It was not entirely fantastic to visualize the ninety thousand Jews of Iraq escorted across the Euphrates and told to run the gauntlet of the desert to this Palestine of theirs."

The scene in the Mas'uda Shemtob Synagogue in January 1951, where I signed off my Iraqi nationality, was, admittedly, nothing resembling ninety thousand men, women, and children being herded across the river and into the desert. Nevertheless, Edmonds's apocalyptic vision was ulti-mately to come true—though instead of being dispatched on foot, the 110,000 Jews of Iraq were in the end carried "on the wings of eagles," in an operation named after Ezra and Nehemiah, who, according to the ac-count in the Bible, presided over the migration of a number of Babylonian Jews to Palestine, there to take part in rebuilding the First Temple and with it the sovereign Jewish entity.

ZIONISM IN BAGHDAD

I cannot say that I really hoped to find out something concrete by way of an explanation about how an ancient and so solidly established ethnic group like the Jewish community of Iraq was so hastily and easily to come to such a panicky end. Nevertheless, I did make the attempt — half-heartedly to be sure — one afternoon in those far-off days of the early 1960s, when my involvement in the communal problem in Israel was steadily deepening. At that time it was already fashionable to argue about such matters as whether Oriental Jewries had contributed to the Zionist movement and to the building of the state of Israel. As expressed in private conversations, clear insinuations in public appearances (especially abroad while on fundraising missions), and occasionally the printed word, a good segment of the Israeli population, including people with authority who should have known better, seemed to believe these Jewries had no history, or at least not much of a recent history, and certainly no Zionist history of record.

It was with such uninspiring thoughts that, that evening in August 1963, I made my way to a certain lecture hall in Tel Aviv. It was as hot and as damp as only Tel Aviv evenings can be, but where I went a small crowd was already gathered to celebrate the twentieth anniversary of the founding of the Zionist *Halutz* movement in Iraq.

In the course of the evening, I was to learn that, well, it was not exactly the twentieth birthday, since the *Halutz* (vanguard) movement held its first congress in Baghdad in 1942. It was not, either, as if the *Halutz* movement's first congress marked the beginning of Zionist activity amongst the Jews of Iraq, as both Zionism and immigration to the Holy Land had started decades earlier. But apparently it was still a good occasion to celebrate an anniversary.

Speaking for myself, I did not quite feel at home in that gathering and had first to overcome a certain feeling of unbelonging. I must have been the only person present that never belonged to a Zionist movement, in Iraq or anywhere else. I never studied the Hebrew language in clandestine classes in Baghdad homes, never carried or hid any arms, never did night guard duty in the Jewish quarters of the city, and never tried to cross the border illegally on the way to the Promised Land. If I knew or recognized any of the faces of the young and not-so-young men and women present that night, the acquaintances had not been made within "the movement" (*ha-tenu‘ah*).

What was it that made the Zionist movement grow and prosper in Iraq in the early 1940s — and especially its spectacular success amongst youths of certain age groups and not others? Looking back to those days with some tranquility, one imagines one can put one's finger on some of the primary causes of this phenomenon. The late 1930s and early 1940s found the Jewish community of Iraq—and Iraqi society as a whole—in the throes of a profound socioeconomic upheaval. By that time, fully two generations of Iraqi Jews from various social classes—though primarily from the upper ones—had gone through the cultural transformation of Westernization provided by such educational institutions as the Alliance Israélite Universelle, the American School, and the English-speaking secondary schools established with the help of Anglo-Jewry. It was because of this that the *Halutz* movement and the Haganah, and the Zionist movement in general, when they finally came in an organized form, landed on very fertile soil.

This point may need some elaboration. The crying discrepancy between the concepts and ideals on which two generations of educated Iraqi Jews were brought up and the reality of Jewish social life and institutions as they then existed in Iraq was becoming intolerable. If the fathers somehow could manage to make ends meet culturally and socially, their children could not. The contrasts were many and quite sharp sometimes: Secular education at school versus the home's traditional Jewish ways; romantic ideas of love and marriage contrasted greatly with the age-old devices of the matchmaker and the huge dowries; and "liberty, equality, fraternity" found no expression in the drab reality of political corruption, graft, and competitive minority existence.

It can thus be said that, more even than nationalist movements, the *Halutz* and the Haganah in Iraq represented a sociocultural revolution among the young. At the gathering in Tel Aviv that evening, Mordechai Bibi, a veteran of the *Halutz* movement, said that he found it remarkable that young Jewish girls, whose parents and brothers would otherwise never have dreamt of allowing them to go out at night without at least knowing their whereabouts, used to stay out all night in defiance of all accepted social norms, motivated by no other cause than that of the movement. Surely, however, it would at least be as true to put it the other way around—that is, that were it not for the sense of freedom and liberation it served to give them, these young women would probably never have dreamed of joining the movement.

For the crowd assembled there, however, these were not the crucial questions and they certainly did not constitute the main worry. One point on which all the speakers dwelt was what they considered the sorry fact that up to that date not a single work of history, autobiography, or fiction had been produced to tell the heroic and deeply human story of a pioneer youth movement which, in the space of less than a decade, managed to assume virtual leadership of an ancient and solidly established Jewish community in a period of transition and sociocultural upheaval.

Listening to the speakers, however, I could not help thinking that such works, had they been written, could indeed have been far more than mere monuments to the *Halutz* or the other Zionist movements in Iraq. They would have provided a direly needed education—for the Israeli public as a whole and even for many in the Iraqi community itself—in the life and recent history of one Oriental Jewry. In his own address, Bibi related how, back in 1950, a very highly placed Israeli personage enquired whether the Jews of Iraq had heard about the establishment of the State of Israel! This seemed to me to suggest that the history of the *Halutz* movement in Iraq, and the recent history of the Iraqi Jewish community as a whole, was a history neglected, a history almost willfully ignored.

VARIETIES OF HARASSMENT

Ambiguity and paradox are almost inseparable features of all Jewish history. Few episodes in recent Jewish history, however, are as shrouded in ambiguity and paradox as the mass emigration to the newly established state of Israel of Jews from Middle Eastern and North African lands. The ambiguity here is apparent on more than one level, but it is especially noticeable in the sphere of motivation. What was the motive force behind this mass exodus? What made well-established and well-adjusted Jewries like those of Yemen, Morocco, and Iraq decide to pack their belongings and make their way to Israel, many of them leaving behind comfortable homes, prosperous businesses, and neighbors and friends with whom they maintained close and intimate ties?

In Israel of the 1950s and 1960s it was the fashion to speak of mass *aliya* from Muslim lands as "rescue immigration," implying that these ancient Jewish communities were virtually ejected from the lands of their birth and had the good fortune of having loving and benevolent brethren in *Eretz Yisrael* who gladly provided them with a haven and new homes. What the historical record says, however, and what some of the people directly involved in those mass population movements testify, seems clearly to contradict this conveniently simple version of the situation.

Some time in the spring of 1964, when Israel celebrated *Aliya Beth* year (*shnat hapalah*), in an attempt to do for themselves what the powers-that-be failed to do for them, former activists of the Zionist movement in Iraq staged a sort of protest. In an impressive gathering in Tel Aviv Iraqi "illegals" celebrated their own *shnat hapalah*. Again, I went there to see for myself, and I thought I detected a trace of bitterness in the tone of some of the speakers, who openly deplored the fact that what they considered a heroic chapter in the history of the Zionist movement was not being given its due in the annals of that movement.

One of those present was Shlomo Hillel, who himself was an architect of the mass exodus of Jews from Iraq. In his address, Hillel pointed out that the omission of the Iraqi episode from the *Aliya Beth* year constituted a historical injustice not so much to those responsible for organizing the emigration as it was to the young generation of Israelis, who were entitled to know what had been done in that particular sphere of Zionist activity.

There were three other speakers, all of them in one way or another actively involved in the founding, organization, and growth of the Zionist movement in Iraq, and subsequently in starting what had come to be known as Operation Ezra and Nehemiah. Shaul Avigur, who organized *Aliya Beth*, reminisced about the beginnings shortly after the *farhud* of the clandestine Zionist cells in Baghdad. Israel Galili spoke of the impressions brought by emissaries from Palestine about the devotion and fervor of the Iraqi Jewish youth enrolled in the three branches of the movement— Hebrew teaching, defense, and illegal emigration; Bibi recalled the days when, before the Iraqi government decided to allow the Jews to emigrate, the country's borders were systematically forced open to make way for hundreds of illegal emigrants; and Hillel told of his efforts in Baghdad, acting in the guise of a representative of some fictitious foreign airline, to see to the organization of the mass transfer of close to 120,000 Jews from Iraq to Israel.

Listening to these speakers I thought it was rather curious that, while at least some of them would still speak of "rescue immigration," all were agreed that it was as a result of intensive Zionist activity inside Iraq that the authorities finally allowed Jews to emigrate—provided, of course, they surrendered their Iraqi nationality.

Naturally there were pressures and "pushes" on the part of the authorities. When the Palestine war broke out in 1948 the Iraqi security forces, who could not have been ignorant of Zionist activities in the country, made many arrests involving persons more or less—and sometimes not at all—engaged in those activities. In the process, however, the authorities soon turned to penalizing the whole of the community in various devious ways. No Jew who had ever been involved in "politics" of any kind was immune to one or another of the variety of rough and arbitrary harassments practiced by the police and the makeshift military tribunals. One glaring example, incredible for sheer transparency, was the way in which active anti-Zionist Jews were apprehended, brought to trial, and convicted on charges of *Zionist* activities.

The story of the Anti-Zionist League started shortly after the United Nations General Assembly approved the plan for the partition of Palestine on November 29, 1947. The event was a signal and in many ways a pretense for street demonstrations staged by radical groups among college students, disaffected elements both of the left, the right, and Communists, many of whom were Jews, convinced anti-Zionists to the man.

These Jews, many of them college students and high school graduates, had applied for a license to found an organization of their own, for which they chose the innocuous name of 'Usbat Mukafahat Al-Sahyuniyya (literally "League for Fighting Zionism"). The permission was granted early in 1946 by the government of Tawfiq Al-Suweidi, seemingly overlooking the fact that the applicants were all Communists who sought both to prove their loyalty to their Iraqi-Arab allegiances and to create a front organization for the clandestine Communist party.

In June 1946, the league took the initiative. It organized a peaceful demonstration, ostensibly directed against "oppressive" rule in Palestine. The Communists, however, who were denied permission to organize their own party, used the league to promote their own cause, and this became obvious in the course of the demonstration. The government—headed then by Arshad Al-'Umari—suspecting the demonstration was directed against it, ordered the police to disperse the demonstrators by force, which resulted in the injury of five, one of whom died of his wounds.

Eventually, the Anti-Zionist League had to suffer a sorry fate, which, if it were not sad, would be uproariously funny. The league "for fighting Zionism," because of the somewhat ambiguous nature of its Arabic name, was accused of being a Zionist organization, fighting for rather than against Zionism. Its leading members were actually prosecuted and imprisoned on these grounds; it did not take the authorities much time or trouble to prove that they were leading members of the Communist party. They duly joined their Muslim comrades for long terms in jail. The anti-Jewish operation, which sometimes looked like a form of revenge the Iraqis were taking for the humiliation their forces suffered at the hands of the Zionists, was waged mainly on the following "fronts":

Employment: Practically all Jewish government employees were given the sack—together with those working for state companies, certain foreign establishments in which the government had obvious interests, and banks both local and foreign who simply took the hint.

Trade and Commerce: Business licenses, permits for exports and imports, foreign currency transactions, and all other business transactions that needed official approval were denied to Jews.

Censorship: At some date following the adoption of the Palestine Partition Plan the post office stopped delivering letters coming from Palestine. Later, when the wave of harassment and trials began, the accumulated sacks were opened and all Jewish addressees were summoned to the CID building individually. Without exception they were charged with "contacting the enemy" and invariably sentenced to imprisonment or a high fine. The security forces also had a look into their records and located Jews who had visited or stayed in Palestine at some earlier date—and these too were summoned and in many cases similarly tried and sentenced.

Students: Jewish students and high school pupils who had ever been caught taking part—or in any other way involved—in demonstrations were subjected to harassment and trial. Usually this took the form of search warrants which the police brought with them to the house of the "suspect" and on the strength of which a search was conducted, the person in question taken for further investigation, and then a trial was staged in which no one was ever on record as having been acquitted. Evidence or no evidence, the person in question was almost invariably sentenced to two years in prison or a fine of two thousand Iraqi dinars—then the equivalent of two thousand pounds or eight thousand dollars and a lot of money by any prevailing standard. One had the distinct impression at the time that, were they not quite certain that the Jews would somehow find the money to pay the fines rather than go to jail, the courts would never have passed so many prison sentences. There were simply not enough prisons to accommodate them all.

On the strictly factual level, these measures notwithstanding, it was ultimately the pressure exerted by the Jews themselves, encouraged and led by the Zionist movements, and the fact that the borders had been forced open—often with the help of high security officials who were not above accepting bribes—that finally forced the hand of the authorities. Once they were allowed to leave Iraq, the Jews showed an eagerness to emigrate that surprised both the Iraqi and Israeli authorities.

To the speakers of the "illegals" gathered in Tel Aviv that evening, however, the point was not an academic one. Fourteen years after the successful conclusion of Operation Ezra and Nehemiah, the Zionist leadership of the Jewish community of Iraq still failed to make its presence felt, or acknowledged, in representative Zionist bodies, or for that matter anywhere within the Israeli political-cultural establishment.

How was one to explain this? One explanation, surely, lay in a certain ambiguity that has always struck me as besetting the subject of emigration from Middle Eastern and North African countries—a certain subtle but highly significant difference between what in effect are two distinguishable approaches to Zionism. Obadia Sehayek, who together with his eight brothers and sisters is said to have formed the core of the *Halutz* movement in Baghdad back in the early 1940s, put it this way: "Our father is an observant Jew and he gave us a religious education. But for us there was only one religion—Zionism."

The fact is that for the Jews of Iraq, and no doubt also for those of Yemen and Morocco, Judaism and love of Zion were inextricably associated with the idea of Jewish statehood in *Eretz Yisrael*. In this messianic, almost mystical concept of a state, political organization and party wranglings played no part whatever, and the result was that these Jews came to Israel totally unequipped for the kind of political power struggle which awaited them.

I am told on very good authority that David Ben Gurion once described the *Halutz* movement in Iraq as "primitive." It is obvious that, to the extent that this movement and its leaders failed to assess coldly and methodically the Israeli political scene—and to draw equally realistic conclusions from that assessment—Ben Gurion was fully justified in his appraisal.

END OF A FRIEND

By the end of the year 1950 only a few, a very few, of my Jewish friends were in Baghdad. Naim Kattan followed Elie after a year or so, first to Paris and subsequently to Canada; Isaac Khedhouri made it to the newly established Jewish state by illegal routes, having been suspected of membership in the Zionist underground; Jacob Mu'allem was among the first to surrender Iraqi nationality and head for Israel—and so did Naji 'Abboudi and Gurji Tchweila.

Among those of my friends who stayed was Edmond Samuel, who survived the great exodus and the turmoil and went to Paris to study, with a proper Iraqi passport, but never made it back to Baghdad. Another was Charles Horesh, a friend I had met through Edmond and other relatives of his who were also friends and acquaintances of mine. The last time I saw Charles was one dry, cold Baghdad morning late in January 1951. It was a few days before my scheduled flight to Israel, and we were bidding good-bye.

Charles was then in his late twenties, unmarried, and working as a senior clerk for a British shipping firm with premises in the commercial center of the city. Among many other things, we spoke about the situation "over there" and the few bits of information then circulating amongst the Jews of Baghdad, anxious as most of them were to know what lay in store for them when finally their turns came and they landed in the Promised Land. By that time letters arriving via London, Paris, and New York from relatives and acquaintances who had already left gave all sorts of hints that the lot of the new arrivals left much to be desired. "Don't come until Ivonne is married"; "under no circumstances ought you to take up that new job"; and "do not move house" were some of the favorite devices, calculated to warn kith and kin against taking the plunge. But it all sounded rather incredible. "What has happened to Maurice, writing like that," Ivonne's father would reflect aloud, realizing that his eldest son's message meant that the family should stay on almost indefinitely, since Ivonne was then just over two years of age!

But it was not such thinly disguised warnings that prevented Charles from registering for emigration, though he did get similar advice from his two younger sisters who had already arrived in Israel and were living in a kibbutz. As a matter of fact I never managed really to fathom his thoughts on the subject; nor did I ever press him. I genuinely respected what I took to be his hesitations, and for the following years between that January morning and the morning of January 27, 1969 — when Charles's dead body hanged in mid-air in Baghdad's largest square — I heard of him only occasionally from relatives and mutual acquaintances. He had left his job and set up business on his own; he had married, had a daughter and his wife was expecting a second child; he had become fairly well-to-do and acquired excellent connections. His appearance, to judge from the photograph released by the Iraqi authorities of him and sixteen others in the defendants box during their collective trial, did not change much.

Except for the word *spy*, attached to his name on a placard hanging from the neck of his hanging body, I never managed to know what precisely were the actual charges on which Charles was condemned. I looked through Baghdad's two leading newspapers, *Al-Jumhuriyya* and the *Baghdad Observer*, of January 18–24, but failed to find even his name mentioned in the proceedings. All that was there were vague, rather trivial tales of how one accused had received a letter from another for delivery to a third; how one of the accused asked another "to mobilize some seamen at ships anchoring at Basra for purposes of espionage"; and how "secret information about men and equipment in an army camp near Basra" was passed to "Israeli agents." My worst suspicions were amply fulfilled a few days later, when I read in the papers on February 7 that the president of the "Revolution Tribunal" that had passed the verdicts and the sentences told foreign correspondents in Baghdad that all material evidence — such as documents and wireless transmitters and other such espionage equipment — had already been "destroyed"! Just like that! Not only the hangings, the manner in which they were carried out and the fanfare that accompanied the operation were offensive. The whole trial now sounds like being one big fabrication lacking even the saving grace of good planning and careful execution.

What had happened? What could Baghdad's motives have been for a deed so clumsy and so shocking that it brought public condemnation even from Arab capitals, including Cairo? Before we set out to answer this question it must be pointed out that hanging is the normal method of carrying out the death penalty in Iraq, applicable to all but the military. Public hanging, with or without pomp, is relatively rare. As far as I recall, only on three occasions did such hangings take place in Iraq during the 1940s. The first was in June 1941, when two Muslims accused of taking part in the *farhud* of May 30–31 were hanged publicly and with the stated intent of serving as an example and a lesson. In 1948, shortly after hostilities broke out in Palestine, four Communist leaders, one of them a Jew, were hanged in four central places in Baghdad, also as a warning and an example.

Later in the year a well-known Jewish merchant, Shafiq 'Adas, was hanged in Basra after being condemned for "dealing with the enemy." This last hanging was attended by such a large and frenzied crowd — it is told — that the executioner had to unveil the condemned man's face so that the spectators be assured that they were getting the same ware they had been promised and not some replacement.

| $\mathcal{F}$AREWELLS AND REUNIONS

O n March 2, 1950, the Iraqi minister of interior, Salih Jabr, introduced to parliament a draft law by virtue of which Iraqi Jews were to be permitted to leave the country provided they gave up their nationality. Jabr told the deputies that the government was prompted to take this measure owing to the mass exodus of Iraqi Jews by illegal means. He explained that, since martial law was lifted on December 17, 1949, illegal emigration increased, and it was "not in the public interest to force people to stay in the country if they have no desire to do so."

It was the government headed by 'Ali Jawdat that had lifted martial law—and it was in that brief period of three-and-a-half months that the illegal traffic in Jews departing for Israel intensified. These were mostly young men and women seeking an outlet for their energies, continuation of their studies, work to do, or just the plain "life" of freedom and social and political liberties that many of them were taught was theirs to lead once they had landed in the Promised Land. But there were also parents who decided to join their sons and daughters already there, and children sent by parents to join relatives, brothers, or sisters who had left before.

All illegal emigration was directed to neighboring Iran, from whence the emigrants were taken to Israel. The crossing to Iranian territory was relatively a simple operation. It was done either via Kurdish territory in the north or from Basra across Shatt el-Arab and into Muhammara (now Abadan) in the south. The movement was organized and supervised by emissaries of the Jewish Agency and the various kibbutz movements, each with its own political party affiliation. These emissaries, helped by local activists, worked through Muslim "contractors"—Kurds from the north, Arabs from the south—who against payment of a certain sum per head undertook to transport to specified points on the other side of the border caravans or boat-loads of emigrants, there to be received by people from *ha-tenu'ah* ("the movement," the collective name by which the Zionist organizations in Iraq were known locally) and transferred to Teheran.

The law introduced by Jabr—and approved despite some isolated protestations to the effect that it was not consistent with Arab interests—became known as *qanun tasqit al-jinsiyya* (literally, the nationality-abdication law). It had three short provisions:

Article One empowered the Council of Ministers to deprive any Iraqi Jew of Iraqi nationality "who, of his free will, chooses to leave Iraq for ever, after he shall so signify in writing before an official designated by the Minister of Interior."

Article Two decreed that any Iraqi Jew who leaves Iraq or attempts to leave the country illegally "shall be deprived of Iraqi nationality by a decision of the Council of Ministers."

Article Three provided that any Iraqi Jew who had already left Iraq illegally "shall be regarded as though he has left Iraq for ever unless he would return within two months from the time this law shall become effective"—otherwise his Iraqi nationality shall be dropped.

Making preparations for emigration posed no difficulty—except where the books I wanted to keep were concerned. Having packed these in small parcels to be mailed to Elie's address in Oxford, I managed to send only about a third of the packages when the time came for me and Mother to leave. Whereupon I consulted my good friend Gurji Rabi', who had a shop on Al-Rashid Street selling spare parts for cars and lorries, and he generously agreed to store the remaining packages in his shop and promised to take them to the post office, one or two at a time and with decent intervals. It was not a difficult thing to do since the parcels were all carefully packed, addressed, weighed, and stamped.

However, Gurji was unable to do the errand. On March 10, 1951, a month to the day after my flight to Israel, Nuri el-Sa'id's government passed a law freezing the assets of all the Jews who had registered for emigration to Israel. The law was rushed through parliament on the grounds that the Jews had smuggled large portions of their wealth out of the country. This, of course, was quite true. My $750, though a negligible sum, was a case in point. A friend of mine was then working as accountant in a Jewish export-import firm owned by three brothers named Mukammal. When I spoke to him about my problem, he immediately offered to arrange the matter through the firm: I paid the money in Iraqi currency, the equivalent of $750, and the firm advised one of the brothers who by that time had established a business in the Brazilian capital.

All I had to do was write to him asking him to please send me the 750 grams of coffee at a specified address in Israel—the coffee device being meant to sidetrack the Israeli authorities, who would otherwise have bought the dollars at the official rate which eventually came to amount to about a third or less of their worth on the black market. In the event — as I was to learn later to my great surprise — it was to one of the many government "brokers" that I finally sold the dollars, the Israeli Finance Ministry having had decided that there was no way of acquiring Iraqi immigrants' dollars and pounds sterling other than by buying the precious currency from them at black market prices, with commission duly paid to the go-betweens, every single one of them an Iraqi himself!

In Baghdad, in execution of the new law, the Iraqi minister of finance ordered all banks and money changers dealing with foreign currency exchange to stop their transactions forthwith, so as to prevent Jewish accounts being withdrawn and smuggled out of the country. What was even more terrible for some of the Jews about to leave for Israel, the land registry office too was ordered to stop registering transactions in which a Jewish party was involved. Many well-to-do and middle class Jews who had joined the registration stampede only lately had sold their homes and other immovable property and were about to complete the deals by going to the land registry office. My brother Eliahu, for one, lost practically his all as a result of the new law. Having invested all his savings in a family house in Bustan el-Khas, and having waited until the last moment before he was finally prevailed on to register for emigration, he sold the house late in the day and the sale was to be finalized the very same morning the new law was to be put into effect.

There was absolutely nothing to do — nor was there any possibility to recover whatever money he had in his bank account. He and his family — his wife, three sons, and three daughters — came to Israel completely penniless. It was a heartbreaking experience for me when, a few years later when my own economic situation looked fairly stable, he came to me with a request to contribute toward renting for key-money a ground-floor flat in a slum neighborhood in Ramat Gan.

The fate of Jewish stores and goods was similar. The office of the public custodian, allegedly responsible now for surveying and administering frozen Jewish assets, locked and sealed all Jewish warehouses and businesses — including those belonging to people who had not registered for emigration — on the grounds that their owners might illegally remove the contents thereof. Gurji's small car spare parts shop was one of the businesses that were sealed and locked — and that was the last anyone had seen of the rest of my precious book packages.

"A CRANK IN ISRAEL"

The decision to give up my Iraqi nationality and head for the unknown was not an easy one to take, nor was I free of premonitions. About Israel, its society and its culture all I knew came from books. Arthur Koestler's *Thieves in the Night* was a source, mainly because of the high esteem the writer enjoyed thanks to his *Darkness at Noon, Arrival and Departure,* and his many contributions to *Horizon,* including a first and horrific account of the extermination camps. I remember that Elie and I were greatly impressed on reading something Koestler had published in *Horizon* with the title "A Crank in Israel." At the time we found the story fascinating and the account well written, so much so that in our letters we used to joke both about the idea and the context.

When my decision was finally taken, and with the dearth of reliable material about my future country of adoption, I often thought about the tale of that luckless crank and what I took to be Koestler's fundamental point—namely that Israel, and the Jewish society of prestate days, were a sort of breeding ground for cranks. The tensions, the complexities, the grudges, the sharp contrasts, the sheer variety, I was beginning to feel, all put together were easily conducive to crankiness, especially where thinking, intellectually inclined people were concerned.

To refresh my memory I managed later on, when already firmly settled in Israel, to locate the article and read it again. It transpired that Koestler was not the real author, only the translator. Published in the June 1949 issue of the monthly, Koestler in a "Translator's Note" writes about its author: "Dr. Jacob Weinshall is a General Practitioner in Tel Aviv, who has published several works in modern Hebrew. His specialty is political cranks." I had never been aware—and, truth to tell, am still not aware— that political cranks were a "specialty," and one treated by "general practitioners" into the bargain.

Be that as it may, the article was presented as the case history of Weinshall's patient B, written at Koestler's request in the form of a letter addressed to him during a recent visit in Tel Aviv "in search of material for a book on Israel." It should be borne in mind, Koestler concludes, that B died in 1945, and the events refer to a period even earlier than that date— "the troubled years of gestation of the new state."

The way the case history was written tended to show the extent to which Weinshall empathized, understood, almost identified with his patient, whom he calls "my friend" throughout. "An aging man with the glamorous past of a near-millionaire in Vienna, who had lost, like the rest of us, his possessions . . . he felt utterly useless in this country of ours," he writes at one point. "History, like nature—and being part of nature— has a horror of the void," he reflects in the course of his case history. "A new society like ours is incomplete and bubbling with voids—like air-holes which make you seasick on a flight." At one point he quotes "one particular outburst" of "my poor friend B":

> A nation of half a million people which knows no other invective than *chamor* (donkey); and whose entire vocabulary for erotic and flirta-tious purposes consists of the abstract statement "I love you"—such a nation has no identity. Just look at the names of our streets! How can you talk of a nation with an identity in a town where Ferdinand Lassalle Street crosses Greengrocers' Lane, and Socrates Mews end in some Rabinowitch Avenue? Believe me, doctor, we have no iden-tity . . . Of course we are all Hebrews, we all speak Hebrew and worship our Prophets and Rabbis. But what sort of Hebrews are we, of which period in History? [Haim] Weizmann thinks we live in the era of Ezra and Nehemiah, of the return from the Babylonian Exile; our socialists in the settlements think we are peasants of the time of the first Mac-cabean dynasty; [Menahem] Begin thinks he is a reincarnation of Bar Kochba who led the revolt against the Romans. At what precise mo-ment did the clock of our history stop? . . . What is it that we have undertaken to continue? The traditions of Flavius Josephus who ca-pitulated and made his peace with the Roman procurators, or of Rabbi Akiba who was a philosopher and yet the leader of a hopeless rebellion against Rome? That is the question!

The manner in which B met his death was as sordid as it was dread-ful. "Seized by an attack of persecution mania he rushed naked into the street. Some young men gave chase, threw stones after him, bruised and scratched him and dragged him by his hair along the pavement. He died in hospital from the effects of the beating he had taken in the street and at the police station."

For a sympathetic, if highly skeptical, observer like myself, with no particular ideological affinity with the newly established sovereign Jewish entity, the story of B, his loud reflections and premonitions, and his shock-ing end could not have provoked anything but somber thoughts. Not that my expectations had ever been especially high. Considering the mass im-migration and the armed conflicts that had just been ended, one knew that the new state's material difficulties must have been quite staggering.

Nevertheless, optimism was widespread amongst the prospective emigrants, especially the younger ones, though few even tried to elaborate.

YUSUF EL-KABEER

Among the few I decided to see shortly before our departure, men whose opinion I held in high esteem and to whom I felt I must bid farewell, was Yusuf el-Kabeer, a prominent lawyer and a highly respected member of the community (in which, however, he never agreed to hold an official position). I had first seen el-Kabeer during the first years of World War II hunting books and magazines in the few foreign-language bookstores I used to frequent, mainly the leading Mackenzie Bookshop. It took a while for us actually to meet and talk, and in the years I spent running Al-Rabita Bookshop and writing book and movie reviews for the *Iraq Times* I often ventured a conversation with him or sought an opinion from him, aloof and reticent though he always was.

It was the first visit I was to pay el-Kabeer at his office and it came at my own request. He knew about the closure of the bookshop and couldn't have helped noticing the absence of my reviews from the *Times,* of which like many of the Westernized Jews of Iraq he was a regular reader. It was thus somewhat obvious that I was getting ready to leave the country permanently, and my host — who was not known for his Zionist leanings and had always counseled integration of the Jews into an Iraqi nationality — made no attempt to dissuade me even though he evinced no special enthusiasm. By that time things were happening with such speed and the number of prospective emigrants was increasing at such a rate that no one even tried to slow down the avalanche.

The only part of our conversation I now remember clearly was his caustic comments — made, it must be added, in sorrow rather than in ridicule — on the attitudes and the high hopes the emigrants were holding as to their prospects in Israel. Especially astonishing to him was the alacrity with which they were rushing to sign away their Iraqi nationality. "In one respect, at least, they are making a grave mistake," he said in his always quiet manner. "They seem to think that emigration amounts to no more than a stroll down the banks of the Tigris (*tisyagha 'al shettani*)."

Yusuf el-Kabeer came from one of the wealthiest and most influential Jewish families of Baghdad. He was the youngest of three brothers, the others being Hesqail and Ibrahim, who both left books of memoirs still available only in manuscript form.

Hesqail al-Kabeer, who left Iraq for Paris as early as 1932, gave his work the title *Relations Between Arabs and Jews*. Ibrahim, who was destined to hold a number of key government posts starting almost with the birth of the Kingdom of Iraq, retired from public service in the mid-1960s and eventually emigrated to France, wrote two volumes of memoirs — *My Communal Life: The Death of a Community* and *My Government Life: The Story of a Dream*.

Yusuf el-Kabeer remained in Baghdad for fifteen years following the mass exodus of the Jews to Israel, leaving his native land for Paris in 1966. Aside from a few scattered articles and letters to the editor he published in the *Iraq Times* in the course of three decades, he seems to have left some memoirs of his life and work in Baghdad that remain unpublished. Nor was he or either of his two brothers known ever to have visited Israel.

BAGHDAD AIRPORT TO LYDDA AIRPORT, FEBRUARY 10, 1951

I still shudder when I remember that flight — and I continue to consider it a miracle that in the end we landed safely in Lydda airport. The old plane with the wooden seats puffed and tumbled and literally crackled, and at one frightening moment midway it took such a plunge I thought it would be the end. I don't recall seeing any stewards or stewardesses, and the passengers were shivering from cold and used whatever they could lay their hands on to wrap themselves. The noise the engine made was so great no one could hear a word.

Although we left Baghdad airport before sunset, it must have taken us several hours to reach Lydda airport, for what I remember is that we landed when it was still dark but soon it was daylight. The way in which we were received already made people grumble, although I thought it was not surprising in the circumstances. The first thing we were asked to do after the landing was to remain seated just where we were; then a short, bearded fellow who looked somewhat unwashed himself came into the plane and started showering the passengers methodically and row after row with DDT powder — just like that.

There were no audible murmurs or complaints and the whole ugly procedure was eventually to become a standing joke among Iraqi immigrants in Israel. Seen in the perspective of what was in wait for these immigrants, however, it was an omen — a first taste of the sort of attitude the in-group was to adopt towards this segment of the out-group.

The time of departure remains a painful and spine-chilling memory.

February weather in Baghdad is notorious for its shiftiness, but on that afternoon of February 10, 1951, the sky was clear and the temperature mild. The windows of the minibus that was being used for taking departing Jews to the airport were closed with makeshift plywood so that passersby could not see the emigrants' faces. The reason for this particular precaution was never clear but it must have had something to do with "security."

What it meant for the passengers, however, was that they were being denied that last glimpse of their native city, which they knew they were destined never to see again. As the vehicle passed the main Rashid Street and then crossed the bridge on the life-giving Tigris, all I could do was to visualize the places we passed and the landmarks that had become such an inseparable part of my daily life and consciousness. As I did so I found I had to swallow hard and try to prevent tears forming in my eyes.

I was twenty-six then. The fifteen minutes or so which the trip to the airport took were obviously not enough for any leisurely recapitulation; but human nature being what it is I found myself forced to try. Twenty-six years and two months—all, but for a few weeks spent in Kermanshah and a few days here and there inside Iraq, spent in this city.

Things remembered and half-remembered, facts and images and fancies—all came crowding into my head in a merciless assault of mixed feelings of regret and resentment, pleasure and high hopes. The joys and the miseries, the triumphs and the disappointments, the friendships, the books, the sheer atmosphere, the smells, the sounds, and the sights: What was one to make of them when one knew one was saying farewell to all that?

Recalling those bleak moments of uncertainty, confusion, and loss now, fifty long years after, I cannot but repeat T. S. Eliot's lines from "Little Giddings" in his *Four Quartets:* "We shall not cease from exploration / And the end of our exploring / Will be to arrive where we started / And know the place for the first time."

But the die was cast and we were heading to the airport and then in a few hours would be in Israel and starting a new life, and I made an effort to concentrate on that side of the bewildering journey.

BULAND RECALLS THE OLD DAYS

It was largely thanks to Samira Al-Mana and *Al-Ightirab al-Adabi* that contacts were renewed, after forty-four long years of forced separation, with at least two long-lost friends of my youth. Both Buland al-Haidari and 'Adnan Raouf had contributed words of appreciation in Najib's memory to the issue devoted to the man and his work on his sudden death, often mixing these with fond memories of the first stages of their friendship with the deceased, Buland going so far as to mention other members of "the gang" (*al-shulla*), the days spent in Baghdad cafes and coffee shops, the meeting place that was Al-Rabita Bookshop and "the Jewish young man who ran it and whose name was Nissim Rejwan."

Eventually, taking my address from Samira, Buland wrote an extremely touching first letter in which he assured me that "what we had started as brothers, as writers, as aspirations, as dreams, cannot but reunite us in the assurance that we are larger than to let passing events separate us."

Moreover, despite the reputation he had acquired in the course of the years as a lazy sort of person—a reputation, by the way, that had nothing to justify it in a man still so active in his late sixties—he passed my address on to 'Adnan, who hastened to write saying, "You no longer have to ask for news of me from Buland. Here I am taking the initiative." This too marked the start of a long correspondence and a constant exchange of things the three of us have written these past four-and-a-half decades and of which we had had the chance of seeing only a tiny bit in books and periodicals that came our way. (Except, I might add, for Buland's work: I still had the thick and indifferently produced and printed bound volume of his Collected Poetry, published by Dar Al-'Awda, Beirut, as *Diwan Buland al-Haidari*.) There is also an English rendering of a long poem of his, "Dialogue in Three Dimensions," in which the chorus sings:

O Lord! . . .
Blame not the witness for the crime he saw,
Nor the hearer for the crime he heard,
For by the ear Thou gavest our hearing,
By the eye Thou bestowedest our sight,
And the eye has never enough of seeing,
The ear of hearing.
By Your will
We speak the truth.

'ADNAN RAOUF IN SEARCH OF OLD MATES

Eventually, I sent Samira three short fragments from my memoirs, which she translated and published in *Al-Ightirab* under the general title "Al-Rabita and After." I am told by Samira and her husband, the poet Salah

Niyazi — the editor — that fellow Iraqi émigrés received the series with enthusiasm. One of these, the poet Lami'a 'Abbas 'Amara, was especially moved by my depiction of those far-off days when she herself was in her early twenties. As luck would have it, it transpired that Lami'a had taught in the same high school in the southern town of 'Amara as did Norma (Nuriyya) Bar-Moshe, and that they became very friendly in the suffocating atmosphere of a small town where young women were hardly allowed to move after sunset. When Samira wrote to tell me about Lami'a's reaction to my memoirs, she gave her address in California as well, which I passed promptly to the Bar-Moshes, and a moving reunion was effected by letter, fax, and phone, with the promise of a forthcoming meeting in person.

In his first letter to me, from Limassol, in Cyprus, where he was spending his retirement years with his wife Sumayya, 'Adnan enquired about Jewish members of our circle and how they were faring. 'Adnan knew of Elie, who left Baghdad in 1947 and thus spent only little time with the circle. He also mentioned Naim Kattan, who now lives and works in Canada and with whom he said he tried unsuccessfully to establish contact. Of the two remaining Jewish members of our circle and about whose whereabouts he enquired, I wrote 'Adnan I had passed his address to Isaac Khedhouri (Bar-Moshe) and told him about Naji 'Abbudi's death in Milan nearly ten years ago.

Buland wrote in one of his letters to tell me he had passed my address to 'Adnan in Limassol, adding that two members of our gang had died in London, and how grievous it was for him to see them buried in a foreign soil. He himself, he said, was not in the best of health though he was still very active in the ranks of the opposition to the present regime in Baghdad. Apart from editing a broadsheet in Arabic reporting the activities of opposition circles, he also travels extensively in Arab capitals to keep in contact with fellow Iraqi opponents of Saddam Hussein now scattered all over the world. (It is estimated that there is today a total of 3 million Iraqi émigrés, exiled and self-exiled — a number which I find mind-boggling in that Iraq's whole population totaled less than 7 million when I left that country in 1951.)

I passed Buland's address to Isaac Bar-Moshe and his wife Norma who, being more energetic than I and my wife Rachel are, in the meantime visited Buland and his wife — the sculptress Dalal al-Mufti — while in London. The Bar-Moshes also flew to Limassol for a reunion with 'Adnan, where they were received with typical Iraqi hospitality by him and by his wife.

Buland, who is now considered one of the foremost contemporary Arab poets, also told me his sole source of income now is the pay he draws from the London-based Saudi-owned weekly *Al-Majalla* for his regular contributions to its literary pages. Early in 1996, the Israeli Arabic monthly, *Masharif*, founded and edited by the late Emil Habibi, published two new poems by Buland. One of them, a long evocative poem with the title "We Were Four," is dedicated "To my dearest brother, Nissim Rejwan."

I and some friends at Haifa University were trying to persuade Buland to spend some days in Israel as guest of various Arabic literature faculties when news came of his death at a London hospital following an open-heart operation which, though successful, led to certain complications because of the diabetes from which he also suffered. He was seventy.

Contacts with 'Adnan lasted much longer. Rachel and I visited him three or four times in Limassol and got to know his charming wife Sumayya better. We even planned a Mediterranean cruise together, and letters kept being exchanged between us regularly—long letters reminiscing about the old days and commenting on current Middle East preoccupations and the seemingly endless peace process between Israel and the Palestinians. Finally in late summer 1998, 'Adnan's health started deteriorating and he was admitted to a Limassol hospital, where he died on the morning of November 29. He was buried in a small mosque in the city, where his two sons, daughter, and two sisters—all living in the United States and France—attended. Sumayya decided to settle in America near the sons and their families.

| THE JEWS OF IRAQ: A BRIEF
HISTORICAL SKETCH

*J*eremiah, the most tragic of the Israelite prophets and a witness to the destruction of the Temple and other ominous events, gave this rare piece of advice to the elders, the priests, and the common people who had been exiled and carried off to Babylonia in three deportations — in 733, 731, and 586 BCE:

> Build houses and live in them; plant gardens and eat their produce.
> Take wives and have sons and daughters . . . multiply there and do not
> decrease. But seek the welfare of the city where I have sent you into
> exile, and pray to the Lord on its behalf, for in its welfare you will find
> your welfare (Jeremiah 29:5–7).

The exiled Jews of Babylonia took the prophet's advice with alacrity and energy; they sought and worked for the welfare of the place and duly found their own welfare therein. Though elsewhere in the Bible we learn of the Jews of Babylonia sitting "by the rivers of Babylon" and weeping in memory of Jerusalem, the overwhelming majority of those Jews continued to rebuild their homes and their lives — and worked hard, prospered, and multiplied.

Since those far-off days, for close on twenty-eight centuries, a Jewish presence was maintained uninterruptedly in the Land of the Twin Rivers (Mesopotamia), now known as Iraq. In today's Republic of Iraq, however, only twenty to thirty Jews remain in the capital Baghdad. As their ancestors had done from time immemorial, these Jews keep praying for "the welfare of the city," as well as saluting the ruler of the day — Saddam Hussein.

The Babylonian Exile, which started with the first wave of deportees early in the eighth century BCE, was not the Israelites' first encounter with that land. In a sense, indeed, the deportations were themselves in the nature of a "return." For it was from Ur of the Chaldees, in Sumer, that Terah, the father of Abraham the Patriarch, took off with his family and members of his clan. After a long and hard journey, they eventually settled in Jericho in the Land of Canaan—by which time Terah had died and the succession fell to Abraham.

This emigration is invested in the Bible with the character of a religious movement, since the Terahites, in leaving Ur, left behind the gods they and their fathers had worshipped. On succession to the clan's leadership, moreover, Abraham—who unlike his father was a monotheist—promptly broke with idolatry and turned to the service of the one and only God whom he recognized as the creator of heaven and earth and who, unlike the deities worshipped by other religions of the period, was neither a nature god nor a territorial one. He was essentially an ethical God to whom justice and righteousness were of supreme concern.

Forty-seven years after the third, massive deportation, in 539 BCE, Babylonia fell to the Persians, and its conqueror, King Cyrus the Great, promptly issued a royal decree granting permission to the Jews to return to Jerusalem and rebuild the Temple. He also decreed that the sacred vessels of the Temple, originally carried by the Babylonians back with the deportees, should be returned to the Jews.

While they were overjoyed and their hopes revived, however, the Jews of Babylonia hesitated, and in the end the overwhelming majority decided to stay, having in the meantime become prosperous and well established in business and farming. The journey to Judea, they found, was long and hazardous, and life there would obviously be rugged and full of hardships. Moreover, the Jews of Judea were poor, and it was necessary to take considerable amounts of money for the rebuilding of Jerusalem and the Temple.

It was remarkable, these factors notwithstanding, that the caravan which eventually left Babylonia for Jerusalem consisted of 42,360 souls, not counting 7,337 slaves. The returnees took with them all their worldly belongings, as well as the contributions of gold and silver made not only by the Jews who chose to stay behind but also by the king out of his treasury. Though the act of return proved to be extremely difficult and the returnees were soon to become disappointed and exhausted after years of hard work, the modest Temple was duly completed, in 516 BCE, and the Jews in both their habitats rejoiced.

With the Temple completed, the Jews of Babylonia were beginning to feel that, unlike themselves who were finding it hard to lead a full Jewish life in a foreign land, their brethren in Judea were leading a full Jewish existence. In the event, however, it was in Babylonia rather than in Jerusalem that the Jewish religion was preserved and codified. Moreover, the work of restoration "back home" was itself made possible thanks largely to the continued efforts and the assistance furnished by Jews of the Babylonian diaspora.

For the next eleven hundred years or more, with the land coming successively under Greek, Roman, Seleucid, and Sassanian rule, the Jews of Babylonia still managed to keep their Jewish identity intact, and weathered the storms that swept Palestine and other lands where substantial numbers of Jews lived. Indeed, while Palestine was struggling, first to stave off the dangers of Hellenization, then to liberate itself from the yoke of Rome, Diaspora communities became increasingly important for the maintenance and survival of Judaism and the Jewish way of life.

To achieve this while living as a minority among a non-Jewish majority, the Jews of Babylonia successfully fought a threefold struggle: They strove to preserve themselves, to gain the goodwill of their neighbors, and to live in accordance with their faith and their traditions. The only major Jewish community not under Roman rule, Babylonian Jewry, for almost two centuries, appeared dormant, lying low and waiting for the storm to pass. Eventually, with the steady deterioration of conditions in Palestine, and after the last vestiges of Jewish independence were crushed there with the fall of Masada in the spring of 73 CE, Babylonian Jewry assumed a far greater role in Jewish life than it had had at any time in the past.

This centrality was nowhere better expressed and preserved than in the compilation of the Talmud, an immense task started at the Academy at Sura circa 367 CE and concluded some 130 years later. It has been said, with justice, that no book—with the exception only of the Bible—has played so important a role in the history of the Jewish people as the Talmud in both its versions, the Jerusalem or Palestinian Talmud and the Babylonian Talmud. The latter is available today in the original in twelve fairly unmanageable tomes and in an English translation in almost three times as many volumes.

If the Talmud can be said to have one quality that overshadows all others, it would be the quality of pragmatism. The rabbis of the Talmud were not philosophers, nor were they concerned with theories. They were practical men whose main concern was conduct. Their practical approach to matters of religion and religious doctrine is so intrinsic to their work, indeed, that it extended even to the paramount subject of belief in God. The rabbis taught that faith is extolled only insofar as it leads to right actions—and that to profess belief in God and to act as if He did not exist was of very little value indeed. To know God and not to act in accordance with His will, they taught, is worse than to deny His existence.

The ways in which Jewries, scattered all over the world in later centuries, put the Babylonian Talmud to good use were many and varied. As new situations arose and as new needs were created, the Jews turned to the Talmud for guidance. Although in many cases they did not find there duplicates of, or exact analogies to, the conditions confronting them, they nevertheless found parallels. This is what led to the writing of so many commentaries to the Talmud, and to the many different codes of law based on it.

The immense influence that the Babylonian Talmud came to have over the dispersed Jewish communities dates from about the end of the seventh century CE. This period coincided with the end of the Sassanian rule in Mesopotamia. Shortly after, the armies of Islam began marching triumphantly to the conquest of large segments of the then civilized world, Mesopotamia being one of their earliest achievements. There is reason to believe that the Jews of Babylonia, as well as Jews elsewhere, welcomed the new masters with a deep sigh of relief, as the Sassanians at that time had started on one of their periodic waves of harassment and persecution against their Jewish subjects.

By the time Muhammad's successors and generals started on their spectacular series of conquests, the most important center of Jewish life as well as the most populated was situated in Mesopotamia. The ancient schools and academies still flourished; the memory of the Talmudic era was still fresh; and the office of the Exilarch (Head of the Exile), both the symbol and the main channel of Jewish self-government, was still functioning despite the many ups and downs it had experienced during the previous few decades. It was, therefore, natural for the new conquerors to turn to the Exilarch of the day, having learned from their short experience as rulers in foreign lands that it was best to make use of existing institutions rather than waste precious time trying to impose their own ways and mores.

Despite the burdens involved in being *dhimmis* (people with whom Muslims had made a covenant and toward whom they had an obligation), the Jews of Mesopotamia welcomed the change to Muslim rule, mainly because the new masters left them very much to themselves. The various aspects of discrimination enumerated in the so-called Covenant of Omar, and which were mostly social in character, were only sporadically enforced and were often even completely overlooked. In everyday practice, *dhimmis* were in fact not only tolerated but in some areas enjoyed almost full equality before the law. In any case, what with their cultural and religious activities remaining very much their own concern, and with their internal affairs run in accordance with their own laws and customs, the Jews felt that their lot was better than it had been under the tottering, often bigoted Sassanian rulers.

In the eighth century Baghdad became the center of gravity not only of the Muslim Empire but also of Babylonian Jewish life and learning. Shortly after its emergence as a capital and a metropolis, the city gradually became the seat first of the Exilarch and then of the Geonim, who up till then had resided in the three centers of Jewish learning, Neharde'a, Sura, or Pumbeditha.

The great medieval Jewish traveler Benjamin of Tudela in Navarre was in Baghdad about the year 1168, and his account throws much light on the life of the Jews of the city in the twelfth century. He writes:

> In Baghdad there are 40,000 Jews and they dwell in security, prosperity and honor under the great Caliph, and amongst them are great sages, the heads of the academies engaged in the study of the Law. At the head of the Great Academy is the Chief Rabbi, Rabbi Samuel the son of Ali. He is the "head of the Academy which is the Excellency of Jacob." He is a Levite, and traces his pedigree back to Moses our teacher.

The glory that was Baghdad ended when Hulagu, Chingiz Khan's grandson, marched with his Mangonel hordes toward Iraq, storming the walls of the capital in January 1258. By the 10th of February, as one historian writes, "Hulagu's hordes had swarmed into the city and the unfortunate Caliph with his 300 officials and kadis (judges) rushed to offer an unconditional surrender." Ten days later, however, they were all put to death, and the city itself was given over to plunder and flames. The majority of the population was wiped out of existence.

The slaughter perpetrated by Hulagu's hordes was of such dimensions that the number of victims has been estimated at anything between 800,000 and 2,000,000. Though according to certain Muslim historians the *dhimmis* of the capital, Christians and Jews, were spared, the Jews of Baghdad suffered along with their Muslim neighbors from the destruction and the pillage.

We know very little about the Jews of Iraq under the Mongol khans, whose hold on the country came to an end in 1336. It was only in the mid fifteenth century that the Jews began to rebuild their lives in the capital, during the reign of Uzun Hasan and his successors of the White Sheep dynasty. It is also thought that after the year 1492 a number of Jews who had been expelled from Spain found their way to Baghdad.

On the last day of the year 1534, the Ottoman sultan Sulayman the Magnificent entered Baghdad, accompanied by a number of Jewish scholars and physicians. He is said to have been aided and warmly welcomed by the city's Jewish community. The Turks ruled Iraq through viceroys, known as pashas or *walis*. By the middle of the sixteenth century, the Jewish community of Baghdad started to reassert its existence and early in the seventeenth century, when the Portuguese traveler Pedron Teixeira visited the city, he found there 25,000 houses, some 250 of them inhabited by Jews. Twelve of the Jewish families he talked to told him they and their forefathers had lived in Baghdad since the destruction of the First Temple. The Jews, he also reported, had many synagogues; they earned their livelihood by working in various crafts and by trade; they inhabited a certain part of the city where their synagogue—a reference to the Great Synagogue—was situated.

After a short interlude of Persian rule, the Turks reconquered Iraq in 1638, and stayed there until 1917. Despite the frequent and often arbitrary changes of viceroys, the position of the Jews remained fairly stable throughout this period. Judging by the standards then prevailing in these matters, the Jewish community along with other minority communities lived under a fairly tolerant regime. Baghdad, as one historian observes, was too cosmopolitan, and the Islamic sects themselves were too deeply divided, to cultivate or encourage fanaticism.

Twelve pashas ruled Iraq in the years 1750–1831, and their attitudes to the Jews were by no means uniform. In the first quarter of the nineteenth century the number of Jews in Baghdad was about six thousand. Some of them were wealthy, the majority fairly well-off, and a small minority poor. Most Jews were active in trade, in buying and selling, and in forming business connections that sometimes extended to neighboring countries like Turkey, Persia, Syria, Yemen, and India. Some Jews were craftsmen—goldsmiths, dyers, etc.; a few worked as government officials. They lived in a separate neighborhood that, though inhabited almost solely by Jews, was in no sense of the kind into which their co-religionists in the West were forcibly segregated.

Apart from Baghdad the only other sizable Jewish community lived in the north of Iraq. But the Jews of Kurdistan, though less detrimentally affected by the Mongol invasion, sustained a severe setback five centuries later when, in 1832, their main intellectual and economic center, the city of Mosul, was sacked and virtually destroyed by the governor of a neighboring province who had rebelled against the sultan. This marked the end of a process of decline from which the Kurdish Jewish community did not manage to recover until the twentieth century.

In southern Iraq, the situation differed in that this part of the country was almost without any Jewish settlements since the thirteenth century, with the exception of small communities in Basra, Hilla, and 'Ana. The reasons for this were largely economic and pertained to matters of geography and administration. It was not until the beginning of the eighteenth century that some measure of progress was made, both in respect of numbers and the socioeconomic status of these Jews.

During the reign of Mahmud II, who ascended the throne in Istanbul in 1808, the first reforms were contemplated after two centuries of social, administrative, and moral decline. On his accession the new sultan set out on a course of modernization by opening a school of medicine and a military academy, as well as a number of secondary schools, and he ordered 150 students to be sent to Europe for higher studies. Primary education was made compulsory, a postal service was established, and the foundations were laid for a nationwide police system. The time-honored practice of replenishing the treasury by confiscating the property of officials and private citizens came to an end. As far as the Jews and the other *dhimmis* were concerned, Geoffrey Lewis, a historian of modern Turkey, had this to say:

> The traditional Muslim tolerance, based . . . on contempt for the benighted adherents of other creeds, was to be replaced by a true equality of religions. Mahmud II is reported to have said, "Henceforth I recognize Muslims only in the mosque, Christians only in the church, Jews only in the synagogue. Outside these places of worship I desire every individual to enjoy the same political rights and my fatherly protection."

During the first decades of the nineteenth century, the fortunes of the Jews of Iraq began to improve noticeably, and on all fronts. Their number in the two main urban centers, Baghdad and Basra, increased and improvements in their economic conditions came when they began to assume their old activity as chief bankers and financial advisers after a few centuries of decline. In the sphere of education, too, changes were taking place that were to prove of lasting significance. Changes in the political status of the Jews also occurred during this period, especially after the series of far-reaching reforms incorporated in the Tanzimat (regulations) were proclaimed in November 1839. Fifty years later, when the Young Turks came with their novel concepts of equality, liberty, and fraternity, the Jews welcomed the reforms wholeheartedly — and when a new parliament was convened in Istanbul in 1908 an Iraqi Jewish notable, Sassoon Heskel, was appointed to represent the Jews of the *vilayet* of Baghdad.

Thus a process of radical change in the social, political, educational, and economic conditions of the Jews of Iraq was almost at its peak just before World War I erupted in 1914. It is important to add here, however, that these changes affected only a small proportion of the community, probably the upper 5 percent representing the rich and just a small part of the middle class. In any case, World War I and the British occupation found the Jews well and adequately prepared.

Some indications of Zionist activity amongst the Jews of Iraq can be traced back to the 1890s. This activity increased somewhat in the early years of the century, though it seldom exceeded reading Hebrew periodicals and early Zionist literature. Rather limited in scope, this activity was started on the initiative of local Jews rather than induced from the outside. The reason why it was on such a small scale was twofold — the hostile attitude of the authorities on the one hand and the lack of potential Zionist leaders on the other. Besides, Iraq at that early stage had not begun to witness the rise of an Arab nationalist movement, a state of affairs that tended to delay the emergence of a parallel movement amongst the Jews.

In the early 1920s, when Zionist activity seemed to gather momentum, the Iraqi authorities expressed the wish that the Zionists maintain a low profile, an attitude shared by the office of the British High Commissioner in Baghdad. The leadership of the community, too, was feeling uneasy about the effect Zionist activity was likely to have on the position of the Jews. This is best illustrated by Menahem Salih Daniel, a prominent member of the community, in a letter he sent the secretary of the Zionist Organization in London on September 8, 1922, in which he wrote that the Zionist movement represented to the Jews "a problem the various aspects of which need to be very carefully considered.

"Problems with which none of the European Jewish communities are confronted," he added, "force themselves upon us in this connection." The letter ended with an ominous note. "The opinions expressed above," he wrote, "are my own personal opinions. The community is unfortunately too helplessly disorganized to have any coordinated opinion, and that is why indeed it is the more exposed."

And exposed the position of the Jews of Iraq indeed was — but in the end neither Daniel's pleas nor his analysis proved persuasive either to the Zionists outside or the Arab nationalists at home. As Elie Kedourie observed: "With perspicacious wisdom [Daniel's] letter foresees the danger to its author's community posed by the style of politics which Zionism and Arabism shared in equal measure, a danger rendered all the more deadly by the indifference about public and political affairs which, as he correctly observes, was characteristic of the Baghdad Jews."

Subsequent developments, especially in the 1930s, were to furnish abundant proofs for Daniel's bleak outlook. Matters came to a head in June 1941 when, at the end of a pro-Axis nationalist revolt headed by Rashid 'Ali al-Gaylani, which involved military intervention on the part of Great Britain, the Jews of Baghdad were subjected to a series of acts of pillage and murder for two days in succession. Reference to these acts, better known by the Arabic term *farhud,* is made in the course of these memoirs.

| $\mathcal{A}$ SELECTION OF BOOK REVIEWS FROM THE *IRAQ TIMES*

The Wandering American by Henry Miller
(6 AUGUST 1947)

Henry Miller is an American rebel. He sees in modern American society nothing but ugliness, stupidity and unhappiness. He dreads in it what he describes as a "world suited for monomaniacs obsessed with the idea of progress—but a false progress, a progress which stinks. A world cluttered with useless objects, which men and women, in order to be exploited and degraded, are taught to regard as useful."

Born in New York in 1891 of American parents of German descent, Miller entered the City College of New York when he was 18, only to leave two months later "disgusted with the atmosphere of the place and the stupidity of the curriculum." The partial list of positions he held between his leaving the college and 1920 includes: dishwasher, bus boy, messenger boy, grave-digger, bill sticker, book salesman, typist, adding machine operator, librarian, statistician, charity worker, mechanic, insurance collector, garbage collector, usher, secretary to an evangelist, dock hand, street car conductor, gymnasium instructor, milk driver, ticket chopper, etc. In 1924 he decided to be a writer, had nothing accepted by publishers and "eventually was obliged to beg in the streets." He left to Paris in 1931 and had his first book published by the Obelisk Press there. It was *Tropic of Cancer* which he followed, five years later, by *Tropic of Capricorn*. After the defeat of France he was obliged to return to the States, where he has recently published a book about America which he called *The Air-conditioned Nightmare*. Concluding his Biographical Note, from which the above facts were taken, Miller says: "I want to be read by less and less people; I have no interest in the life of the masses, nor in the intentions of the existing governments of the world. I hope and believe that the whole civilised world will be wiped out in the next hundred years or so. I believe that man can exist, and in an infinitely better, larger way, without civilisation."

Here is a passage from *The Air-conditioned Nightmare:*

This frenzied activity which has us all, rich and poor, weak and power-ful, in its grip — where is it leading us? There are two things in life which it seems to me all men want and very few ever get (because both of them belong to the domain of the spiritual) and they are health and freedom. The druggist, the doctor, the surgeon are all powerless to give health; money, power, security, authority do not give freedom. Education can never provide wisdom, nor churches religion, nor wealth happiness, nor security peace. What is the meaning of our activity then? To what end?

Miller's books were criticized for being chaotic, obscure and ludicrous. They are banned, both in the United States and in the British Empire, on the grounds that they are obscene, indecent and degrading. The read-ing public must have found these books too aggressive and bitter to fit with its refined tastes and high aesthetic standards. Miller, of course, has many faults. He can be repetitive, exaggerating, over-enthusiastic, out-spoken and even, sometimes, sentimental. It may also be said that he puts too much stress on certain unpleasant aspects of life. One thing, at any rate, must go to his credit; he is an honest man and a genuine artist. Like D. H. Lawrence, Miller is passionately interested in the things he writes about; he works as if under an inner compulsion, like a saint, a prophet. The following passage is quoted from his novel *The Rosy Crucifixion:*

The prisoner is not the one who has committed a crime, but the one who clings to his crime and lives it over and over. We are all potentially free. We can stop thinking of what we have failed to do and do what-ever lies within our power. What these powers that are in us may be no one had truly dared to imagine. That they are infinite we will realise the day we admit to ourselves that imagination is everything. Imagination is the voice of daring. If there is anything God-like about God it is that He has dared to imagine everything.

To accuse Miller of writing chaotic, obscure and obscene books would not be so unjustifiable as absurd. He sees life, as it is being lived by millions and millions of people at present — and here quite a number of people may agree with him — as chaotic, ugly and humanly degrading; and to hold him responsible for what he sees would be like getting angry with the mirror for failing to produce a lovely image or blaming a child for inherit-

ing his parents' mental deficiencies. It is part of the tragedy of our age—
of man in fact—that people are determined not to learn the truth about
themselves and their lives. They are scared at it and they may as well be
so. The moment they begin to see the misery, ugliness and pointlessness
of their present condition they may go mad, commit suicide, or—which
is what they seem to dread most—realise that they must do something
about the whole damned lot.

The world cannot reasonably pose to judge Miller or blame him for the
violent and "obscene" character of his works—which is evident enough
—as long as it teems with ugliness, violence, frustration and prejudices.
You can't be judge and defendant at the same time.

Legacy of a Lost Generation:
Dangling Man by Saul Bellow and *Mr. Adam* by Pat Frank
(10 SEPTEMBER 1947)

The two novels under review have in common something more than the
fact that they are both written by Americans. Each of them relates the
history of an estranged and helpless individual during a period of acute
world crisis.

Joseph, the hero of *Dangling Man,* narrates his own story in the form
of a diary. He is, or was, an uncompromising intellectual and a disillusioned Communist. What he wanted, and failed to get, is a "colony of the
spirit" or a group whose covenants forbade spite, bloodiness and cruelty.
Called by the army, he resigned his job at a traveling agency, and at the
time he starts the diary he has spent seven months to put his papers in
order, during which time his wife supported him. These long, idle days,
the greatest part of which he spent alone in his room, and the additional
four months which form the period of the diary, witnessed his dreams
and his private plans crumble before him to the last one . . .

Joseph is characteristic of a whole generation of young intellectuals
striving to create a rational basis for modern life to answer the question,
"How should a good man live, what ought he to do?" Having refused to
accept the world as it is, they are torn between two alternatives: the "ideal
construction" and complete resignation. Pursuit of the ideal construction
takes many different forms: the Socialist utopia, "colonies of the spirit,"
the Superman or complete detachment.

But the gap between these ideal constructions and the real world is
so great and unbridgeable that very few, somewhat abnormal people can
stand the strain. Joseph couldn't. He was for some years a member of

the Communist party; he was offered a successful business by his older brother; he married at the age of 22 and the marriage, though not a complete failure, turns out to be unimportant and unnecessary.

Joseph is one of those who, even when they want it, are not able to close their eyes to reality and live in comfort. He rejects both the Communist formula and the offers of his brother, and he insists on some absolute values. When he is ignored and snubbed by an old party member, he raises a row, insisting that he has a right to be recognised by an old friend. All the time, he keeps reminding himself that he is living off his wife's earnings and would tell anyone how he is dissatisfied with the world and with his own circle.

When a man is forced to such depths of disillusionment and despair, what is he to do? After 11 months of idle and meaningless living Joseph sees to it that he is taken by the army immediately and he ends the journal with these lines:

> I am no longer to be held accountable for myself; I am grateful for that.
> I am in other hands, relieved of self-determination, freedom cancelled.
> Hurray for regular hours! And for the supervision of the spirit! Long live regimentation!

Saul Bellow has seized and recorded, faithfully and skillfully, the experience of a whole generation, the generation that has come to maturity during the Depression, the New Deal, the days of the Popular Front, Munich and the war. His book is a testimony on the psychology of that generation, and it is written with brilliance and integrity.

As a novel, *Dangling Man* suffers from the fact that it is written in the form of a journal. In some places it lacks detail, and the author overlooks many dramatic possibilities, chiefly because he tries to keep the focus on the inner feelings and reactions of his hero. This preoccupation of the author with his hero's limited development makes the movement of the story very linear. But this is one of those books that manages to retain its value and importance despite its technical faults . . .

What Worth Is Man?
Our Threatened Values by Victor Gollancz
(1 OCTOBER 1947)

Those of us who were unfortunate enough to grow up in the troubled atmosphere of the Thirties have been witnessing what is probably the most significant and terrible change in the world's outlook: Man's changed attitude toward himself and his abandoning the basic idea, embodied in the teachings of all the world's religions and emphasised by nearly two centuries of liberal thought, of the sacredness and inviolability of human life.

Ever since the rise of Fascism in Italy and the official murder of the Socialist leader Matteoti in 1924, governments in totalitarian states had made it an ordinary procedure to dispose of — they used to call it "liquidation" — those of their subordinates who dared to raise their voice against the existing regimes. Human life became very cheap indeed. Hitler's "Blood Bath" in June 1934 involved several hundreds of his political opponents; the Moscow trials of 1936–1937 served to settle some differences of opinion between two groups with the Communist party — that simple! — and apparently resulted in strengthening the so-called dictatorship of the proletariat which is, incidentally, nothing other than a dictatorship "over" the proletariat. Franco, aided by Italian and German arms, pursued in Spain a policy of wholesale killing of his opponents which he is still continuing.

During the recent war, disregard for human life and dignity became almost universal and certainly alarming. Hitler's extermination camps which spread all over the Continent of Europe; the indiscriminate bombing of cities; the atom bomb; the mass deportation of Poles — these are things which we have not forgotten yet. The depressing catalogue could be considerably lengthened. You have the trial and the savage term of imprisonment passed on Tanner of Finland; the execution of Mihailovitch of Yugoslavia; and the latest example of legalised revenge — the hanging of the Bulgarian opposition leader, Petkov.

The growing insensitiveness displayed by the ordinary man to these happenings, his lack of feeling and his indifference, are regarded by Mr. Gollancz as symptoms of the denial of the basic values of Western civilisation — a denial which is becoming more frequent every day. The thesis of *Our Threatened Values* is that there are some basic virtues, inseparable from Christianity and liberal humanism, which distinguish Western civilisation. These virtues — mercy, pity, humility, justice — are being progressively weakened. It is not suggested by the author that these virtues have always been practised in the past, but they have been accepted and praised, and sometimes put into practice. Nor is it here implied that their acceptance or praise is dependent on an acceptance of Christianity; only that the central value which these virtues imply is derived from Christianity — the principle of respect for personality as such. Mr. Gollancz devotes the first part of his book to showing the decline in these values and he illustrates his thesis by many significant quotations . . .

A year has passed since the first edition of this book was issued. Re-reading it in this cheaper edition—now published—I find that, far from becoming outdated, it has gained in importance and timeliness. With the subsequent cut in the food rations for the Germans, the danger of a general famine in Europe in the coming winter and the consolidation of totalitarian governments in certain European countries, the contents of this book and what it has to say are now more urgent than a year ago.

There are so many passages which are worth quoting in this book; but one will have to be sufficient here. Concluding Part I, Mr. Gollancz writes:

> Man, said Aristotle, is a political animal. He is that, and much more besides; and Aristotle himself meant something far wider than we mean by the word political. Every man is potentially a political, creative individual creature: his glory is independence and his birthright spontaneity. I want to see the potentiality realised, the birthright accepted, the glory achieved. I want to see a race of MEN, not of domestic animals however "happy"; of self-directing intelligences, not of anthropoid automatons who will do what they are told and think what others prescribe for them. And I say that any ideal pettier than this rests, in the last analysis, on contempt for humanity.

Rex Warner's Version:
The Cult of Power by Rex Warner
(4 NOVEMBER 1947)

The old, long-cherished world values are losing the power they used to exercise over men's minds. Religious and, more important still, humanitarian notions and ideals like tolerance, kindliness, humility, and in general respect for man's personality and the sanctity of human life—values that have more or less guided the actions of individuals and nations for the last thirty centuries or so—seem no longer capable of having any restraining influence on either individuals or nations.

Not only that those standards are being ignored: it is disturbing how indifferently they are being ridiculed and dismissed as signs of sentimentality, weakness, etc., etc. It is neither possible nor necessary to consider here the whys and hows of this state of things. It is sufficient, for the purpose of this article, to call attention to the fact that a whole system of values is breaking up, and that these values have become too weak to inspire respect or enforce obedience. This weakening of hitherto universally accepted standards and their inability to restrain the individual, has resulted in what the author of *The Cult of Power* calls the philosophy of the moral anarchist; in the individual asserting himself against all established ideals and institutions.

But, having accomplished his work in destroying all the holy images and ideals, what is the moral anarchist to do next? This is the crucial problem which is bound to face the individualist who succeeds in setting himself up against the universe; and here the impact of his actions will make itself felt. For he will find himself in a great desert, and to quote Mr. Warner, "his supporters will begin to miss the faces that he has taken from them." For him, "there will be one way of escape, and that is by giving to the mass of the people what they want—a system of ideas by which they can regulate and give meaning to their lives." After having rejected God, he will have to make himself God, to become a "leader."

In more European countries than one, we have been witnessing this same sequence of events. At the root of this cult of power and the worship of violence which characterise Fascism, Mr. Warner points out, is this philosophy of moral anarchism and intellectual scepticism. The intellectual sceptic has turned and is bound to turn into a power-addict, the power-addict into the "leader," and the world in the process is plunged into a devastating war.

Though *The Cult of Power* is a book of essays, it has the rare merit of having one principal theme to give it unity and purpose. Whether Mr. Warner is writing about freedom of expression, Dostoevsky or Aeschylus, his theme is the same, and he always succeeds in making his point clear in an exceptionally graceful way . . .

Yet, Mr. Warner is essentially an optimist. Not that cheap sort of optimist we are used to, who thinks that all will be well when we succeed in overthrowing the social and economic system. He is an optimist in the sense that he believes—or so he seems to do—in the essential goodness of man and in his inexhaustible potentialities for self-betterment. Although he makes no practical proposals, he writes at the end of his title essay:

> Mere reiteration of European ideals of universal love and justice will cut no more ice than they did (in the Twenties). Life will desire to assert itself within narrow and constricted bounds rather than to be swallowed up in the empty sands of unfulfilled promises and generalities that have no apparent application. Nor is the situation likely to be at all helped by bogus religious revivals led by elderly generals. The only reply to the cult of individual or racial power and violence is the actual practice of general justice, mercy, brotherhood and understanding.

Can Men Be Rational?
The Comforts of Unreason by Rupert Crawshay-Williams
(17 DECEMBER 1947)

That man is a predominantly rational being whose thought and whose behaviour are shaped and determined by purely rational motives and considerations is an idea which, like that of inevitable progress, must now be discarded as a 19th century fallacy.

Practically all 19th century writers and thinkers, from J. S. Mill to Herbert Spencer, from Ricardo to Karl Marx, assumed that men, both as individuals and when gathered in groups, were capable of acting and thinking rationally. In an age of industrialisation and relative prosperity, the existence of such optimistic views was hardly surprising.

With the emergence of psychoanalysis and the other schools of modern psychology, and the introduction by the Freudians of more efficient techniques for the study of the human mind and the motivation of human actions, it became quite clear that the motives to irrational thought and irrational behaviour in human beings are more powerful and numerous than those which can enable them to act and behave rationally. This has now become so obvious that hardly anyone working in political, social or psychological research can pretend to deny it.

Although the irrational nature of much human behaviour was an underlying assumption of many a book on psychology and the social sciences, not many books have been devoted entirely to the study and analysis of irrational thought and the motives behind it. In fact, as far as it can be ascertained here, *The Comforts of Unreason,* which is such a study, is the first book to be written in English and to have as its subject the entire field of the motives behind unreason and of their manifestations and workings. The work of Bertrand Russell, I. A. Richards, C. K. Ogden, A. J. Ayer, and a few others was concerned with only some aspects of the subject of Mr. Crawshay-Williams' book—but not with the whole field.

The author of *The Comforts of Unreason* devotes the first part of his book to giving what he considers to be the motives for irrationality, and proceeds in Part Three to reveal the methods by which our everyday irrational thoughts work. In the fourth and last part of his work, he discusses the irrationalities to be found in more complicated kinds of thought —in the work of philosophers, writers, and scientists when they are speaking of other things than their scientific work. The book has also a supplement in which its author discusses the "methods of diagnosis and prevention" of irrationality, gives some tests and points out to some danger signs and traps in which the unwary are liable to fall . . .

Does all this mean that we are incapable of rationality and balanced thinking? Mr. Crawshay-Williams is, to say the least, not clear about this point. On the one hand he tells us (pp. 42–43) that to form a considered and rational opinion about a complex subject "requires more caution and more trouble than we usually exercise." In the Epilogue, on the other hand, the author hardly agrees with what he had just said. Here is the Epilogue in its entirety:

> Whether or not I have made out a reasonable case for the views expressed in this book, I leave the reader to judge, confident that — if I am right — his opinion will probably remain unchanged whatever anyone says.

Even if one agreed that it is possible to form such considered and rational opinions about some subjects, the fact remains that this needs much mental discipline and intellectual detachment, qualities which are very rare even among intellectuals. If we keep in mind that the ordinary man does not even bother his head about these matters, we will not be very far from the conclusion that the chances to attain a rational world are practically nil.

The Strange Case of Mr. Burnham:
The Struggle for the World by James Burnham
(25 FEBRUARY 1948)

In 1941 there was published in the U.S.A. a book which caused something of a stir in political and intellectual circles both inside and outside of America. The book was *The Managerial Revolution* and its author James Burnham.

In that book Burnham set out to explain and establish what he called the theory of the Managerial Revolution. Widely different opinions and criticisms were expressed for and against the book, ranging from strong enthusiasm to outright condemnation. Communists thought, of course, that the theory was based on wholly unscientific and incorrect assumptions, and that it was merely a justification which Burnham had worked out for himself for quitting the proletarian cause (Burnham was an ex-Marxist of the Trotskyite variety). Socialists and organised Labour were, as always, not quite sure, but nevertheless the leftists amongst them dismissed the book on similar grounds. Burnham was further accused of Fascist leanings and a totalitarian outlook, despite the fact that he made it quite clear in the book that he was by no means pleased with his own conclusions, or with the prospect of a Managerial society.

Now it may be correctly pointed out that the theory of the Managerial Revolution contains nothing entirely new. Its main thesis is that while the capitalist system and the liberal-capitalist ideology are disappearing from modern society, they will be superseded, not by a workers' state or a class-less society, but by another ruling class. The Managers, who according to Burnham are the ruling class of the future, are, it may be argued, nothing other than Trotsky's "Bureaucracy" more broadly and methodically de-fined. It remains a fact, nevertheless, that Burnham was the first among modern social thinkers to take his point of departure from the assump-tion that Socialism is not the inevitable successor to Capitalism, while at the same time pinning no hopes on the possible survival of the good old days of free enterprise and laissez-faire.

With this in mind, and with high expectations, one opens *The Struggle for the World* in which Burnham has proposed to analyse, as he says at the end of the first chapter, "in its primary and most fundamental lines, the world political situation as it exists in this period following the conclu-sion of the Second World War; as it exists in reality, not as it is distorted in wishful dreams or in the lies of propagandists." "I propose, further," he goes on, "in terms of the actual situation, to examine the alternatives of political action which are at the disposal of the United States."

One reads, with no little admiration, Burnham's masterly analysis of the situation in the first part of the book: his views on the political and cul-tural "immaturity of the United States," his thoughtful and penetrating examination of the question of the oneness of the world and the problem of the control of atomic weapons. (The analysis of the idea of "one world" leads Burnham to the conclusion that "the world is potentially one in the light of a possible ideal of brotherhood, of common humanity. The world is actually one . . . through the direct or indirect influence of a particular technology and method of economic production. Politically, and, most deeply of all, the world is many.")

Having reached this stage in his analysis, and having decided further, that the control of atomic weapons can be effective only if it becomes a monopoly in the hands of one state, and that there are "just two" serious candidates for the monopoly control of atomic energy, the United States and the Soviet Union, Burnham proceeds to tackle the problem of which of these two states should be entrusted with this task. Since it is impossible for either of these states to control atomic weapons—and thereby save "Western" civilisation from destruction—as long as the other state exists, Burnham proposes that there should be set up an American "World Empire" which, by constituting a monopoly of atomic weapons, will solve this most urgent problem. This follows because, as he sets out to demonstrate, a Soviet or Communist World Empire would be both undesirable and highly objectionable.

It is interesting and, in the light of his theory of the managerial revolution, highly instructive, to see why Burnham objects to a communist-dominated world empire. Burnham is at great pains to show that communists, whatever form their tactics take from time to time, are in the long run seeking world domination. He writes, on page 66: "Communism may be summarily defined as a world-wide, conspiratorial movement for the conquest of a monopoly of power in the era of capitalist decline. Politically it is based upon terror and mass deception; economically it is, or at least tends to be, collectivist; socially it is totalitarian."

Granted! But, one feels entitled to ask, what has happened to Burnham's Managerial Society? In *The Managerial Revolution* Burnham arrived at the conclusion that Nazi Germany, Soviet Russia and Fascist Italy had all accomplished their own managerial revolutions and were building their managerial societies; that capitalist America was fast moving towards a similar fate and showed every sign of developing into a managerial society; and that Great Britain was passing through the same kind of revolution. Now it may be said, on the authority of Burnham himself, that if this was the situation seven years ago, it could not have altered very much since. One can add, again on Burnham's own authority, that if the situation has been altered at all, this change should have taken, in the case of the United States, a more rather than less "managerial" aspect. Leaving Britain out, as Burnham proposes to do, why should one prefer a Managerial America to a Managerial Russia? There is no answer to this question—not in Dr. Burnham's book!

But whether American or Russian, whether managerial or not, a world empire according to the author of *The Struggle for the World* should be created immediately if Western civilisation is to be at all preserved. This is the most urgent task facing the United States today, which he suggests should take the initiative and assume the leadership of a world-wide federation. Granted this, the problem will remain as it is: how to get along with Soviet Russia—or, to put it in a way more in keeping with the spirit of this book, how to get rid of her? Burnham would "prefer that in the Soviet Union the smashing of communism should be accomplished from within, rather than by a war from the outside." Since this is highly improbable, if not impossible, it should follow that war, atomic war, is the only way to get along with Russia. This does not constitute any misrepresentation of Burnham's views, since he's ready to admit that in his opinion peace should not be the goal of policy, and that getting ready for war actually diminishes its possibility.

This Machiavellian argument is nothing new—the new thing in this book is the spectacle of Burnham trying to formulate what he calls the Supreme Object of American Foreign Policy. One can only hope that it will not take a very long time from now to see the author of *The Managerial Revolution* occupying an important office at the State Department in Washington, advising the Secretary of State on how to have a realistic foreign policy. *The New Machiavelli*—at last!

Big Book Business:
The Fate of Writing in America and
The League of Frightened Philistines by James T. Farrell
(17 MARCH 1948)

The current tendency of American book publishing is essentially one of more and more concentration on best-sellers. This fact is of capital importance because no American publisher can stand the strains of rising production costs and fierce competition from the reprint houses if he failed to produce a best-seller from time to time. But to produce a so-called best-seller would require the means to make it one. For it is by now fairly well known that this phenomenon of the best-seller depends on factors which have less to do with the "quality" and the writing of the book itself than they have with purely external causes. To produce a best-seller a publisher should invest considerable sums of money on advertising and promotion work; he should have connections or controlling interests in one of the book clubs (no book is a best-seller which is not chosen by a big book club); and it would greatly help if he has his own reprint house so that he can draw for himself all the profits which could be possibly obtained from the book through all the stages of its life.

If it is true, as a writer in *The Nation* indicated some time ago, that regular book publishing (which excludes reprints, book club connections and best-sellers) is becoming a losing business, and that American publishers are able to keep going only because they produce or hope to produce best-sellers, then the conclusions to be drawn seem to be these. Small independent publishers who care for quality and cannot afford the huge investments required for producing a best-seller will be gradually driven out of the business. The author's lot will be indeed poor. He will have less chances of getting his book published with the number of independent publishers diminishing, especially if he is a new and a serious writer; the new publishing magnates will feel more free to exert pressure on him as to what he should write and how to write it.

The effects which these developments are likely to have on literary values and cultural standards in general are no less discouraging. Already protesting voices are raised against the decline of book reviewing in the American popular press, with the top reviewers occupying the chairs of book club selection committees. As in the case of film audiences, the reading public is being conditioned to accept a certain type of books which are proving popular with book club members and undiscriminating readers of cheap fiction. The whole cult of the best-seller is in fact based on uniformity ("three million of your fellow citizens have bought and read this book; you should therefore read it yourself!") and in literature uniformity is the surest way to kill good, serious writing, which cannot be maintained without variety and scope for experiment. Those books which are receiving the blessings of Hollywood producers are proving the most popular with the public. Mr. Farrell even refers to cases where films which were originally not based on books were novelised!

All this and the Philistine too! We are all familiar with the Frightened Philistine who would call Lawrence a Fascist, blame Proust for the fall of France, accuse Joyce of obscenity, and consider Picasso's drawings mere scribblings of a child or a lunatic. Every country has its own share of this type of middlebrows, thank God. England had her Agate, is still having Elton, Noyce, Lucas, Jay and the *John O'London* group.

James Farrell belongs to the generation of American writers who reached their maturity during the hard times of depression and economic slump. This seems to have influenced his outlook and made him one of the politically conscious, for Farrell is still active in the small group of American Trotskyites. This fact is mentioned here because throughout *The League of Frightened Philistines* one encounters certain references to the works of Marx, Lenin and Trotsky which seem a bit irrelevant and out of place. The efforts which have been made to apply Marxian conceptions to literary criticism have always been unsuccessful. The Marxist critic tends to be too preoccupied with economic and materialistic motives to be able to see other and no less important factors.

But there are some very interesting essays in this collection. The title essay contains a defence of modern writers against the attacks made on them by certain Philistine critics. In another essay, "Politics and Ideology," Farrell again takes these gentlemen to task. It is really hard to see what these critics find objectionable in modern writers like Hemingway, Faulkner, Dos Passos and Farrell himself. They seem to think that these writers, in these critical times, are abandoning the ideas of the past and consequently demoralising the democratic forces. Archibald MacLeish wants these writers to defend ways of thinking, ideas and beliefs which he thinks should be defended. Van Wyck Brooks believes that "modern writers are cynics and that they write out of hatred and a drive-toward-death." It is extraordinary how these critics overlook the apparent fact that it is not Hemingway, Faulkner and Dos Passos who are responsible for the current decline in belief and in greatness, but the age they happen to be living in. After all, these writers, and their counterparts in Europe, are merely trying to see life truly and record their impressions honestly. Why blame the modern artist for revealing the sickness of the age?

Good Dinner or Greek:
The Education of Girls by John Newsom
(14 APRIL 1948)

The education of girls is not as specialised a subject as it would sound. More even than the subject-matter of education proper, it has great relevance to the life and welfare of society, and involves, moreover, the whole question of the relations between men and women and their corresponding social functions.

Apart from this intrinsic interest in the subject of girls' education, what makes *The Education of Girls* even more interesting and readable is that it does not pretend to be a specialist work, and Mr. Newsom, its author, writes with remarkable wit and lightness of temper on a subject about which as an educational officer he has a deep and first-hand knowledge. Mr. Newsom contrives somehow to make his reader feel that the problems discussed, far from being distant academic issues, constitute some of the major problems of modern everyday experience. And, as the argument unfolds throughout the course of the book, one realises that the question is one of the utmost practical importance.

The problem which *The Education of Girls* tries to tackle — and which, as the author points out, is more simply stated than solved — is "to discover how far the present education, and particularly the secondary education, of girls is related to the function of women in modern society." Mr. Newsom sets himself the task of attempting to synthesize these two subjects, women's education and their social function. This involves him in a consideration of the differences between the sexes and he reaches conclusions which he himself is aware will provoke strong objections from his readers, especially women. But before considering his conclusions it would perhaps be of interest to see, first, the assumptions on which the author of this book builds up his argument.

These assumptions are that men and women have marked physiological differences as individuals "even though they have a great deal in common," that "the different roles of men and women in society are complementary and equally valuable," that at the present time education is not taking account of the individual differences between the sexes and their social functions; that methods of education should be judged not by the results on the pupil at the end of her school career, but mainly by what sort of woman she becomes when she reaches maturity; and that the reader appreciates that he — the author — is concerned here not with the small minority of girls who may eventually go to a university but with the 99 per cent who finish their education by the time they are eighteen.

There are very few things which could be more foolish, futile and meaningless than the controversy — which no one knows how it got started — centering on the question of whether men are superior to women and whether, if they are not, women are not "equal" to men. The hopeless inconclusiveness of this controversy is due first to the lack of accurate definitions of what, in this contest, is meant by the words "superiority" and "equality," and, secondly, to the utter irrelevance of it all. For it is very difficult to discover what purpose can be there behind the arguments unless it be, on men's side, to keep woman in what is called her "place," and on women's to prove that her function in society is identical with that of man. Both of which, as can be readily seen, are childish nonsense.

It is not denied here that women have in the past been placed under gross disadvantages and that apparently men, for their part, came to like this state of affairs. It can be argued that men held all the important positions in society and kept their women at home; that they enjoyed every freedom from spending their leisure time as they liked to bigamy, and they denied them to women; and that they assumed to themselves the right to be served and taken care of by women, while forgetting to observe their own duties to the latter. In this connection the implication of Dr. Johnson's remark — quoted in this book — when he says that "a man is more pleased when he has a good dinner upon his table than when his wife talks Greek," if it is to be taken literally, reflects this mentality of men very clearly. And Mr. Newsom, in quoting this "dictum" approvingly is, it is hoped, taking it only metaphorically!

There is no reason whatsoever why, on the one hand, a woman should be made to prefer learning to cook well to learning to speak a foreign or a second foreign language and, on the other, why it should be impossible for her to do both things at the same time!

The Anatomy of Clothes:
On Human Finery by Quentin Bell
(12 MAY 1948)

The view, widely held among "educated" people, that the subject of fashion is either a purely feminine concern or so vulgar that it should be beyond the dignity and refinements of their intellectual pursuits, could not be more superficial and even sometimes snobbish.

Far from being either, the study of fashion constitutes one of the most important and fascinating departments of social history and social research. And it is really surprising that so far it has received so little or no attention which it legitimately deserves from those concerned with the study of the economic, social and psychological aspects of human life and conduct. A quick glance at the origin and development of clothes would suffice to show to what extent they can be regarded as manifestations of other, far more important developments in the social and economic spheres.

For this purpose it would perhaps be essential to refer to authorities other than Mr. Quentin Bell, whose *On Human Finery* is not a history of fashion but, as will be presently seen, an essay on the theory of dress, . . . and specifically on Veblen's theory of dress . . . There are, of course, theories of dress other than the one put forward by Thorstein Veblen. These fall into four main groups which are listed by Mr. Bell as follows: (1) those which explain the changes of fashion as the work of a few individuals; (2) those which see in fashion a product of human nature; (3) those which see in it a reflection of great political or spiritual events; (4) those which invoke the authority of a Higher Power.

One by one and with a clarity and wit which are truly remarkable, Mr. Bell rejects these theories and sticks instead to Veblen's, which, though he develops and sometimes even criticises, he considers to be the only sound philosophy of dress.

According to Veblen, dress serves purposes which are both utilitarian and spiritual. But, and especially among the higher ranks of society, "the need of dress is eminently a 'higher' or spiritual need." Dress is the concern not only of the wearer himself, but chiefly of those who own it, whether worn by themselves or by those who are their dependents (wives, children, servants, etc.). Further, because "good" dress is sumptuous and judged by both its own financial worth and by the proofs it provides of its wearer's indifference to work and other practical (and therefore vulgar) matters, its sumptuosity is demonstrated in the following ways: (1) by what Veblen calls Conspicuous Consumption, which is the use of expensive materials and/or expensive productive processes; (2) by Conspicuous Leisure, which is obtained by making the dress in such a way as to suggest that the wearer is leading an unproductive type of existence; (3) by Conspicuous Waste, which is obtained by designing the dress so as to prove that the wearer indulges in futile (and therefore reputable) activities.

But the most interesting difficulty about dress is not the ways in which it is made or displays the wealth or the futile and reputable existence of its wearer. It is rather how dress "becomes fashionable" and why it goes out of use; who and what "sets the evolutionary process into motion." Veblen, and Mr. Bell, reject every theory of fashion known before them. Their own theory takes as the mainspring of fashion "the Emulative Process" by which is meant that the members of one class imitate those of another (higher) class, who in their turn are driven (being anxious to keep the line separating them from their socially inferior imitators) to "ever new expedients of fashionable change." In this connection the story of the rise and fall of the crinoline is most amusingly told by Mr. Bell here—how even maids wore it, and how, little by little, it began to shrink away till it went out of fashion.

This process of emulation explains, incidentally, why women and even men have never been able to break altogether with any currently prevailing fashion. They may complain, and complain bitterly and endlessly, of the various inconveniences of this dress and that, but they will not fail to be seen in it. Mr. Bell implores us to consider ". . . how many lovely necks must have been hidden by a ruff between 1570 and 1620 . . . what legs have gone unseen to the grave!"

Mr. Bell's own original contribution toward a more comprehensive theory of fashion based on Veblen's ideas consists in adding another way by which he considers the upper classes have demonstrated the sumptuosity of their clothes. Besides conspicuous consumption, leisure and waste, there is what he calls Conspicuous Outrage, which is displayed in the dress by this being designed in such a manner as to mark an indifference to vulgar prejudice. Mr. Bell further asserts that sumptuous dress is uniform: "It must exhibit not only pecuniary strength, but the membership of a reputable class . . ."

There is a chapter in *On Human Finery* on recent trends in fashion. Unfortunately, these trends do not include the most recent one of the long skirt. It would have no doubt been extremely interesting to hear what Mr. Bell has to say about this—all the more so because his analysis of the trends following the First World War are so illuminating. As it is, the book is a most exciting one, and it could never be recommended too strongly.

Cecil Collins—Work, Opinions:
The Vision of the Fool by Cecil Collins
(23 JUNE 1948)

The cycle of paintings and drawings by Cecil Collins which he calls "The Holy Fools" has been getting occasional comments in certain literary journals during the past five years. Those who did not have the chance to see these paintings on show at the Lefevre Gallery have seen a few reproductions of them in some of those magazines.

In *The Vision of the Fool* the whole series of 31 paintings and drawings are reproduced, two of them in colour plates. In addition there is a fairly long introduction written by the artist for these reproductions. This introduction is not intended to be an explanation of the paintings for, as Collins points out, "paintings and drawings cannot be explained; like life, they are unexplainable." The introduction is rather "in the nature of a series of reflections and meditations upon these drawings and paintings." It is of high importance, not only for the views it contains—though these are quite original and thought-provoking—but also because it is the first statement of the artist's attitude to his art and his relation to modern society. It is something in the nature of a manifesto.

Because the work of Cecil Collins belongs to that category of creative art which attaches more importance to content as opposed to form—if these two can possibly be separated—and because, despite what is said to the contrary, his work has a message, it is essential, before looking at his paintings and drawings, to consider what he has to say about his own opinions, about the aims of his work, and about the position of the artist

in society. For what he has to say—though not intended to be an explanation of his work—may nevertheless provide a clue to its significance
and to its "message."

For Collins, the root of the trouble lies in the fact that conscience—
human as well as aesthetic conscience—is universally undeveloped. His
conviction is that the gap in society exists, not between highbrow and
lowbrow—"a false and ridiculous division"—but "between those human
beings who have a conscience about life, and those who have no conscience at all."

By its belief in the finality of the useful and the fecundity of money, and
by its ruining of "the leisure of the soul," modern society has succeeded
in rendering poetic imagination, art and religion, "the three magical representatives of life," a heresy. Even the Church has become the corpse
of Christianity—believing as it does in war in war-time and in peace in
peace-time, and ceasing, consequently, to have anything to do with the
passion of Christ or with his martyrs and saints. The saint, the artist and
the poet have been reduced to a position where they can maintain their
place, if at all, only at the expense of their security and comfort, where
they have to pay for their pride in poverty and loneliness.

Collins's Fool is obviously a symbol, the living symbol of poetic imagination, art and religion. This symbol is being destroyed by modern society. In its place is developing the norm of "the little man," "the common,
ordinary and plain man," the law-abiding, useful, respectable and clever
citizen, who can always be relied upon to do what he is told, to conform,
to abstain from thinking, meditating or asking questions.

This society is becoming increasingly troubled by the inexplicable sor-
rows and joys of the Fool—"the saint, the artist and the poet are all one
in the Fool, in him they live, in him the poetic imagination lives." By its
concentration upon science, efficiency and utility, modern society has
outlawed the saint, the artist, the poet and the Fool, because they desire
the unknown, the marvelous and the poetic.

To Collins these three elements are among the most magnetic attributes
of God. "The saint finds the marvelous, the unknown, the poetic, under
the aspect of charity. The artist finds these attributes under the aspect
of beauty. The Fool finds them in virginity of spirit." The importance of
these things to the life of society is better left to the artist to explain his
views on.

So far for the opinions of Cecil Collins. Only a few words remain to
be said about his work. Collins's Fool belongs to different times and different places. He is sometimes timeless, sometimes he suggests the Eliza-

bethan period, the Restoration period, or modern times. He belongs to both sexes.

Of the 31 reproductions included in the book—all remarkable in their different ways—the most strikingly suggestive are the two colour plates, "The Pilgrim Fool" and "Three Fools in a Storm," and two black-and-white reproductions, "Fool and Flower" and "The Sleeping Fool." The first of these depicts a modern Fool holding the hand of a child and walking away from a burning city that forms the background. "Three Fools in a Storm" shows the three of them dancing joyously, with one of them holding an oil lamp in his hand. The background of "Fool and Flower" is again a burning city, with the Fool trying to pick up a flower placed in the middle of a huge, deserted space; he is picking it with such reverence and respect which—it is suggested—only a Fool is capable of. "The Sleeping Fool" is again a modern one, and the way he looks while fast asleep, the calm and perfect peace of mind, the entirely undisturbed sleep, suggests a complete detachment from what is going on about.

The rest of the reproductions, though not immediately appreciable, are no less suggestive than the four mentioned. Among them "The Peace of the Fool," "Girl Fool," "The Joy of the Fool," "Fool Picking his Nose in Front of a Bishop," and "A Procession of Fools," are most rewarding to look at.

*I*NDEX OF NAMES OF PERSONS

(Note: This index does not include names appearing in the two appendixes nor does it include the names of the author or members of his family.)